tHe OCTOBER faction

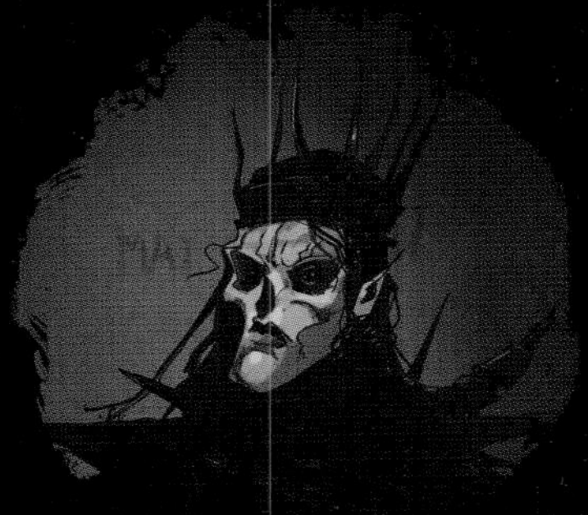

ISBN: 978-1-63140-739-0

19 18

www.IDWPUBLISHING.com

Ted Adams, CEO & Publisher
Greg Goldstein, President & COO
Robbie Robbins, EVP/Sr. Graphic Artist
Chris Ryall, Chief Creative Officer/Editor-in-Chief
Laurie Windrow, Senior VP of Sales & Marketing
Matthew Ruzicka, CPA, Chief Financial Officer
Dirk Wood, VP of Marketing
Lorelei Bunjes, VP of Digital Services
Jeff Webber, VP of Digital Publishing & Business Development

Facebook: **facebook.com/idwp**
Twitter: **@idwpublishing**
YouTube: **youtube.com/idwpul**
Tumblr: **tumblr.idwpublishing**
Instagram: **instagram.com/idw**

Originally published as THE OCTOBER FACTION issues #13–18.

Created by
Steve Niles & **Damien Worm**

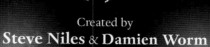

Written by **Steve Niles**
Illustrated by **Damien Worm**
Color Assist by **Alyzia Zherno**
Letters by **Robbie Robbins, Shawn Lee,**
and **Christa Miesner**

Series Editors: **Michael Benedetto** and **Chris Ryall**

Cover by **Damien Worm**
Collection Edits by **Justin Eisinger** and **Alonzo Simon**
Collection Design by **Ron Estevez**
Published by **Ted Adams**

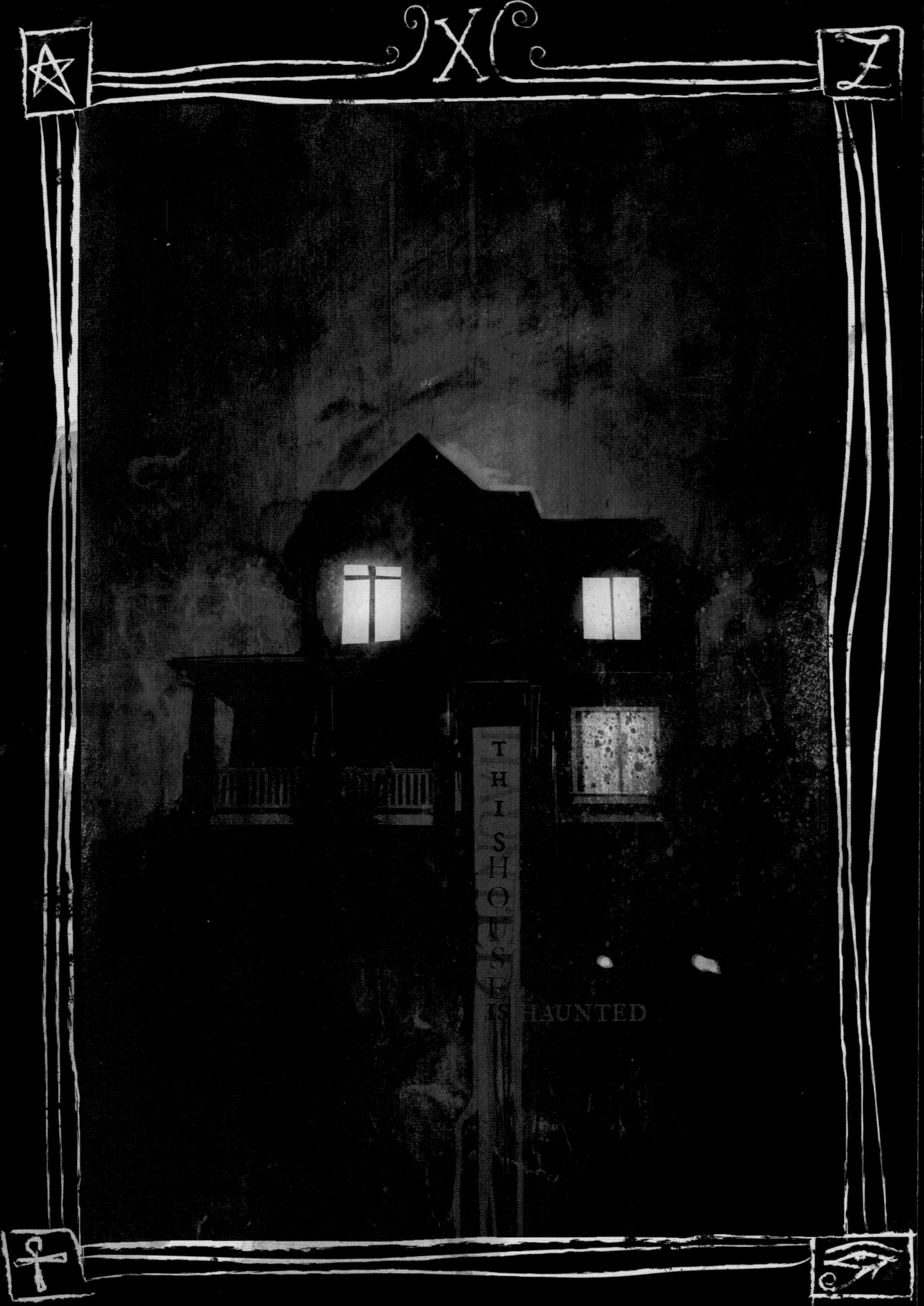
X
THIS HOUSE
IS HAUNTED

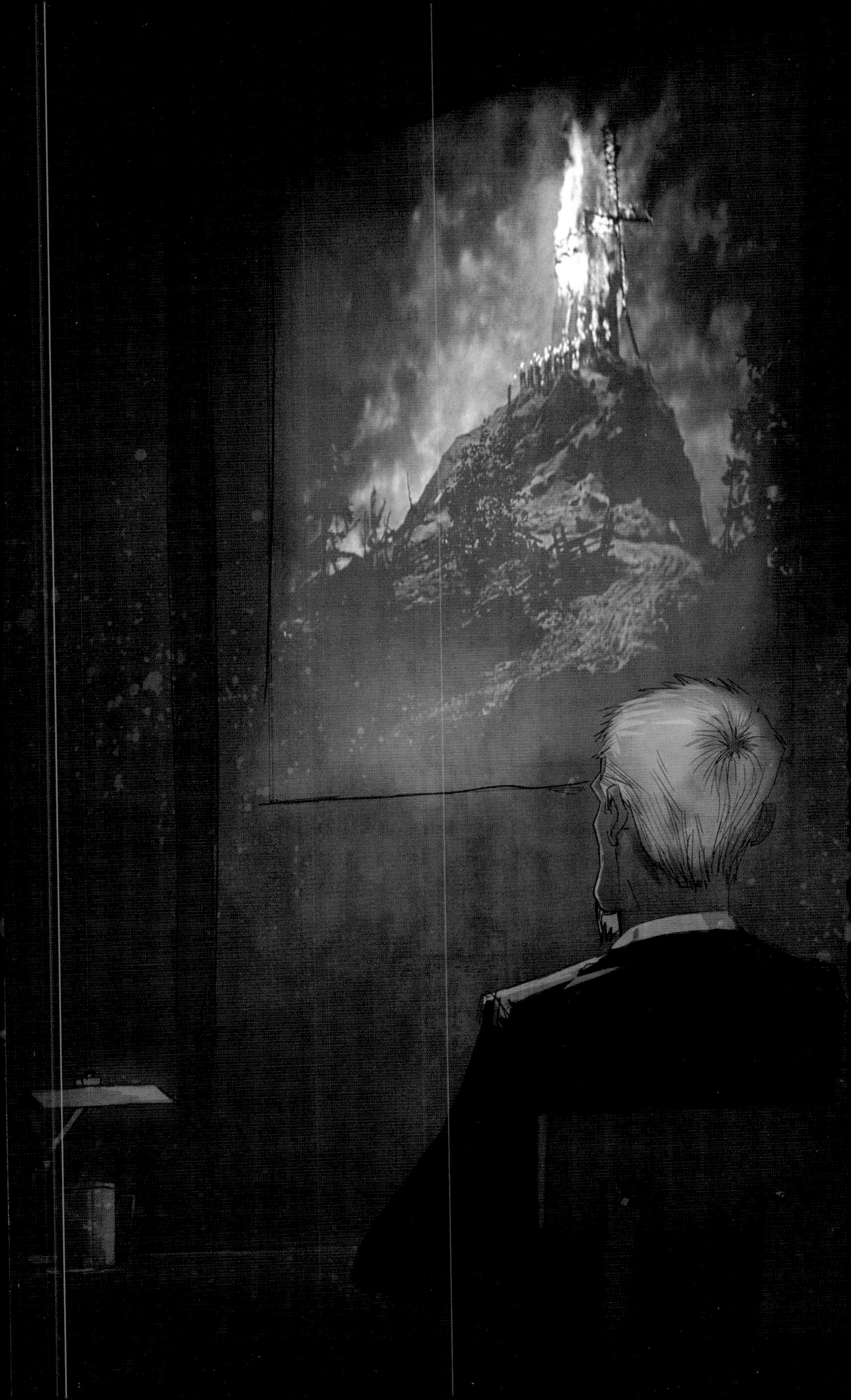

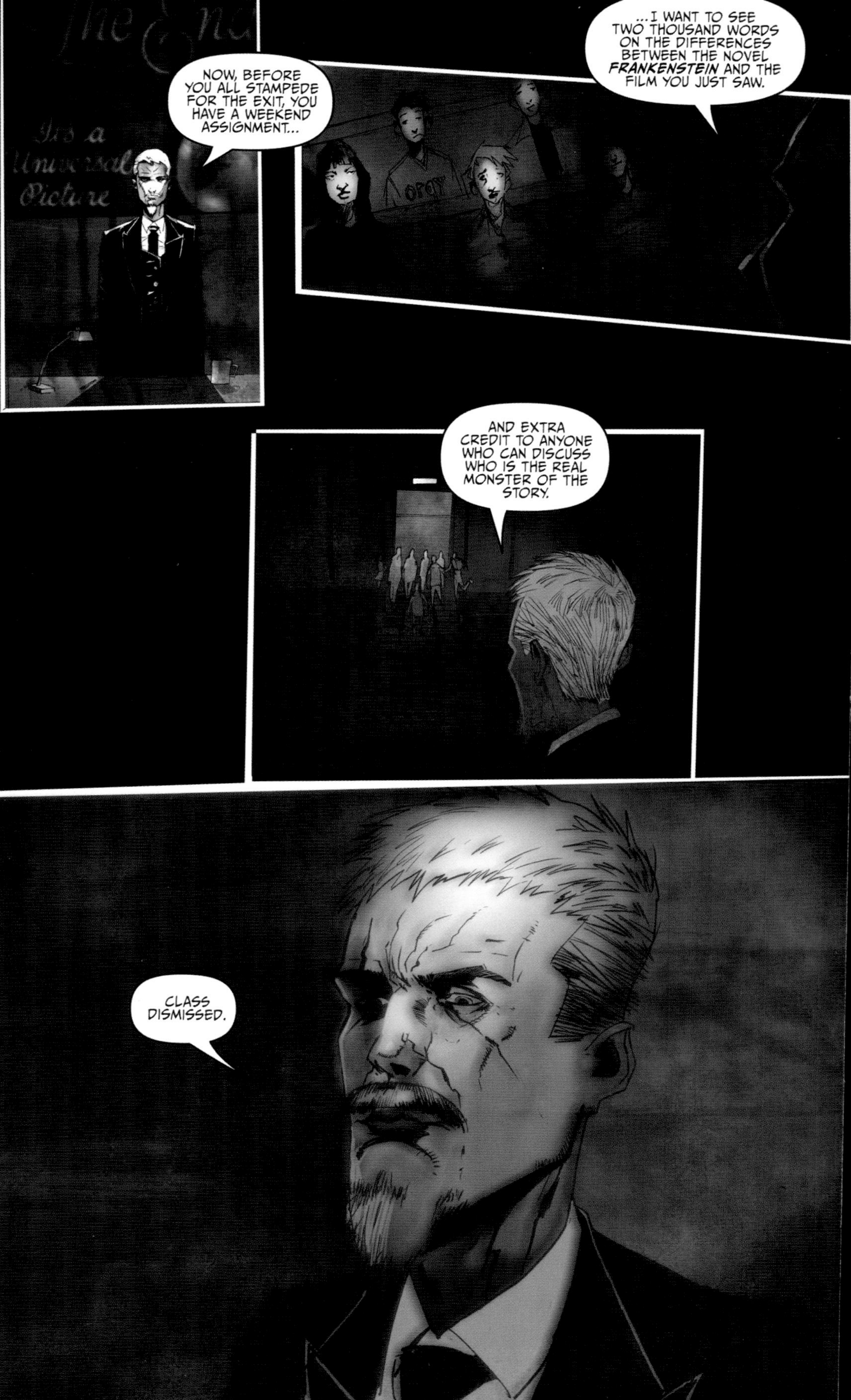
It's a Universal Picture
NOW, BEFORE YOU ALL STAMPEDE FOR THE EXIT, YOU HAVE A WEEKEND ASSIGNMENT...
...I WANT TO SEE TWO THOUSAND WORDS ON THE DIFFERENCES BETWEEN THE NOVEL FRANKENSTEIN AND THE FILM YOU JUST SAW.
AND EXTRA CREDIT TO ANYONE WHO CAN DISCUSS WHO IS THE REAL MONSTER OF THE STORY.
CLASS DISMISSED.

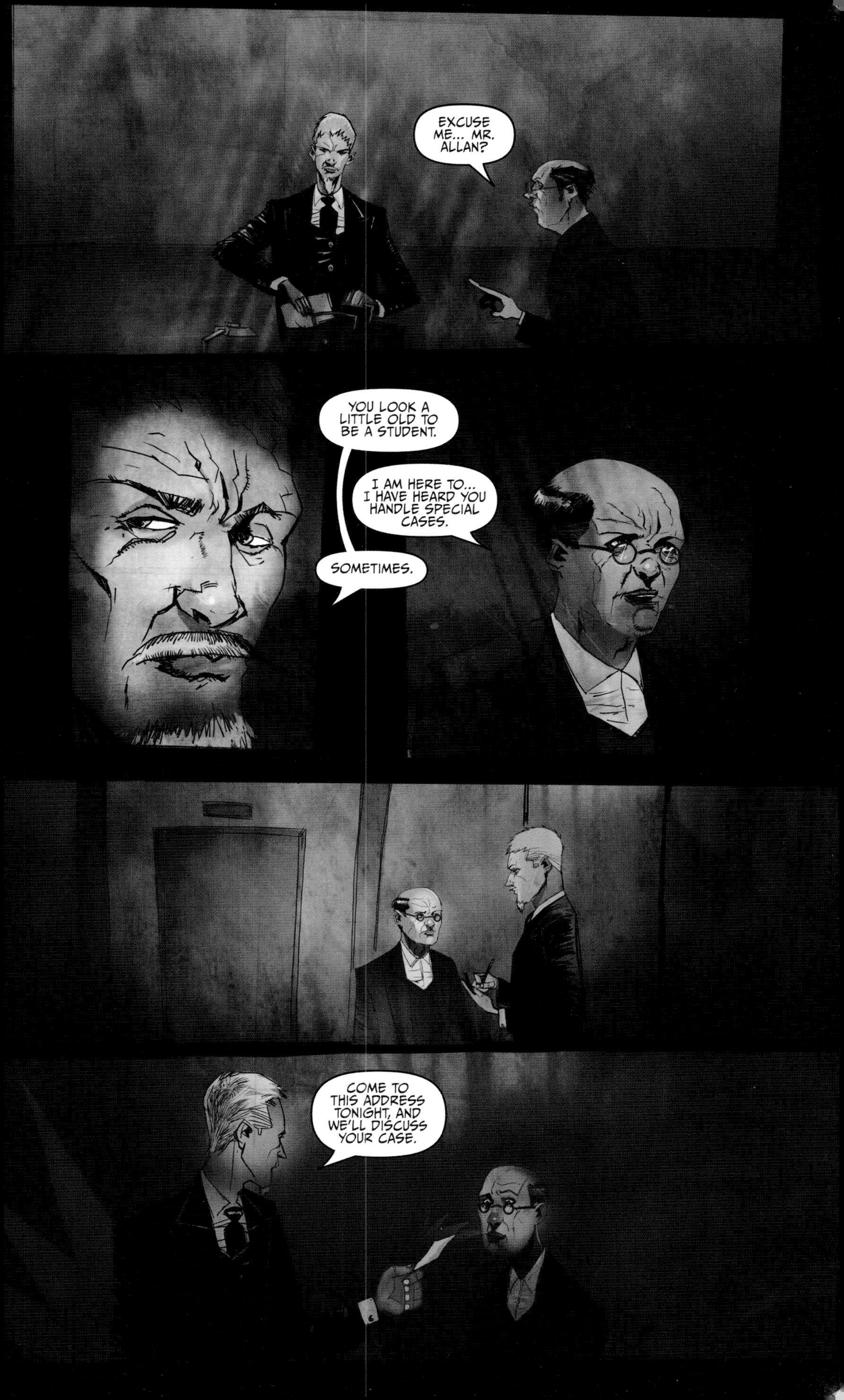
EXCUSE ME... MR. ALLAN?
YOU LOOK A LITTLE OLD TO BE A STUDENT.
I AM HERE TO... I HAVE HEARD YOU HANDLE SPECIAL CASES.
SOMETIMES.
COME TO THIS ADDRESS TONIGHT, AND WE'LL DISCUSS YOUR CASE.

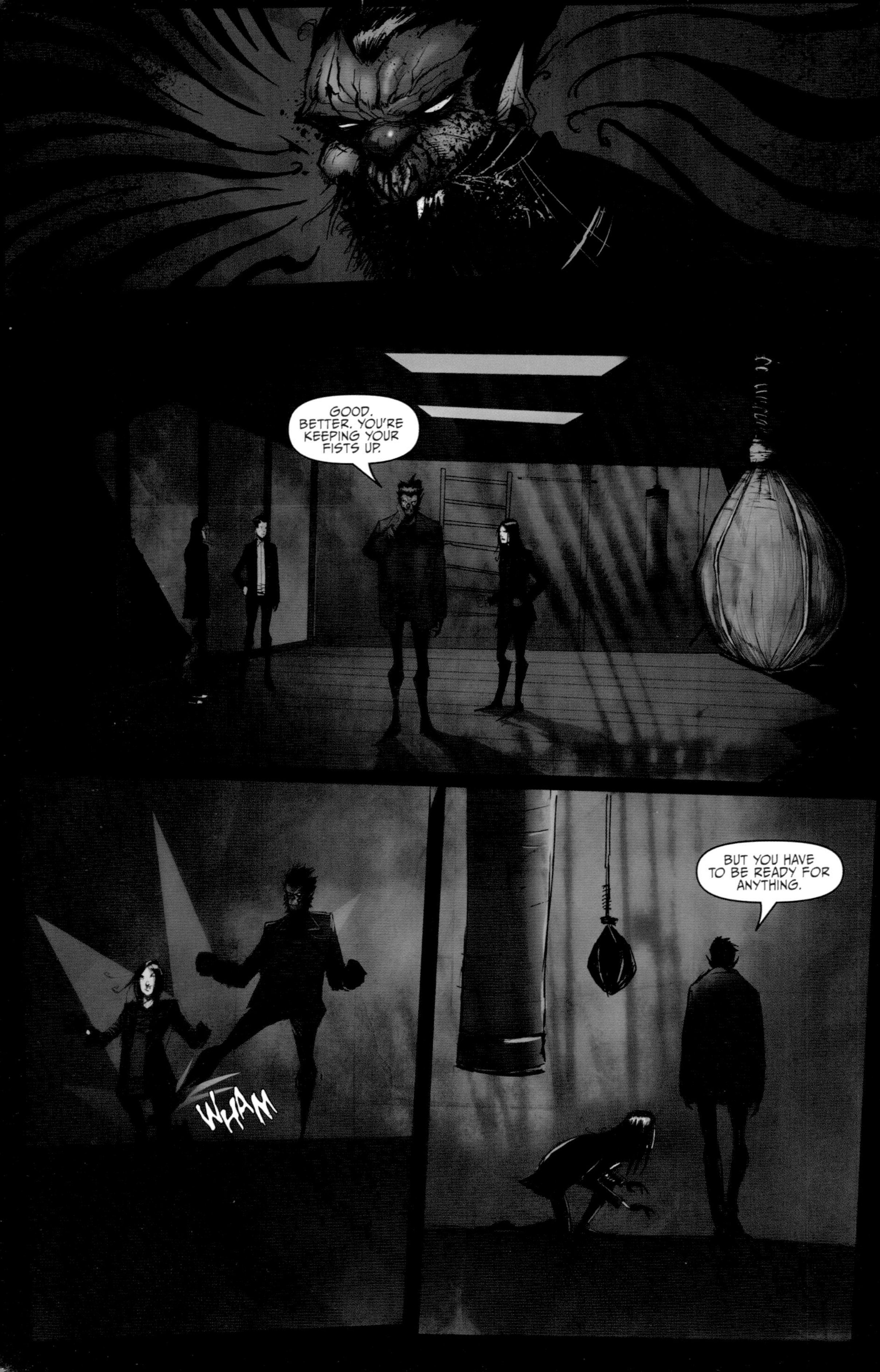
GOOD. BETTER. YOU'RE KEEPING YOUR FISTS UP.
WHAM
BUT YOU HAVE TO BE READY FOR ANYTHING.

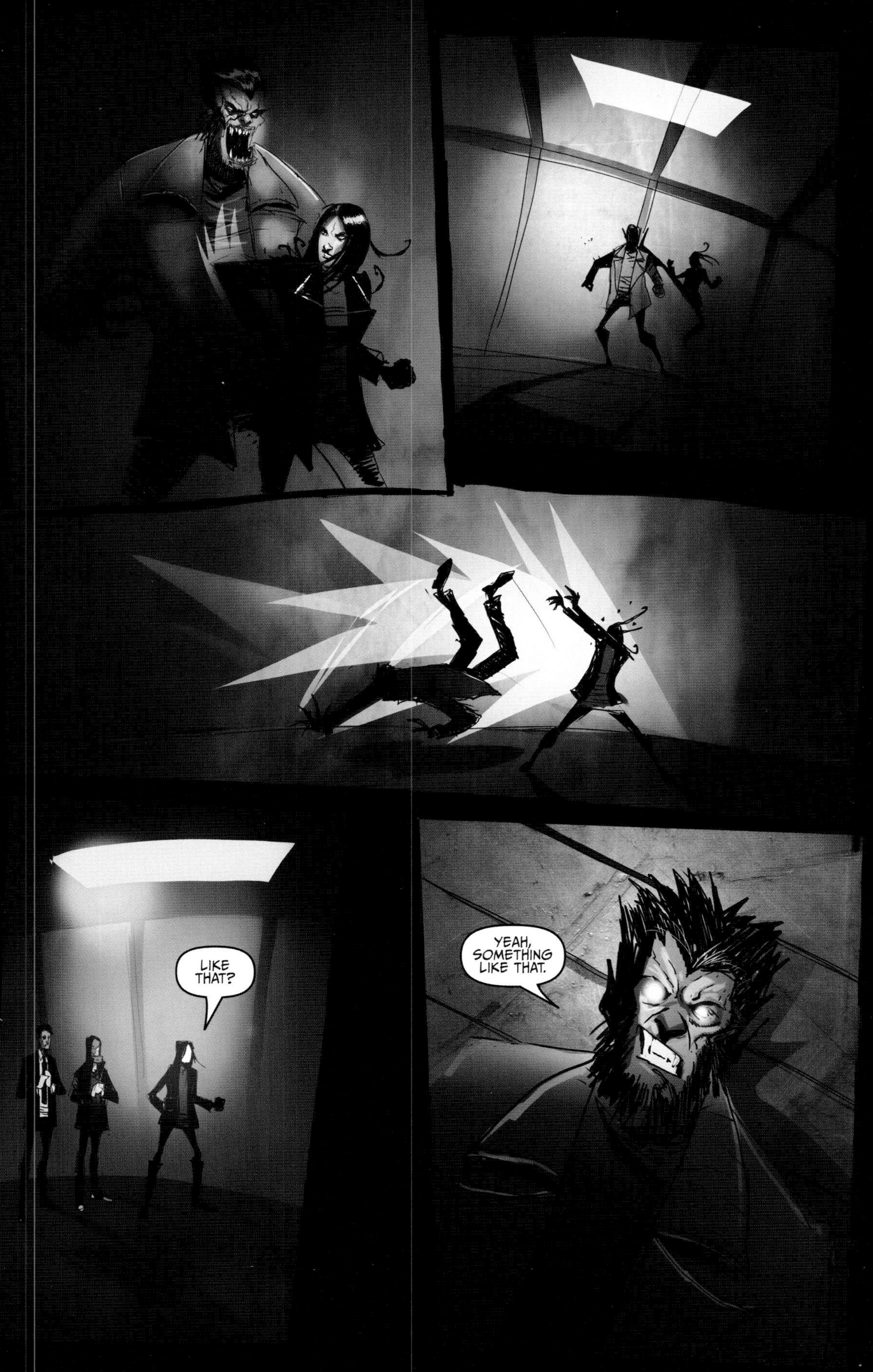
LIKE THAT?
YEAH, SOMETHING LIKE THAT.

LATER THAT NIGHT.
I... I HAVE AN APPOINTMENT WITH FREDRICK ALLAN.
YEAH, SURE, COME ON IN.
THIS WAY.
RIGHT IN HERE.

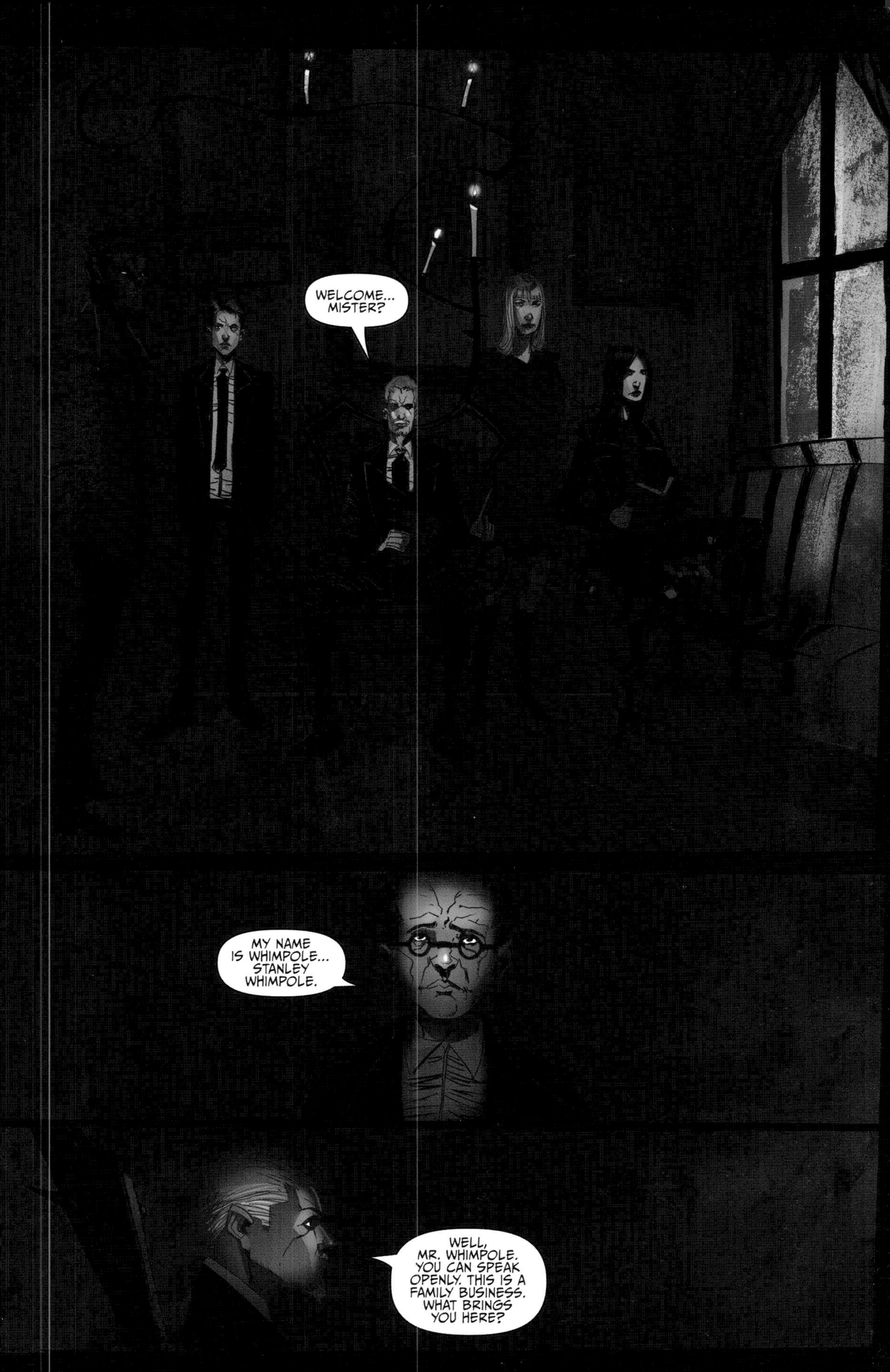
WELCOME... MISTER?
MY NAME IS WHIMPOLE... STANLEY WHIMPOLE.
WELL, MR. WHIMPOLE. YOU CAN SPEAK OPENLY. THIS IS A FAMILY BUSINESS. WHAT BRINGS YOU HERE?

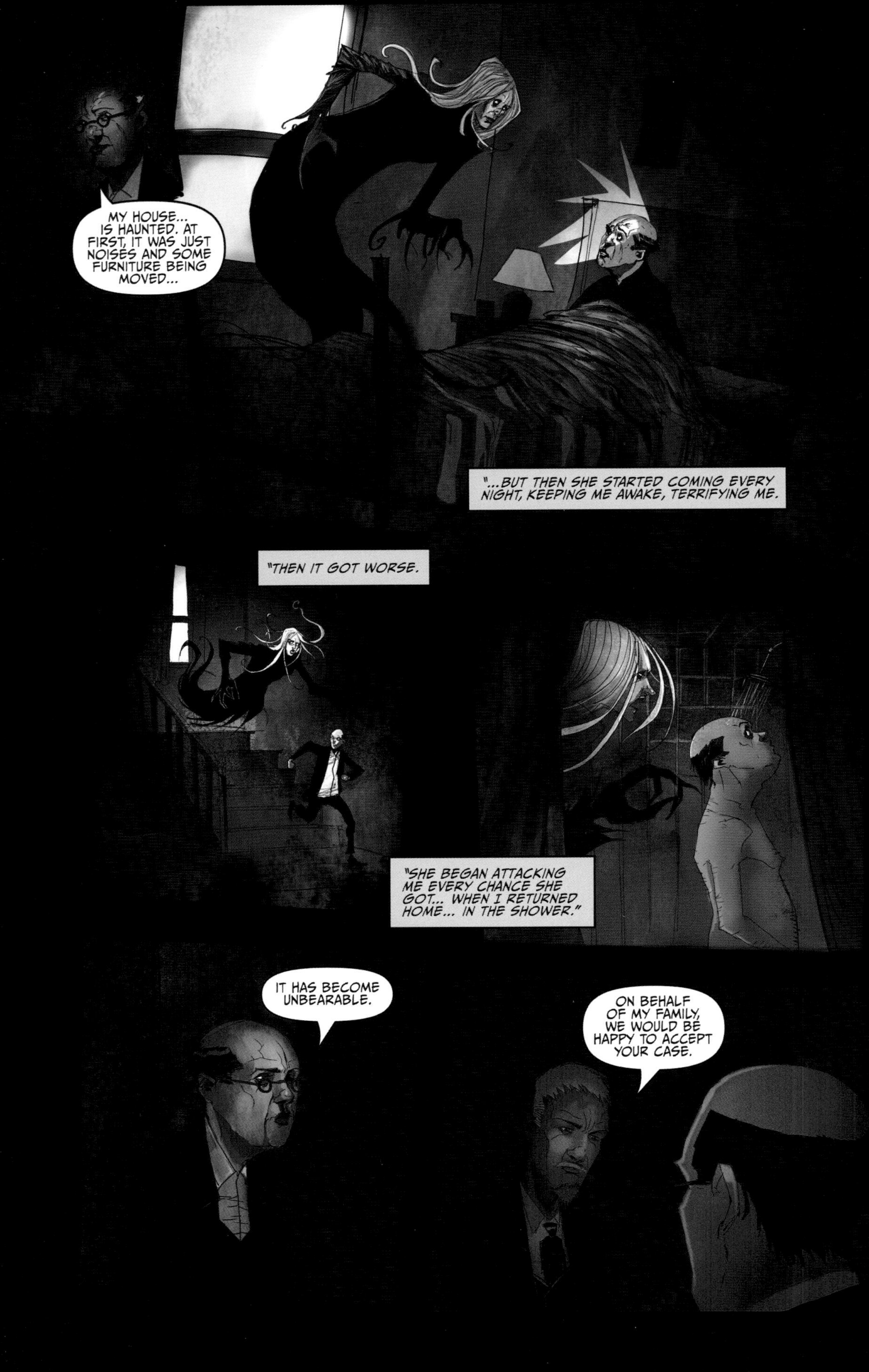
MY HOUSE... IS HAUNTED. AT FIRST, IT WAS JUST NOISES AND SOME FURNITURE BEING MOVED...
"...BUT THEN SHE STARTED COMING EVERY NIGHT, KEEPING ME AWAKE, TERRIFYING ME.
"THEN IT GOT WORSE.
"SHE BEGAN ATTACKING ME EVERY CHANCE SHE GOT... WHEN I RETURNED HOME... IN THE SHOWER."
IT HAS BECOME UNBEARABLE.
ON BEHALF OF MY FAMILY, WE WOULD BE HAPPY TO ACCEPT YOUR CASE.

I THINK THIS IS AN EXCELLENT FIRST CASE FOR YOU KIDS. GHOSTS ARE EASILY DISPATCHED WHEN HANDLED CORRECTLY.
I'VE HAD PLENTY OF TROUBLE WITH GHOSTS. I WOULDN'T BE SO CAVALIER IF I WERE YOU, FRED.
CAVALIER? ME? ALL I'M SAYING IS, IF EVERYBODY DOES THEIR JOB, THIS SHOULD BE AN OPEN-AND-SHUT CASE.

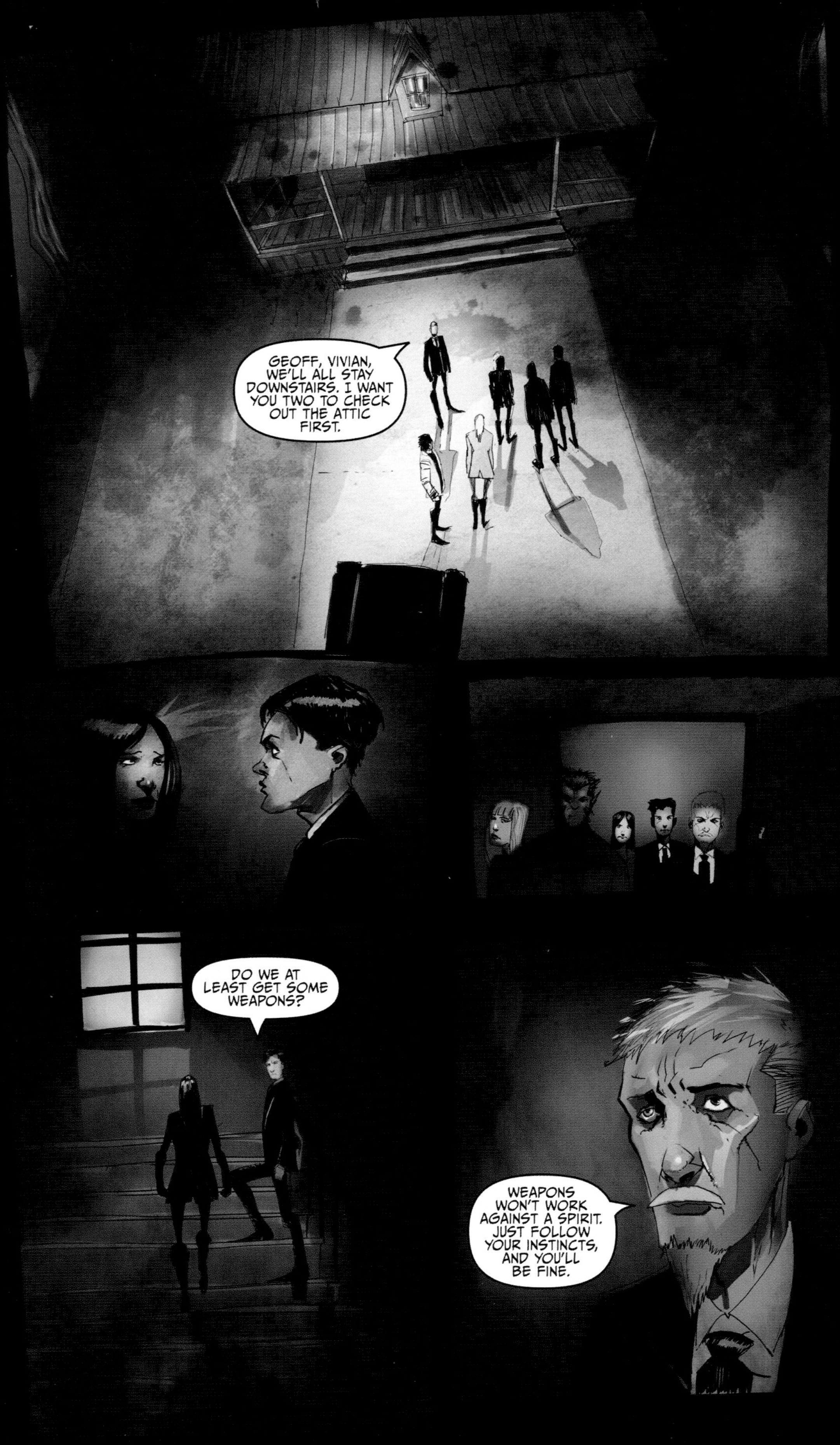
GEOFF, VIVIAN, WE'LL ALL STAY DOWNSTAIRS. I WANT YOU TWO TO CHECK OUT THE ATTIC FIRST.
DO WE AT LEAST GET SOME WEAPONS?
WEAPONS WON'T WORK AGAINST A SPIRIT. JUST FOLLOW YOUR INSTINCTS, AND YOU'LL BE FINE.

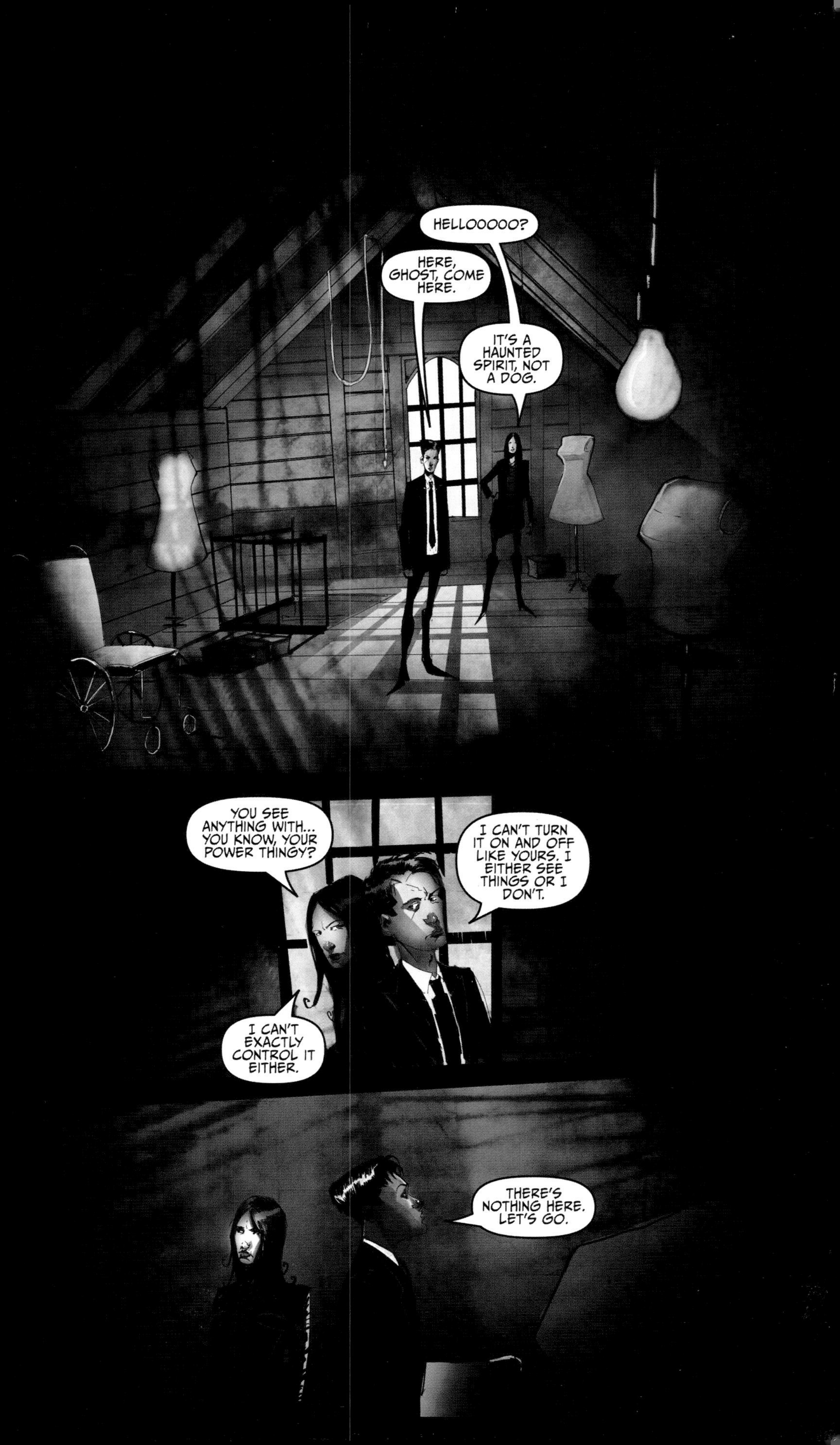
HELLOOOOO?
HERE, GHOST, COME HERE.
IT'S A HAUNTED SPIRIT, NOT A DOG.
YOU SEE ANYTHING WITH... YOU KNOW, YOUR POWER THINGY?
I CAN'T TURN IT ON AND OFF LIKE YOURS. I EITHER SEE THINGS OR I DON'T.
I CAN'T EXACTLY CONTROL IT EITHER.
THERE'S NOTHING HERE. LET'S GO.

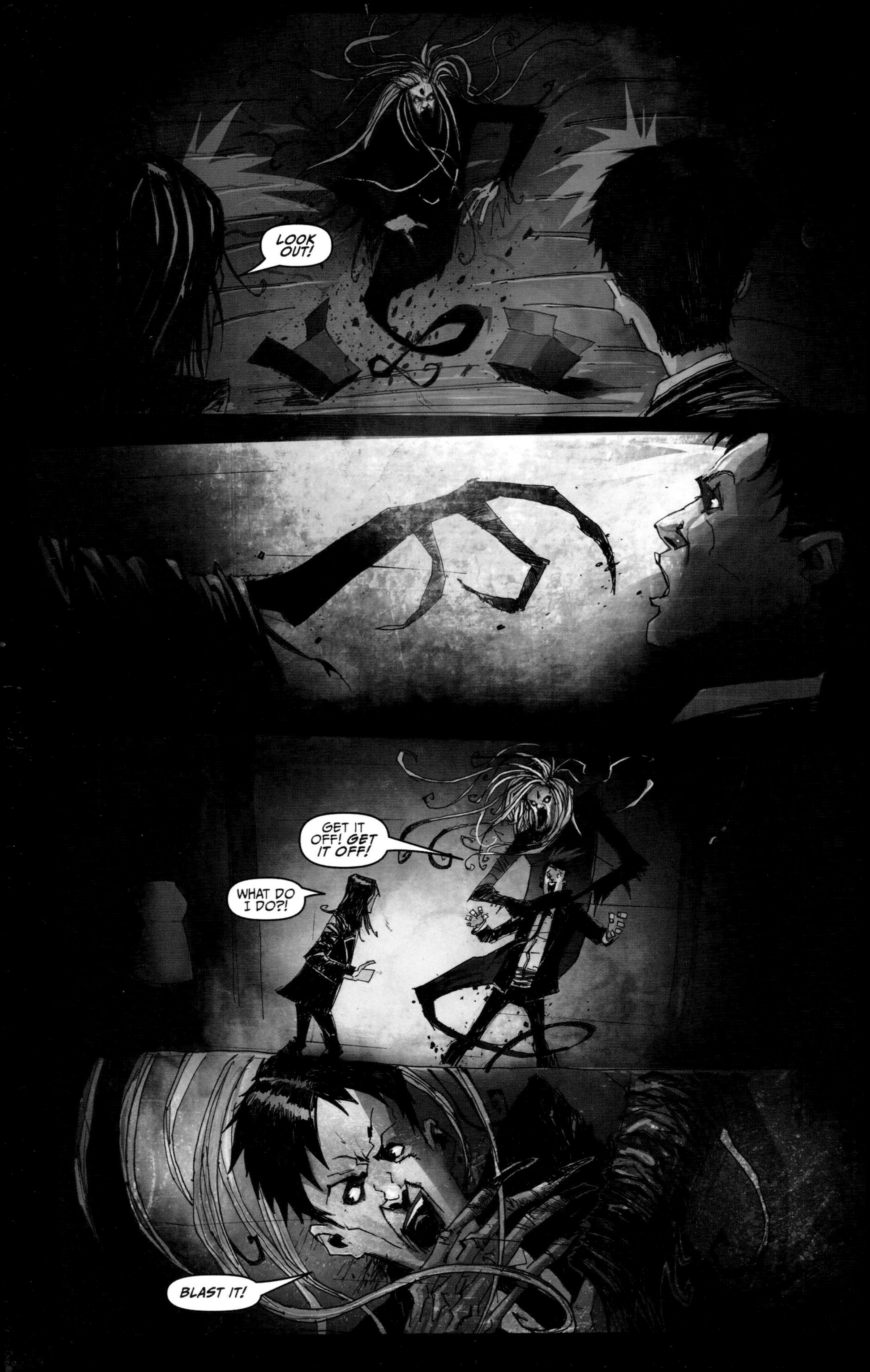
LOOK OUT!
GET IT OFF! GET IT OFF!
WHAT DO I DO?!
BLAST IT!

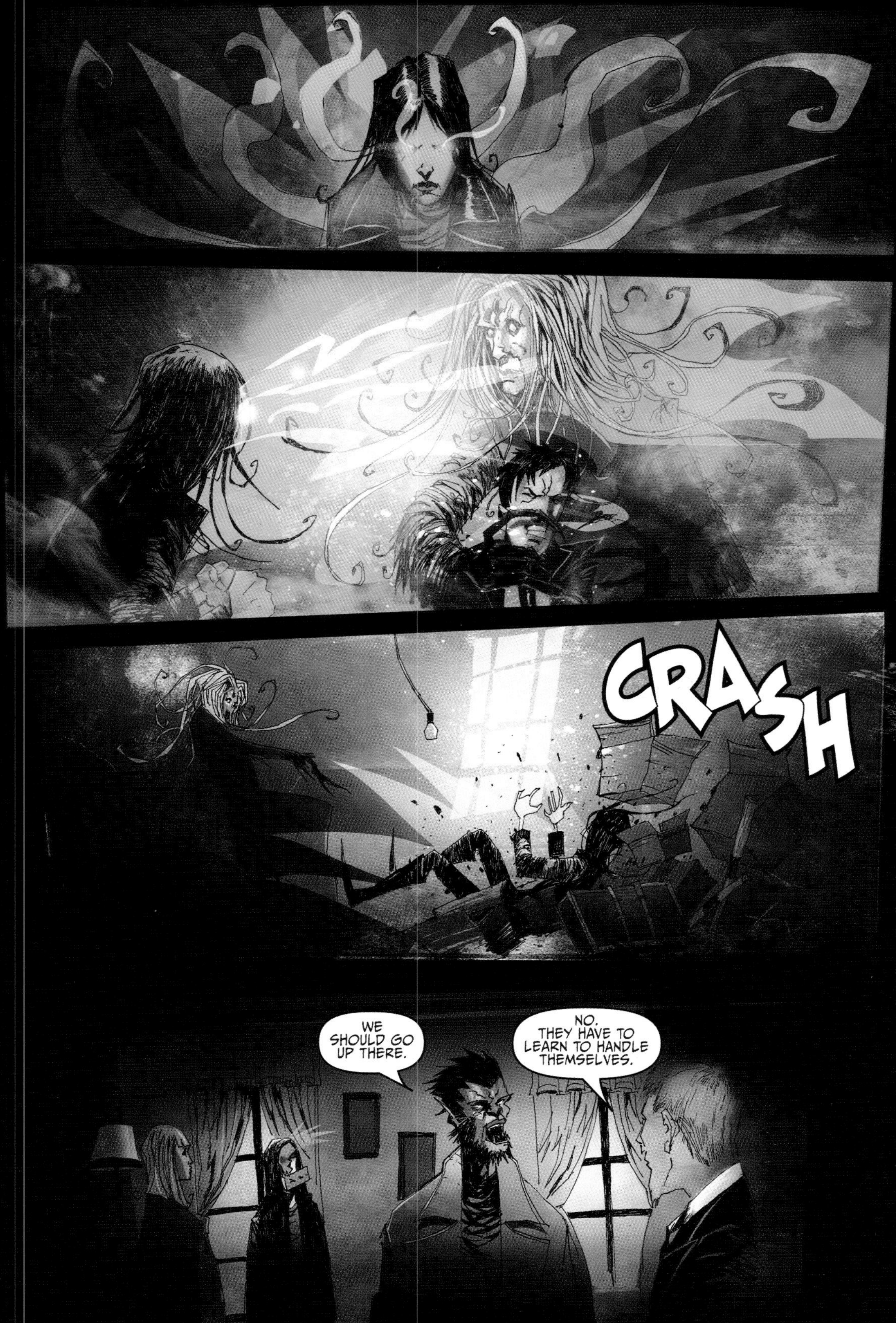
CRASH
WE SHOULD GO UP THERE.
NO. THEY HAVE TO LEARN TO HANDLE THEMSELVES.

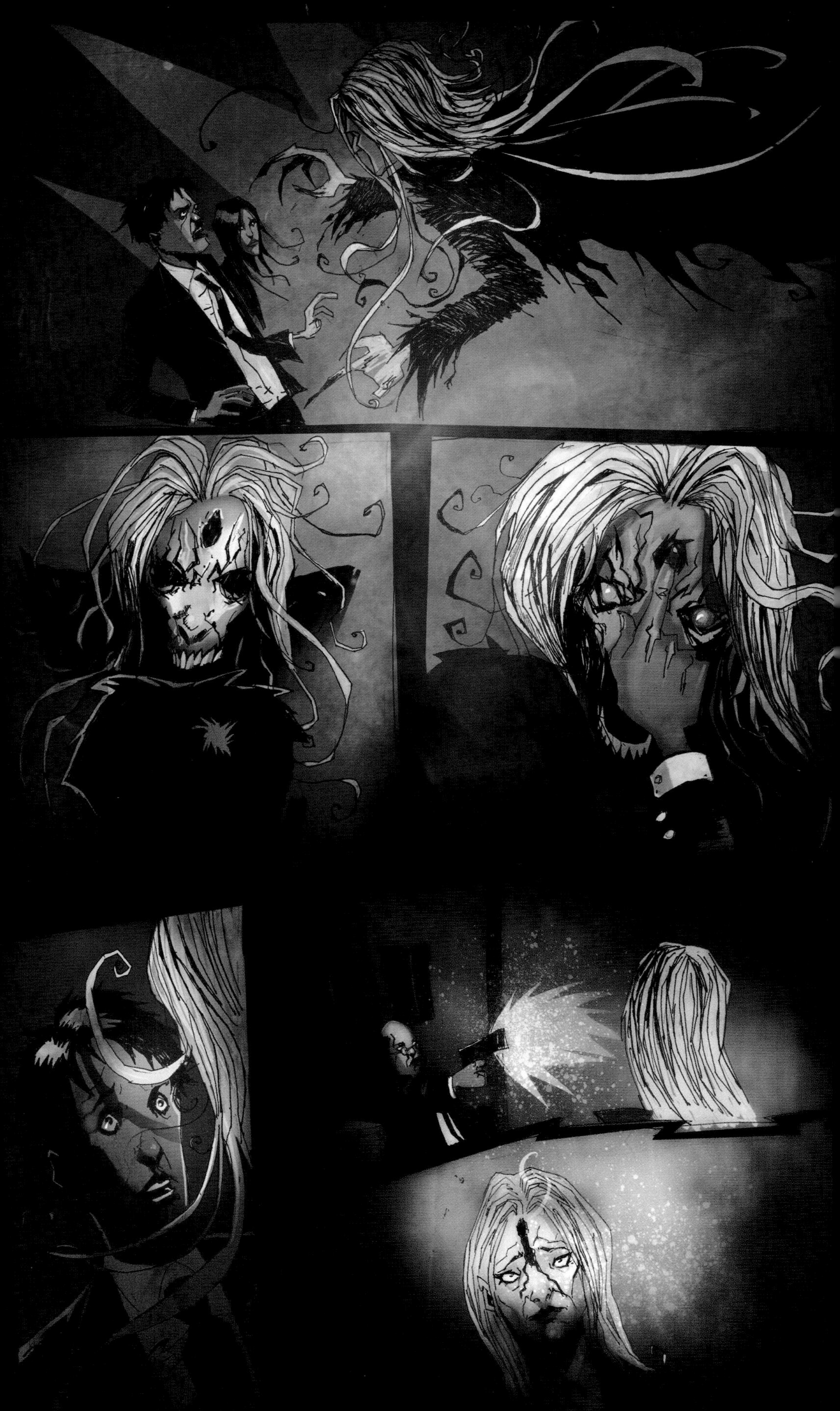

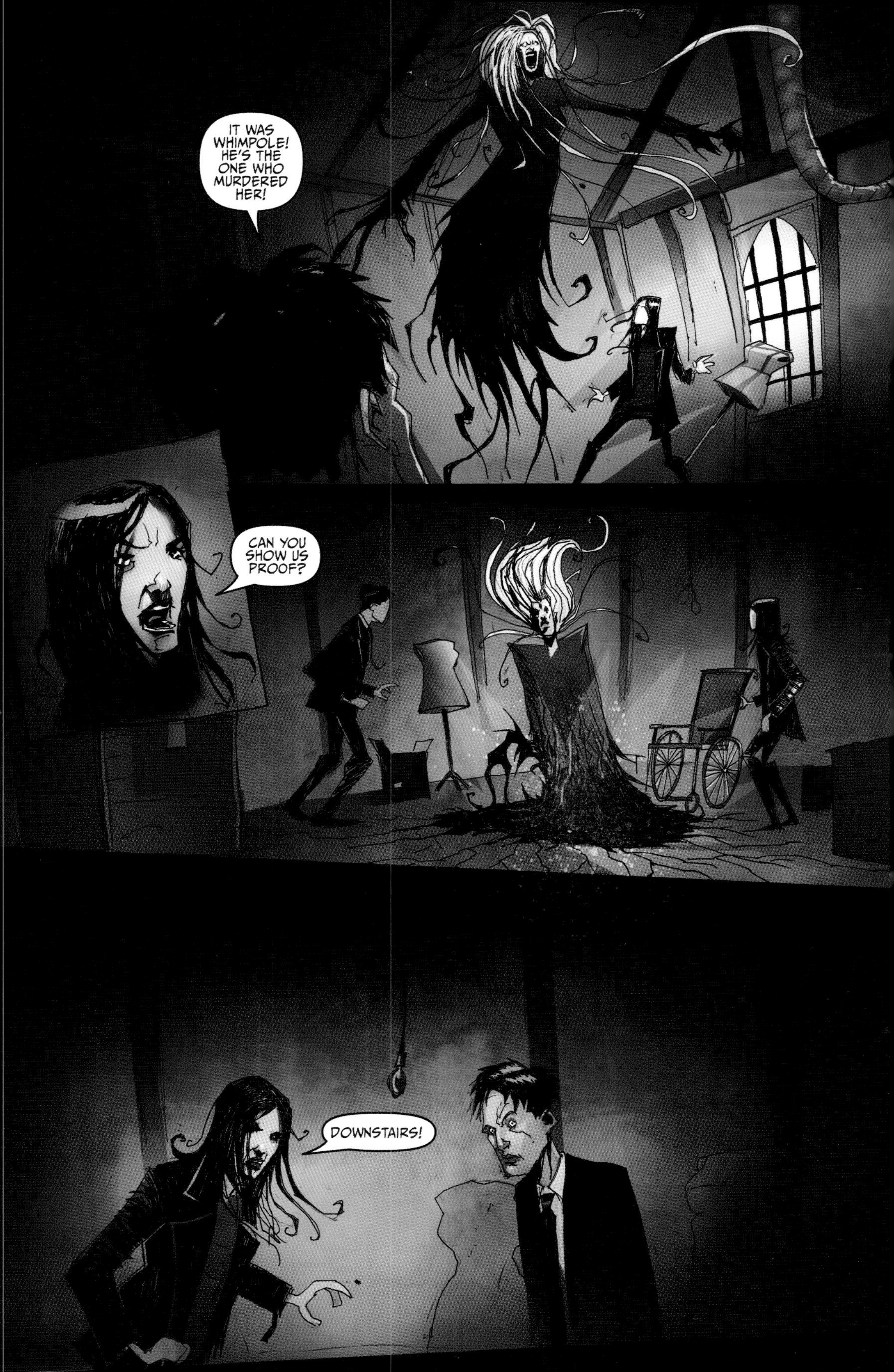
IT WAS WHIMPOLE! HE'S THE ONE WHO MURDERED HER!
CAN YOU SHOW US PROOF?
DOWNSTAIRS!

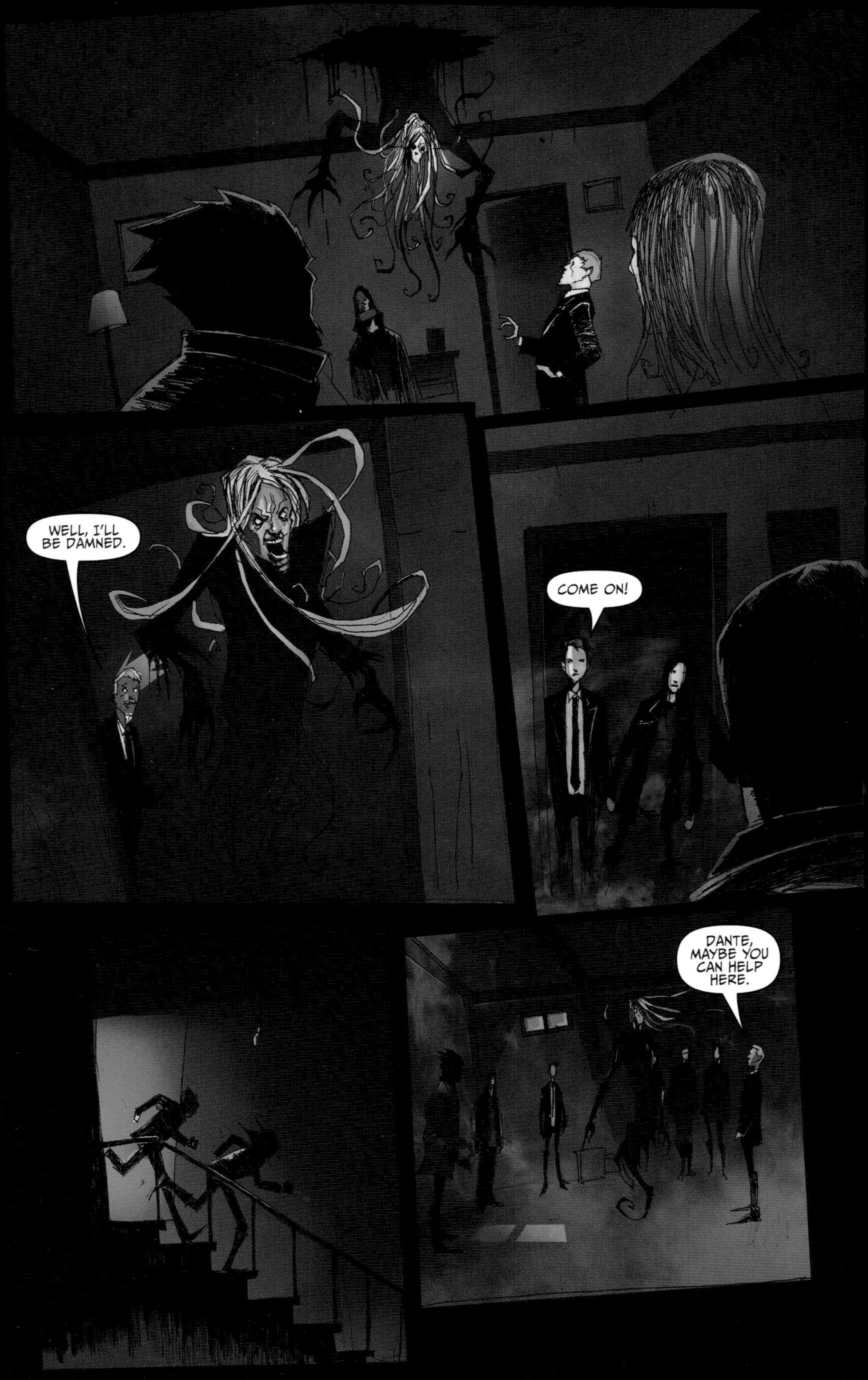
WELL, I'LL BE DAMNED.
COME ON!
DANTE, MAYBE YOU CAN HELP HERE.

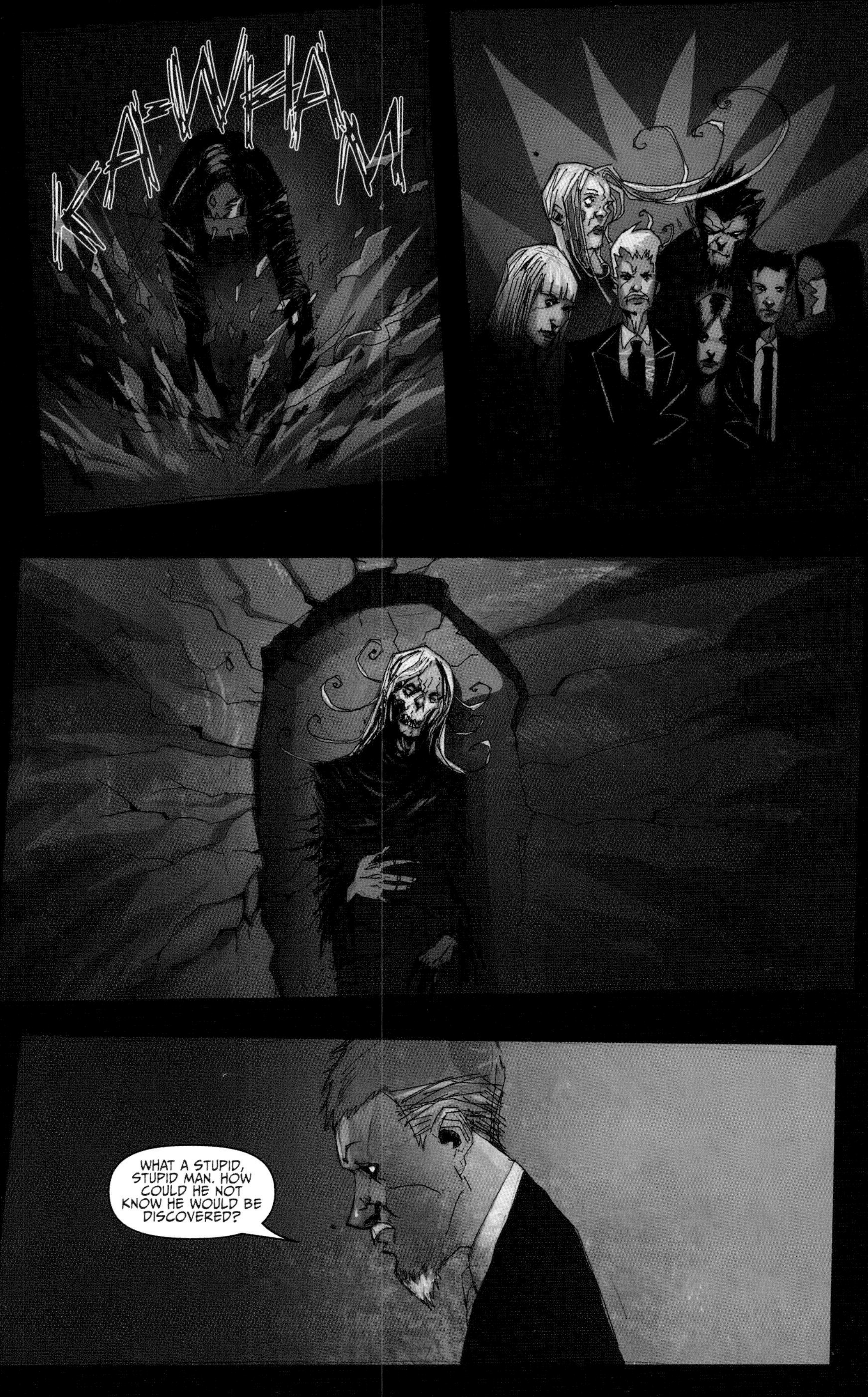
KA-WHAM
WHAT A STUPID, STUPID MAN. HOW COULD HE NOT KNOW HE WOULD BE DISCOVERED?

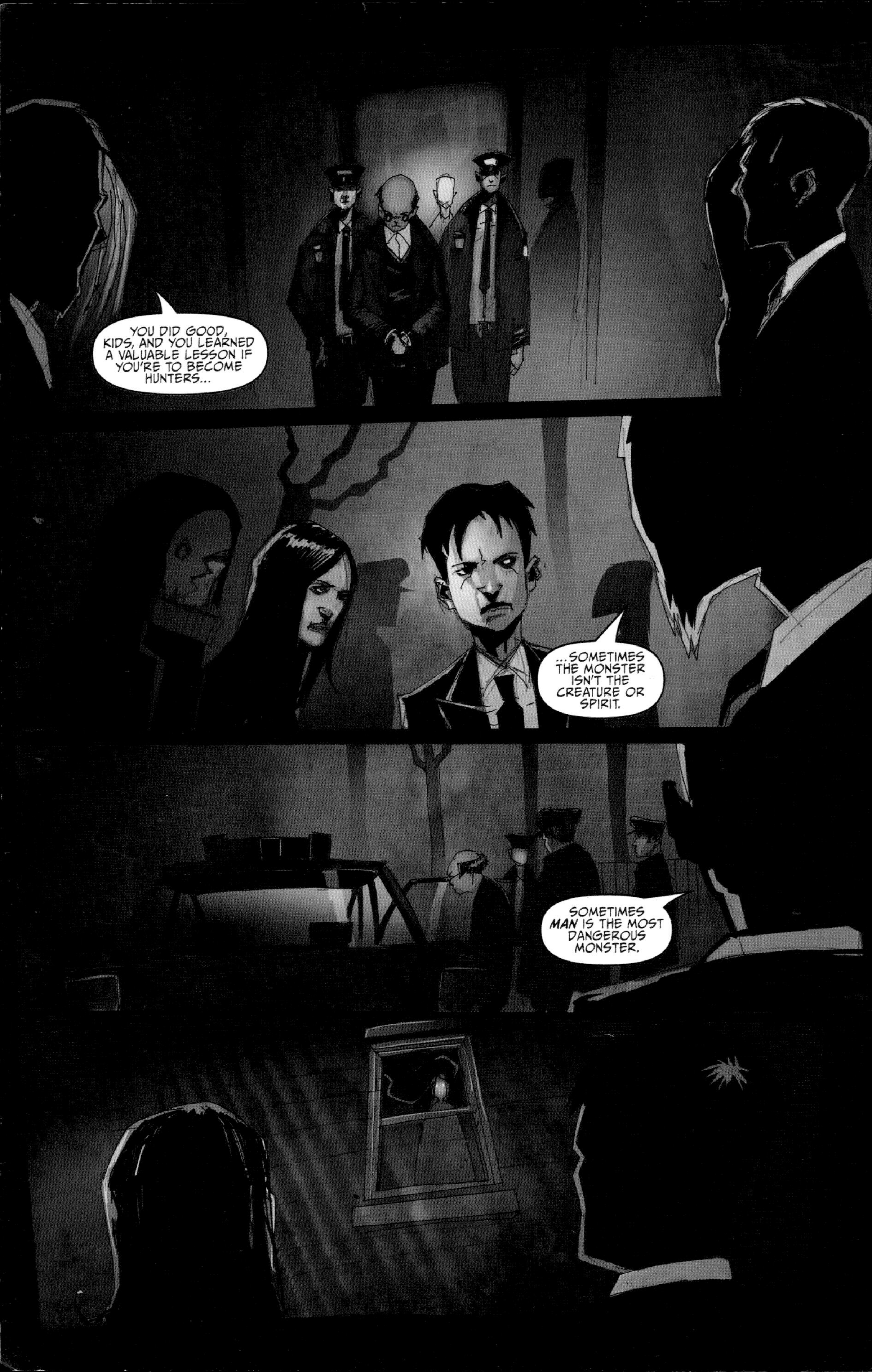
YOU DID GOOD, KIDS, AND YOU LEARNED A VALUABLE LESSON IF YOU'RE TO BECOME HUNTERS...
...SOMETIMES THE MONSTER ISN'T THE CREATURE OR SPIRIT.
SOMETIMES *MAN* IS THE MOST DANGEROUS MONSTER.

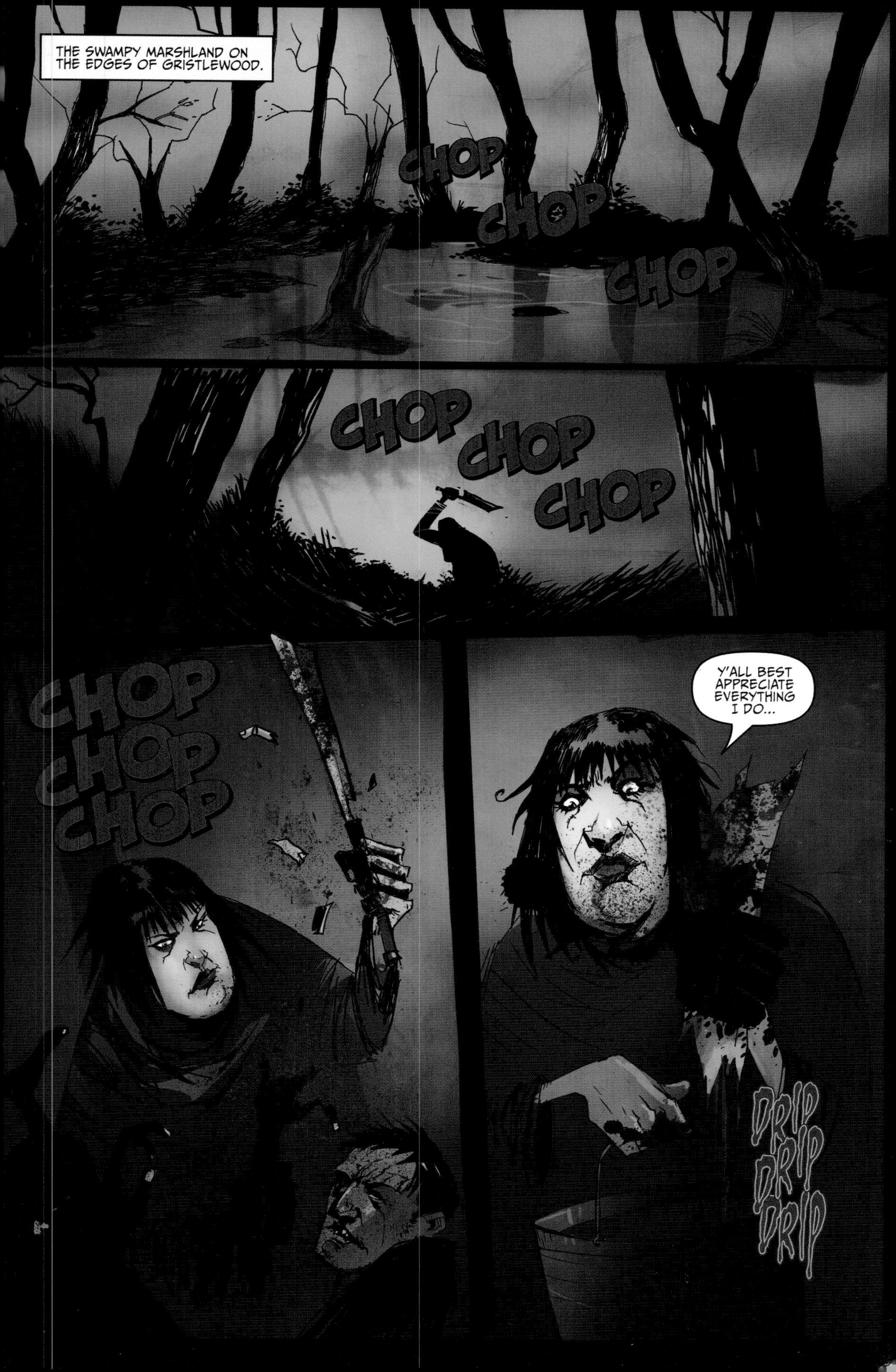
THE SWAMPY MARSHLAND ON THE EDGES OF GRISTLEWOOD.
CHOP
CHOP
CHOP
CHOP
CHOP
CHOP
CHOP
CHOP
CHOP
Y'ALL BEST APPRECIATE EVERYTHING I DO...
DRIP
DRIP
DRIP
DRIP

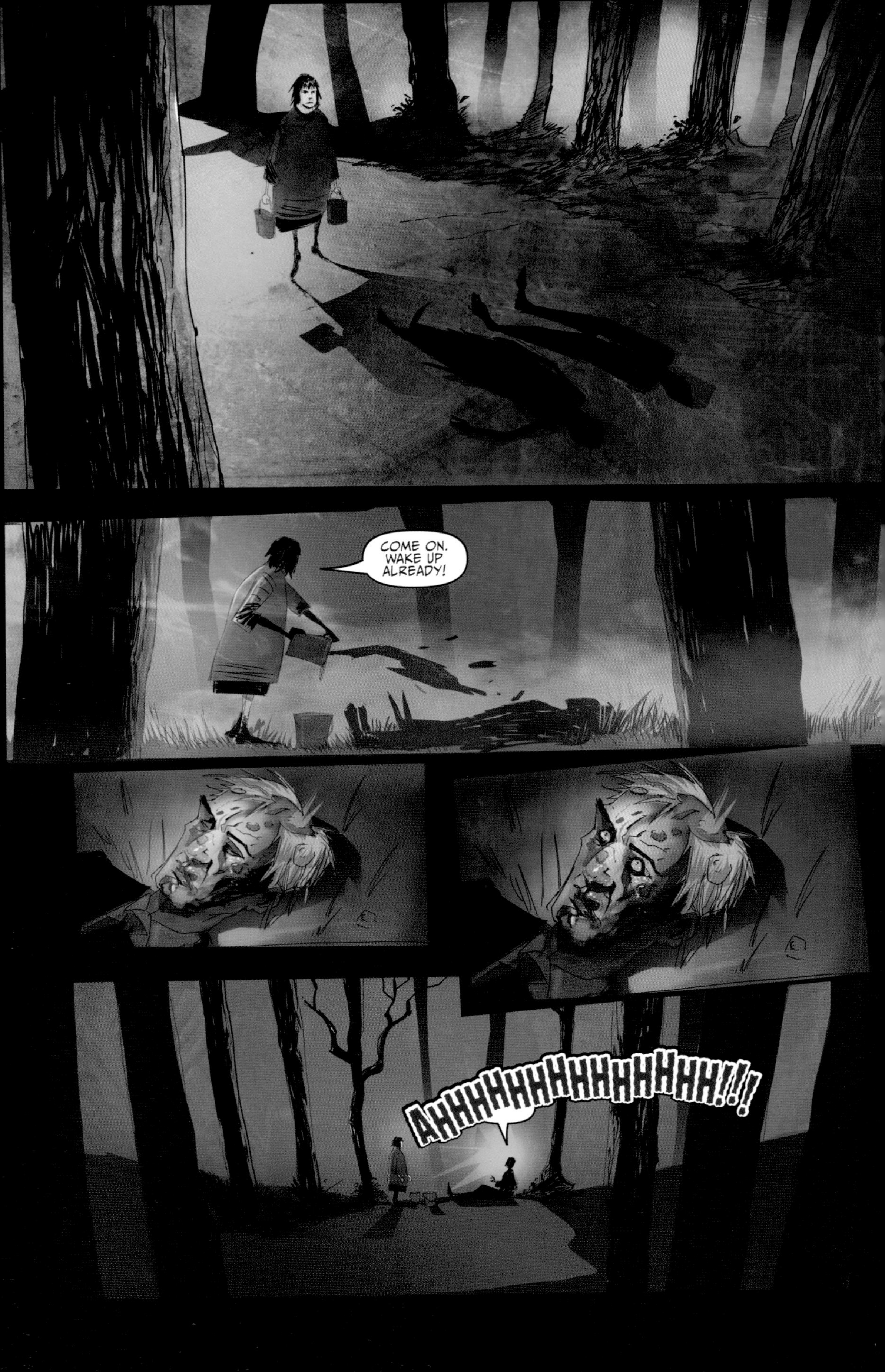
COME ON. WAKE UP ALREADY!
AHHHHHHHHHHHHHHH!!!

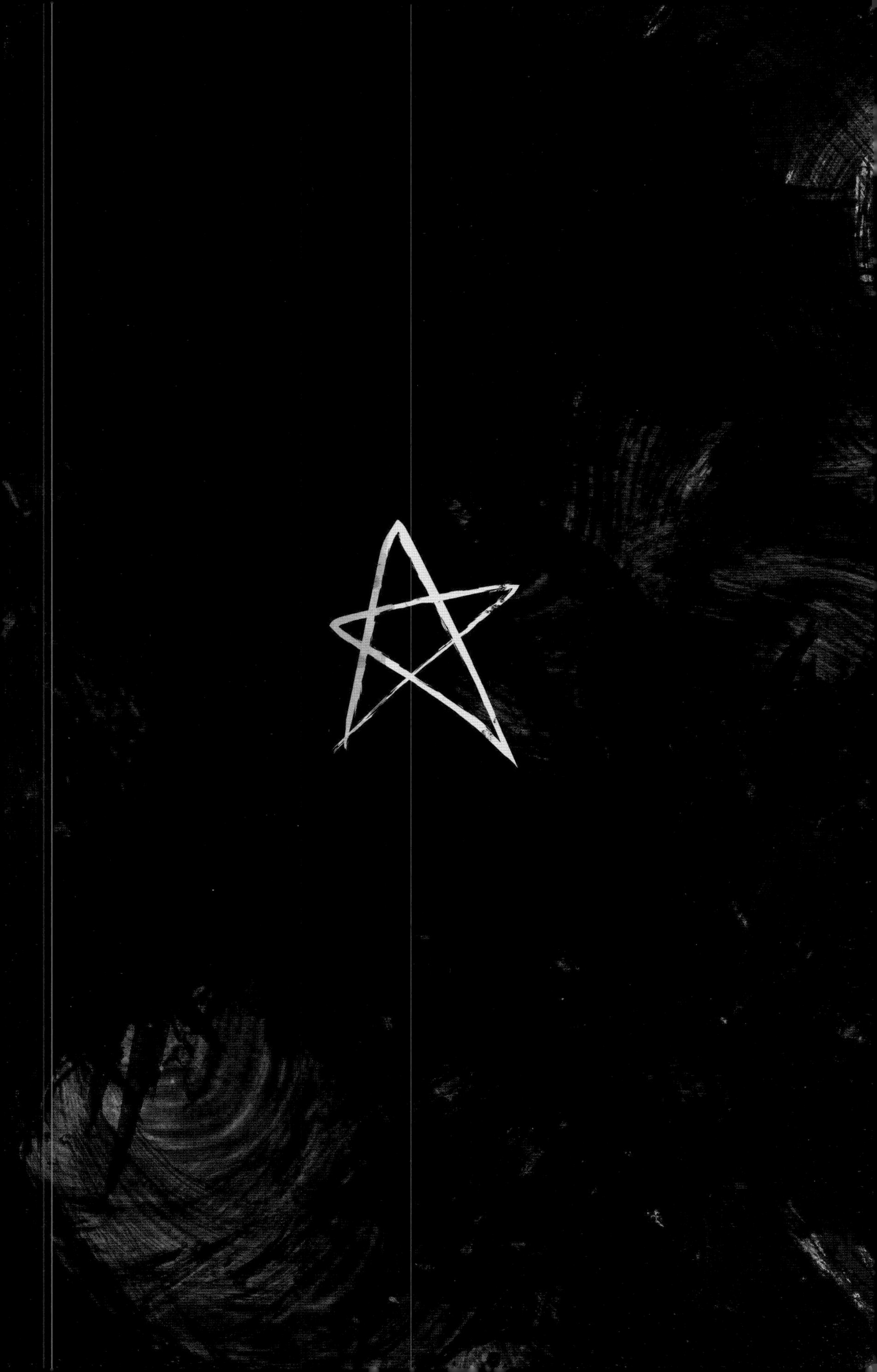

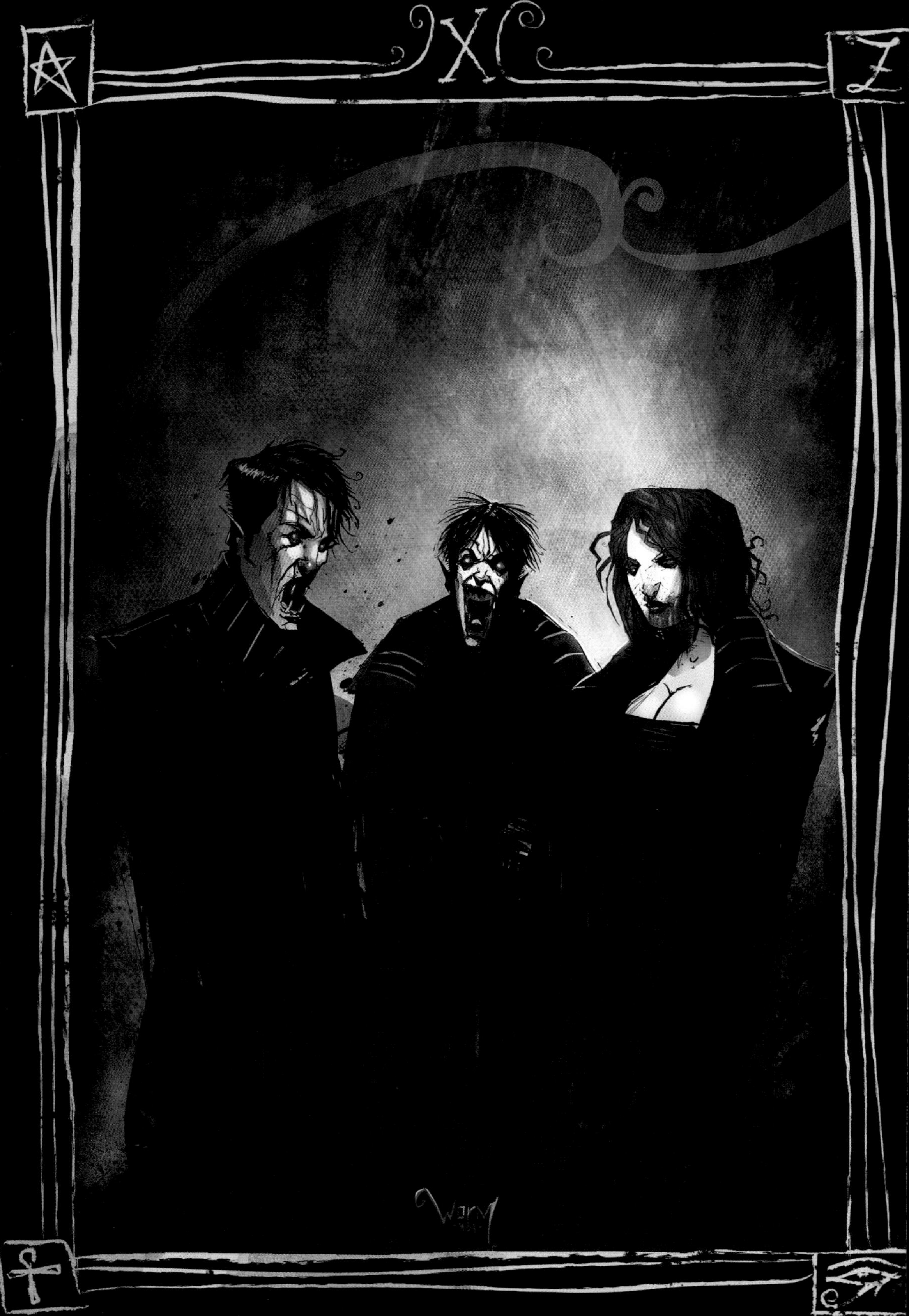

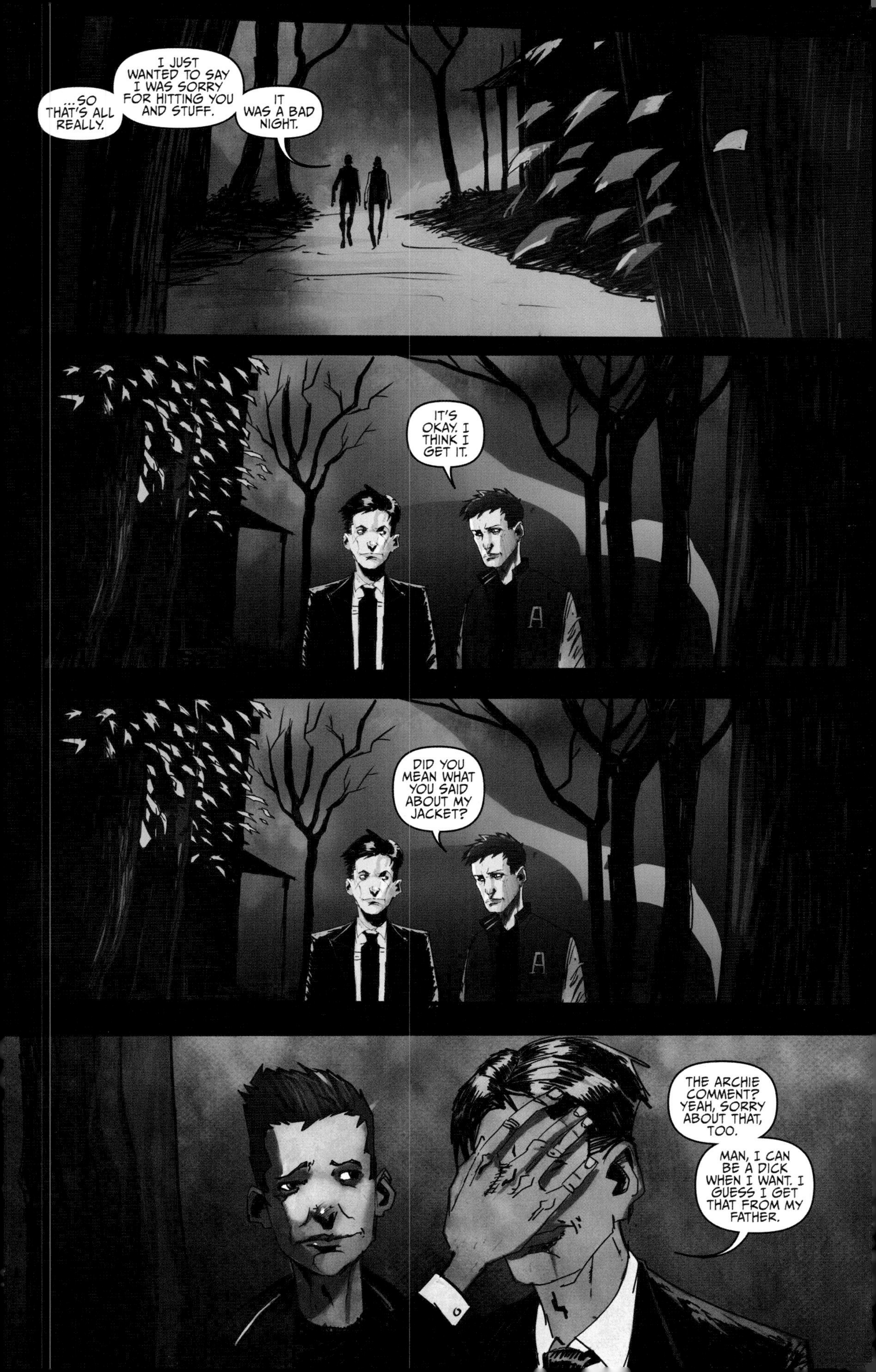
I JUST WANTED TO SAY I WAS SORRY FOR HITTING YOU AND STUFF.
IT WAS A BAD NIGHT.
...SO THAT'S ALL REALLY.
IT'S OKAY. I THINK I GET IT.
DID YOU MEAN WHAT YOU SAID ABOUT MY JACKET?
THE ARCHIE COMMENT? YEAH, SORRY ABOUT THAT, TOO.
MAN, I CAN BE A DICK WHEN I WANT. I GUESS I GET THAT FROM MY FATHER.

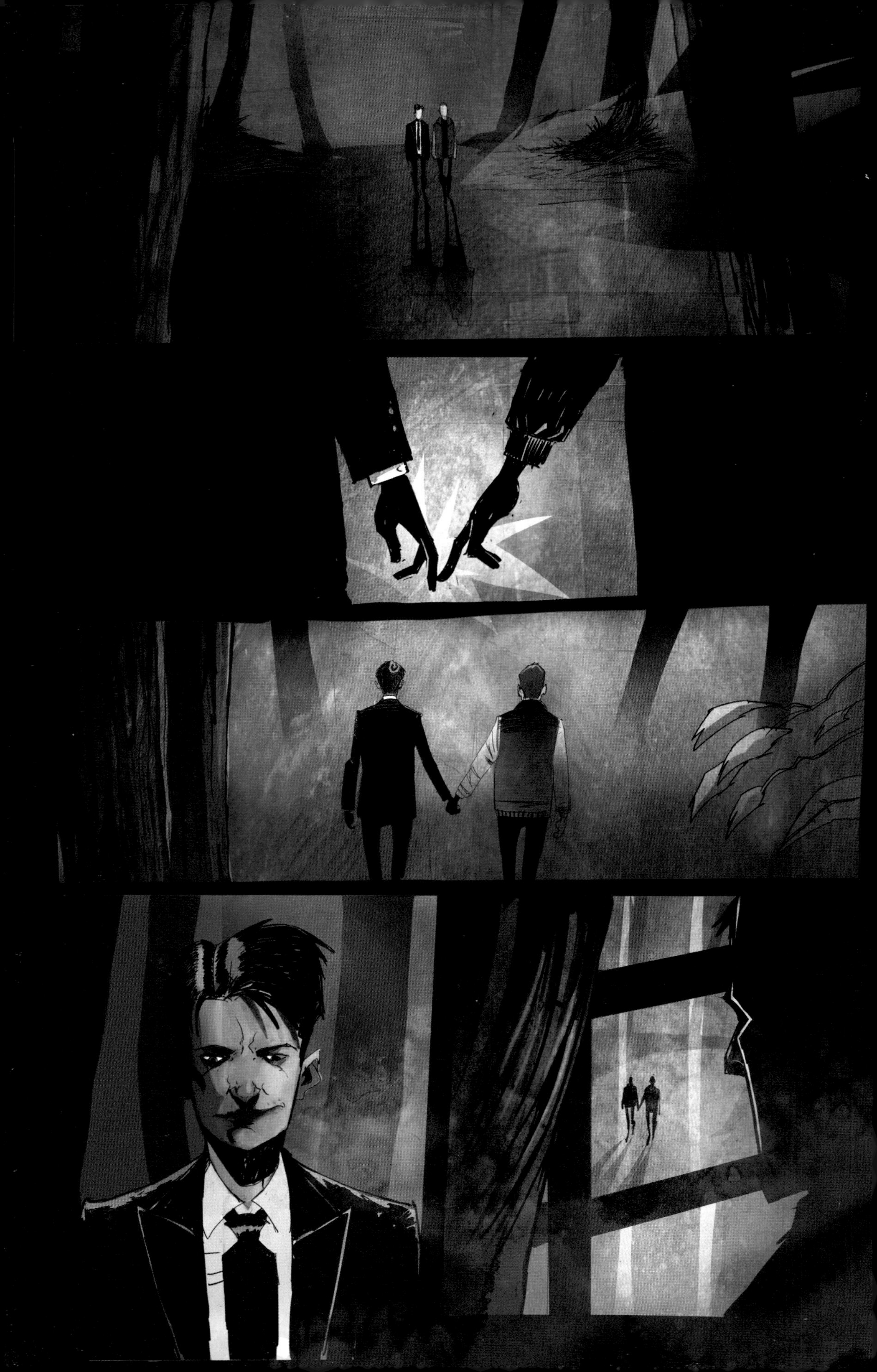

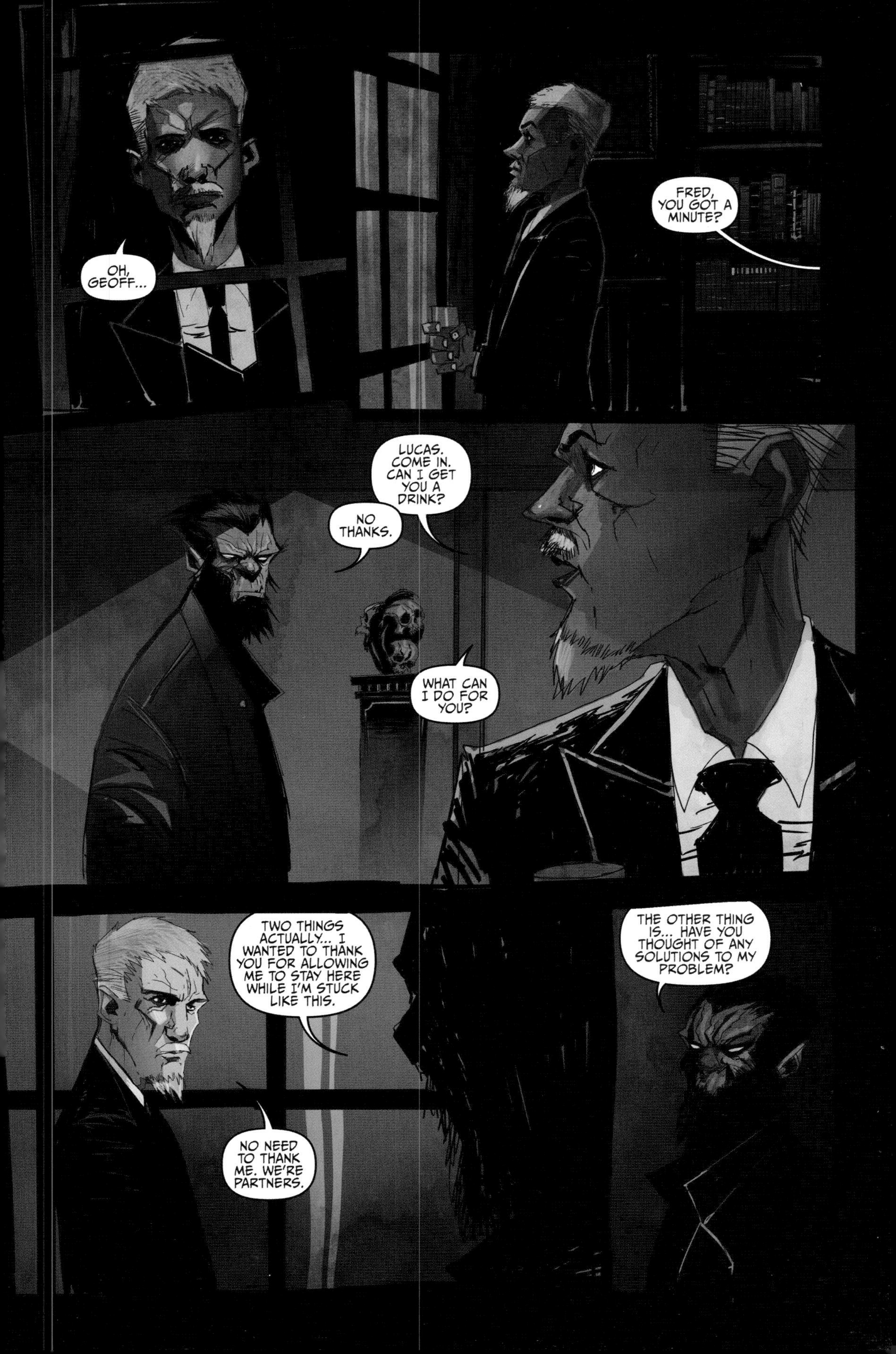
FRED, YOU GOT A MINUTE?
OH, GEOFF...
LUCAS. COME IN. CAN I GET YOU A DRINK?
NO THANKS.
WHAT CAN I DO FOR YOU?
TWO THINGS ACTUALLY... I WANTED TO THANK YOU FOR ALLOWING ME TO STAY HERE WHILE I'M STUCK LIKE THIS.
NO NEED TO THANK ME. WE'RE PARTNERS.
THE OTHER THING IS... HAVE YOU THOUGHT OF ANY SOLUTIONS TO MY PROBLEM?

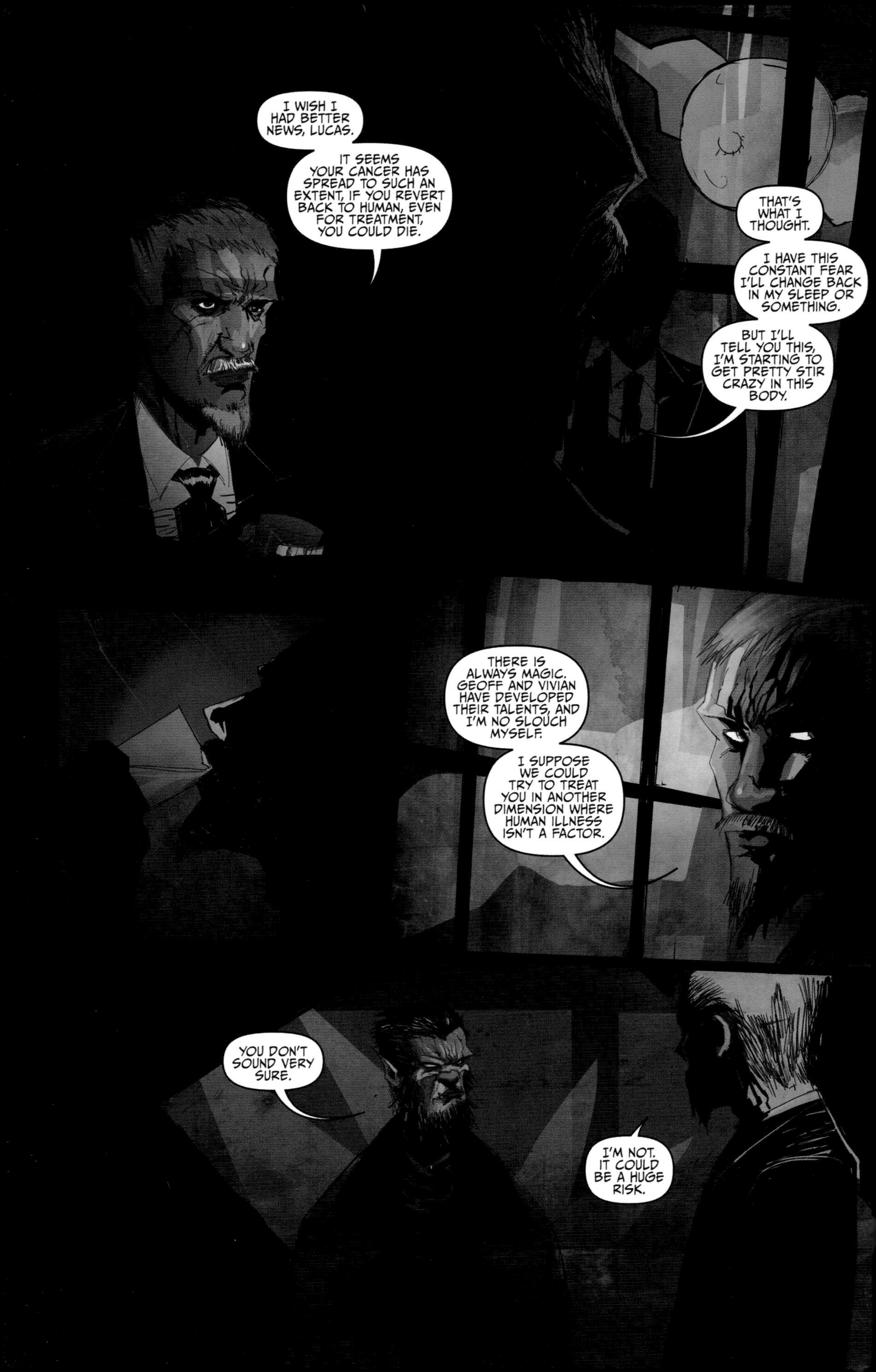

I WISH I HAD BETTER NEWS, LUCAS.
IT SEEMS YOUR CANCER HAS SPREAD TO SUCH AN EXTENT, IF YOU REVERT BACK TO HUMAN, EVEN FOR TREATMENT, YOU COULD DIE.
THAT'S WHAT I THOUGHT.
I HAVE THIS CONSTANT FEAR I'LL CHANGE BACK IN MY SLEEP OR SOMETHING.
BUT I'LL TELL YOU THIS, I'M STARTING TO GET PRETTY STIR CRAZY IN THIS BODY.
THERE IS ALWAYS MAGIC. GEOFF AND VIVIAN HAVE DEVELOPED THEIR TALENTS, AND I'M NO SLOUCH MYSELF.
I SUPPOSE WE COULD TRY TO TREAT YOU IN ANOTHER DIMENSION WHERE HUMAN ILLNESS ISN'T A FACTOR.
YOU DON'T SOUND VERY SURE.
I'M NOT. IT COULD BE A HUGE RISK.

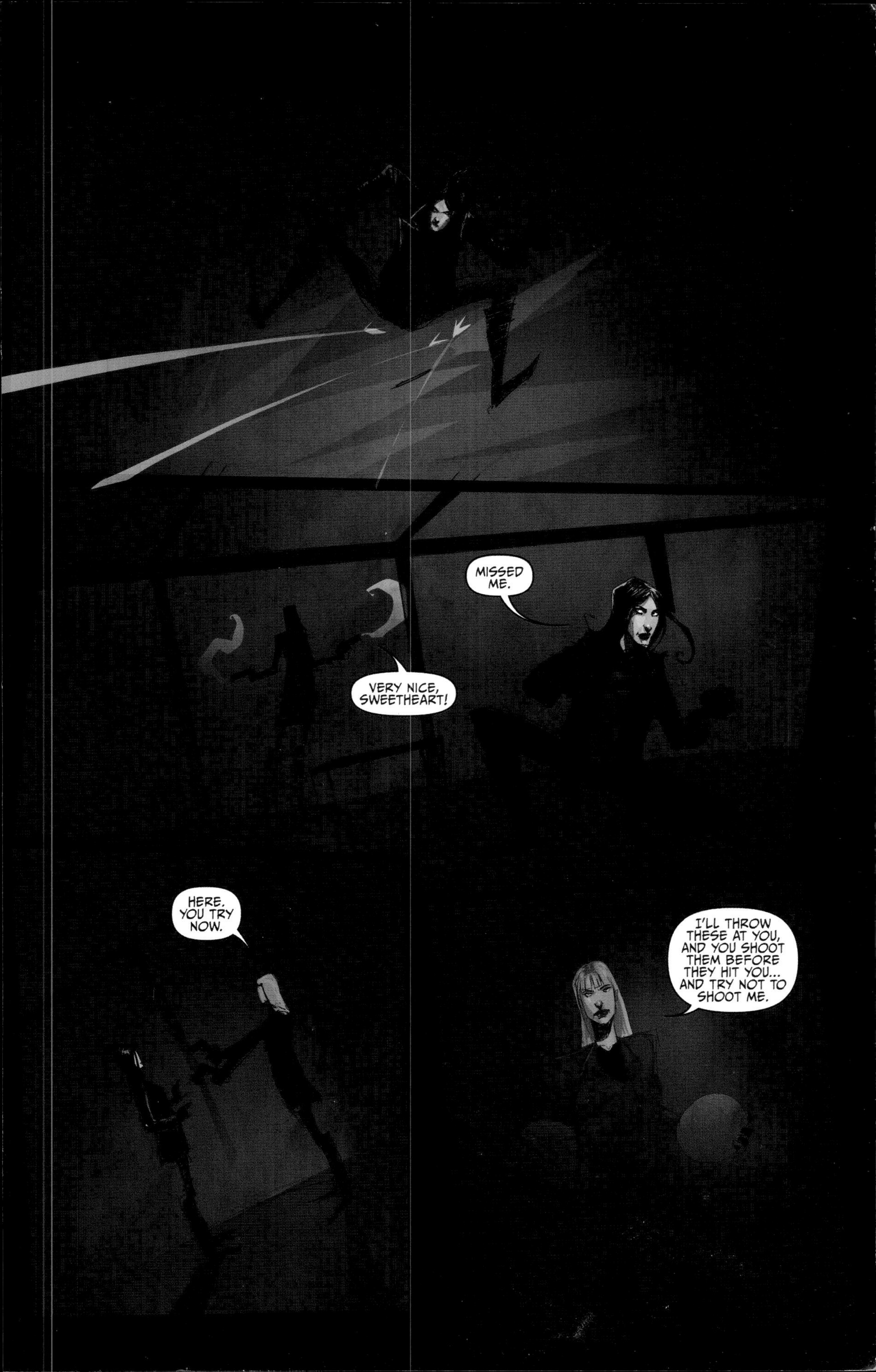
MISSED ME.
VERY NICE, SWEETHEART!
HERE. YOU TRY NOW.
I'LL THROW THESE AT YOU, AND YOU SHOOT THEM BEFORE THEY HIT YOU... AND TRY NOT TO SHOOT ME.

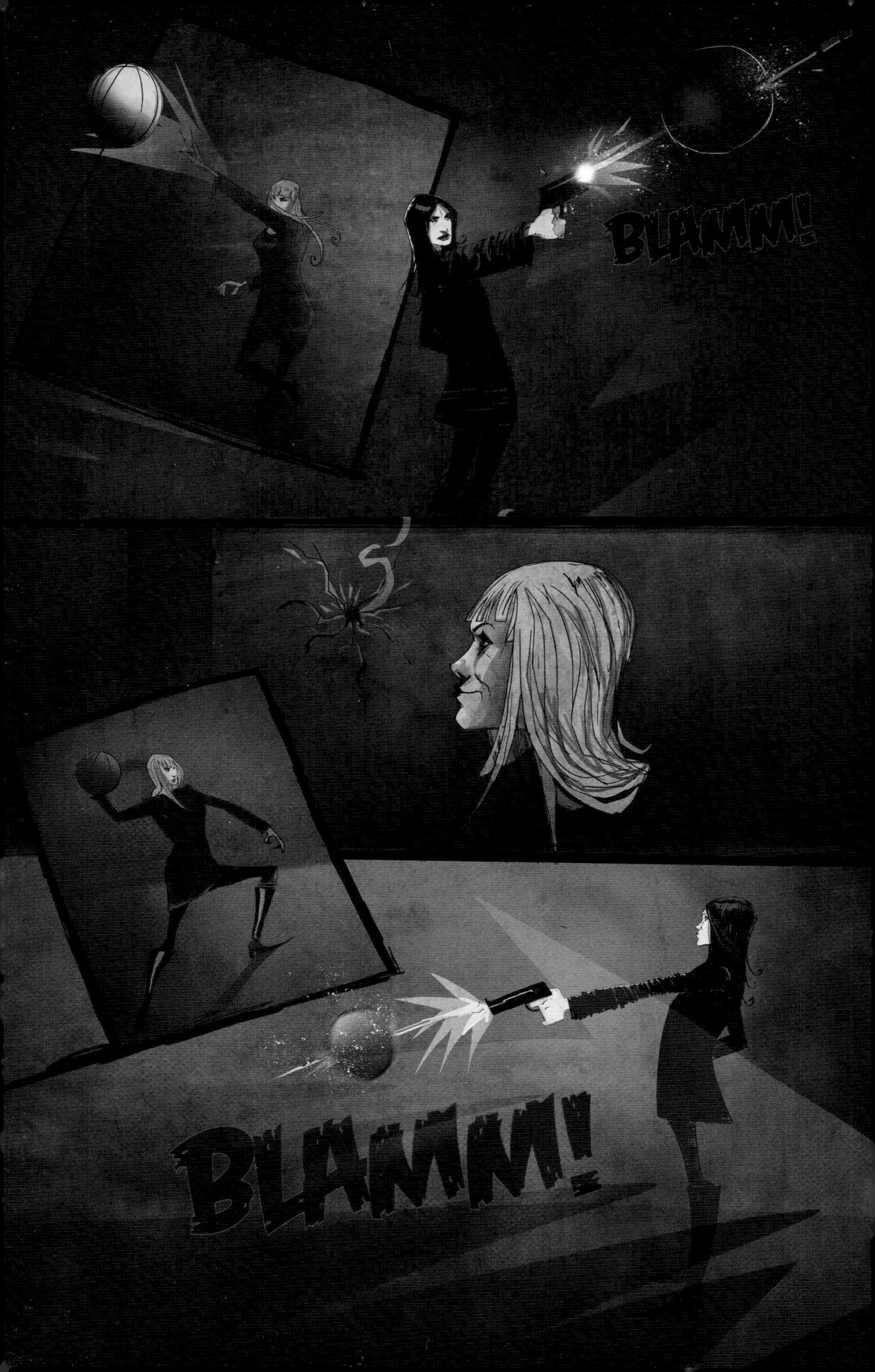
BLAMM!
BLAMM!

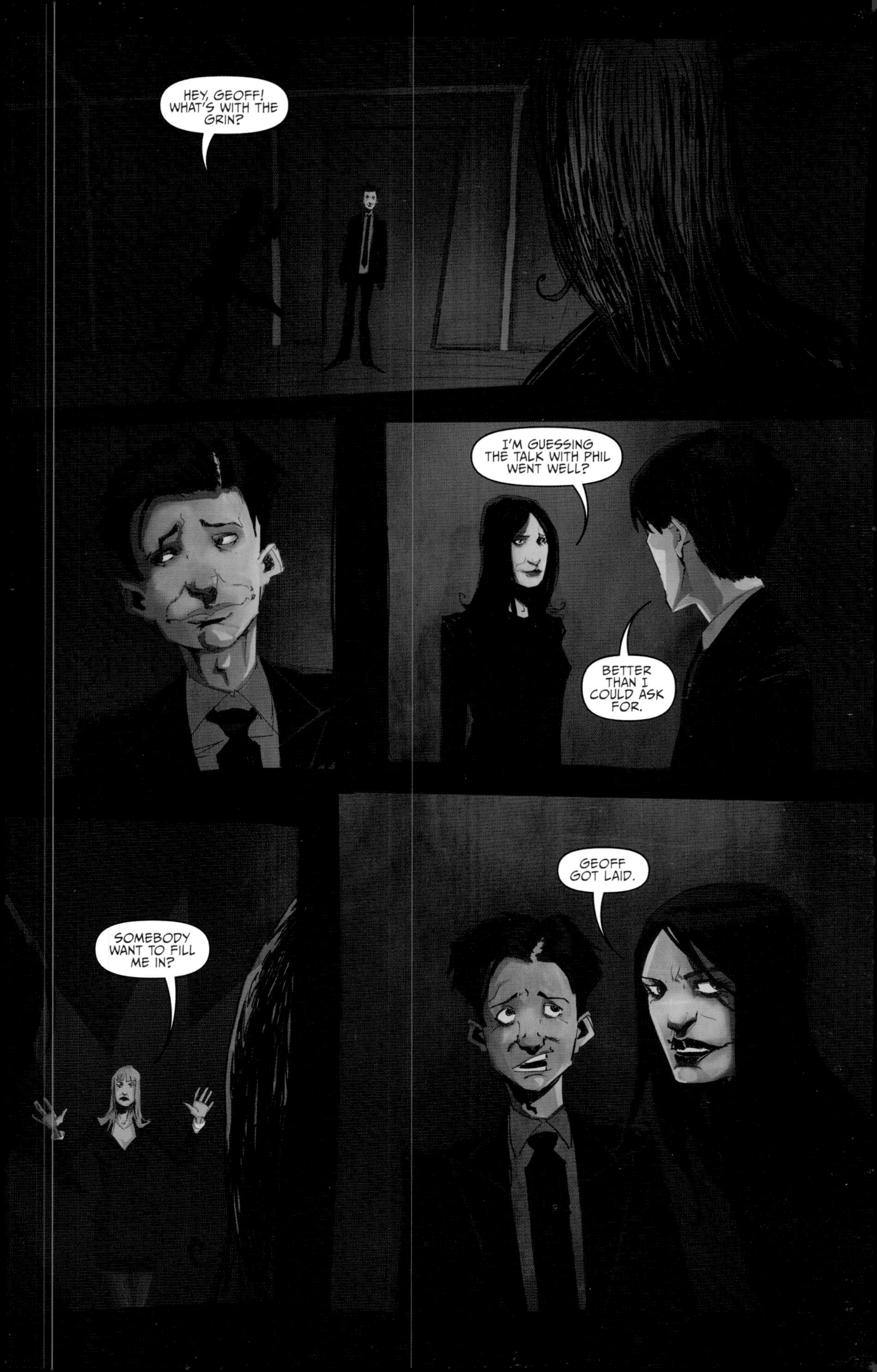
HEY, GEOFF! WHAT'S WITH THE GRIN?
I'M GUESSING THE TALK WITH PHIL WENT WELL?
BETTER THAN I COULD ASK FOR.
SOMEBODY WANT TO FILL ME IN?
GEOFF GOT LAID.

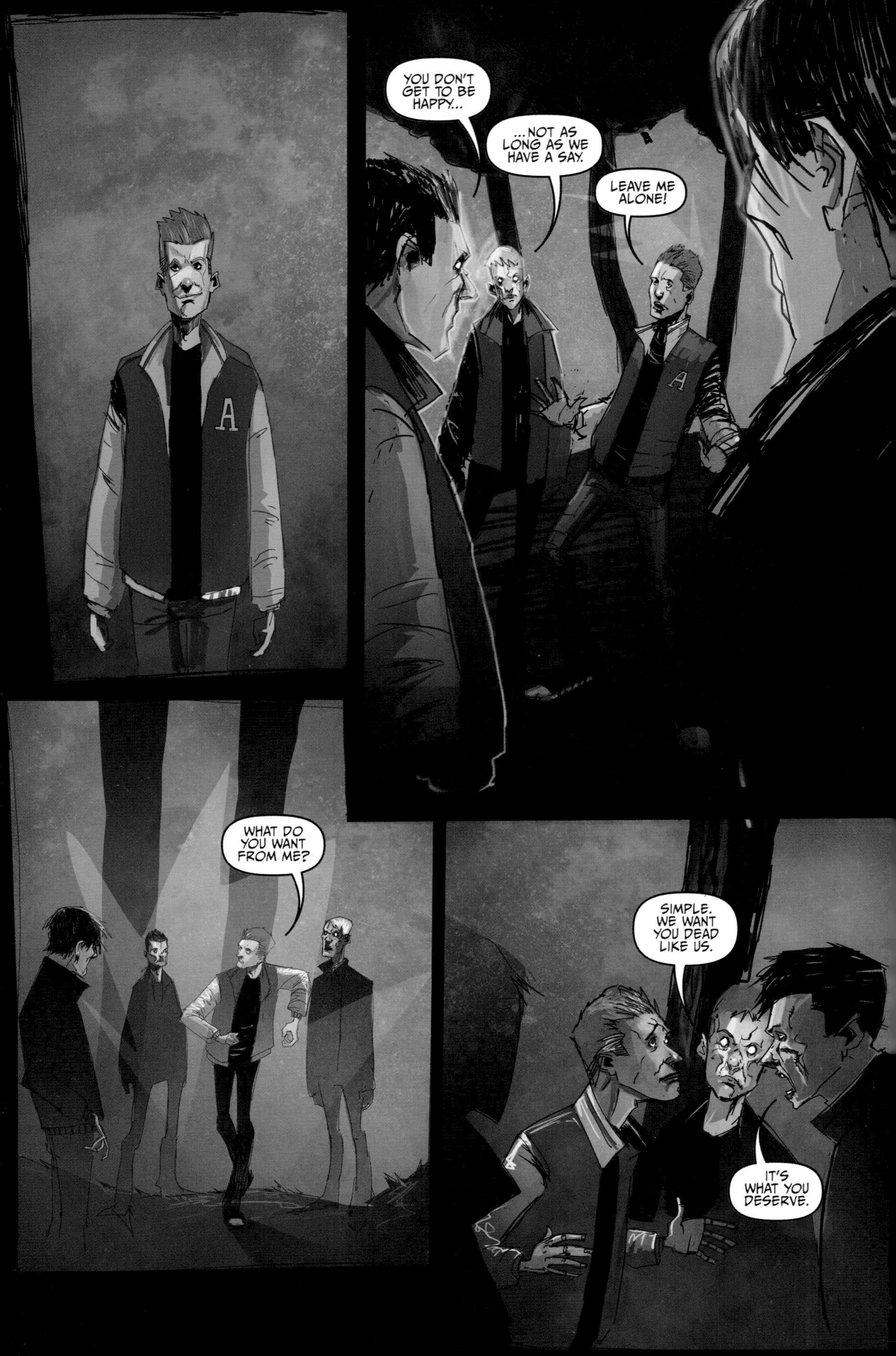
YOU DON'T GET TO BE HAPPY...
...NOT AS LONG AS WE HAVE A SAY.
LEAVE ME ALONE!
WHAT DO YOU WANT FROM ME?
SIMPLE. WE WANT YOU DEAD LIKE US.
IT'S WHAT YOU DESERVE.

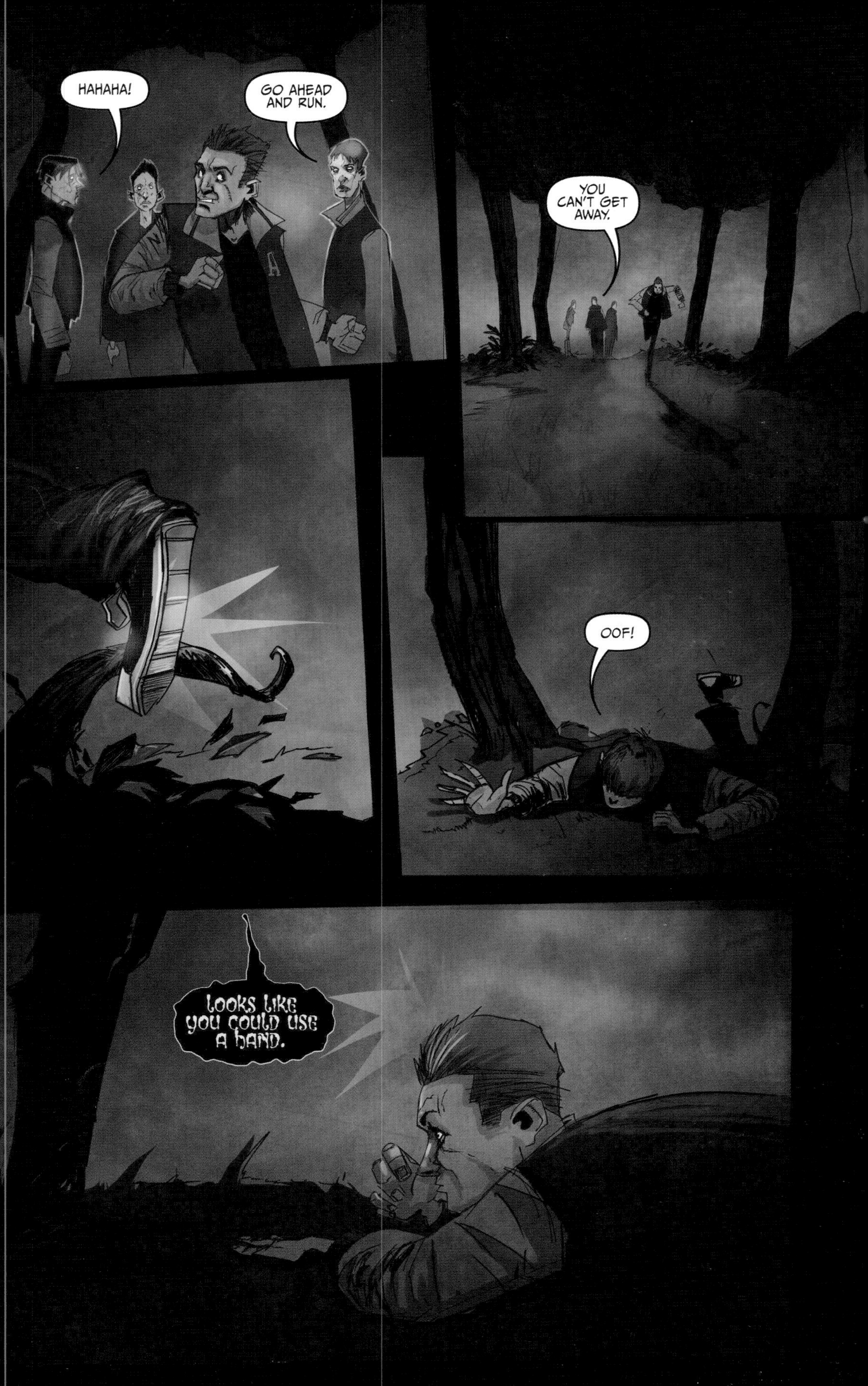
HAHAHA!
GO AHEAD AND RUN.
YOU CAN'T GET AWAY.
OOF!
LOOKS LIKE YOU COULD USE A HAND.

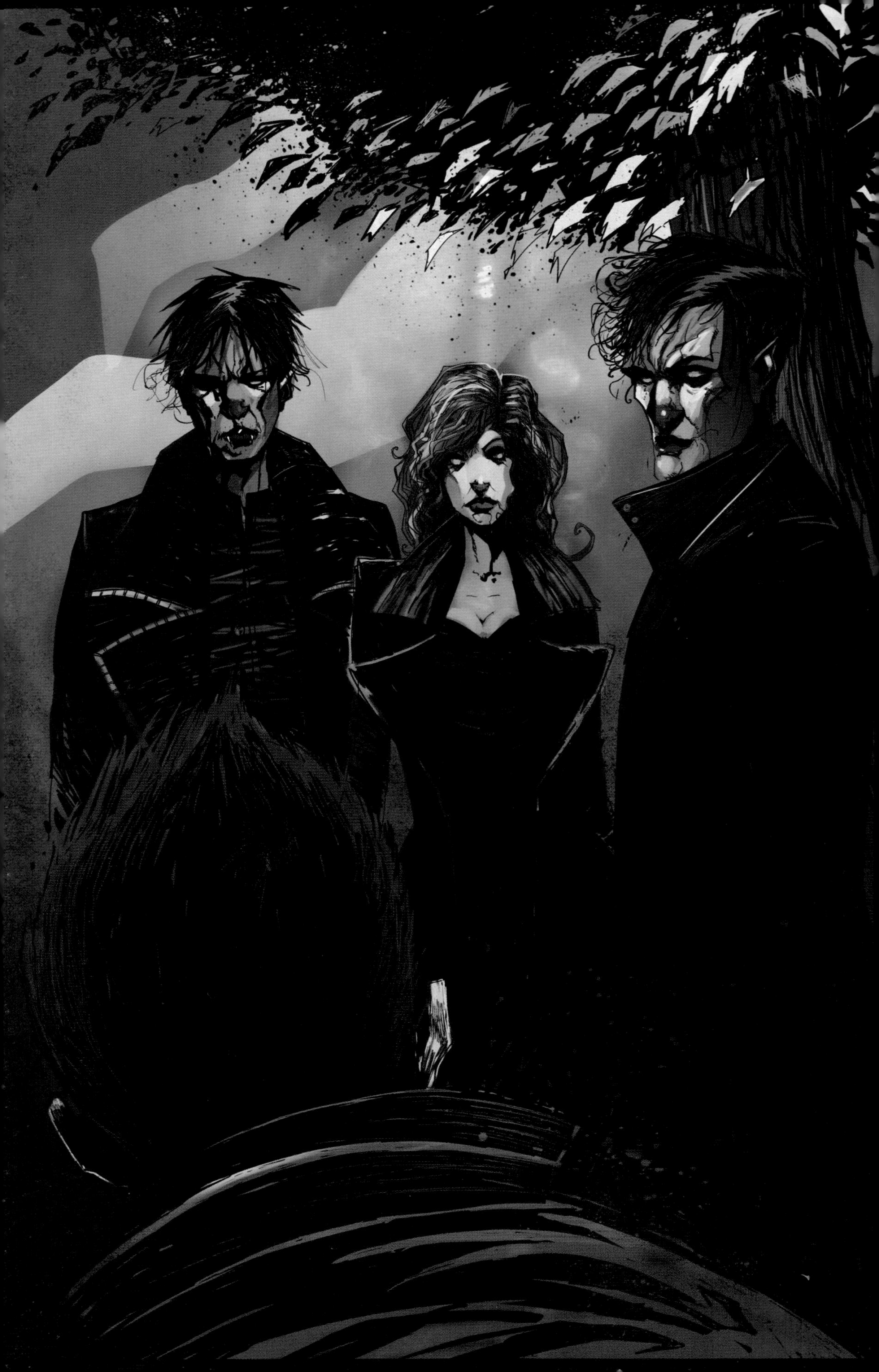

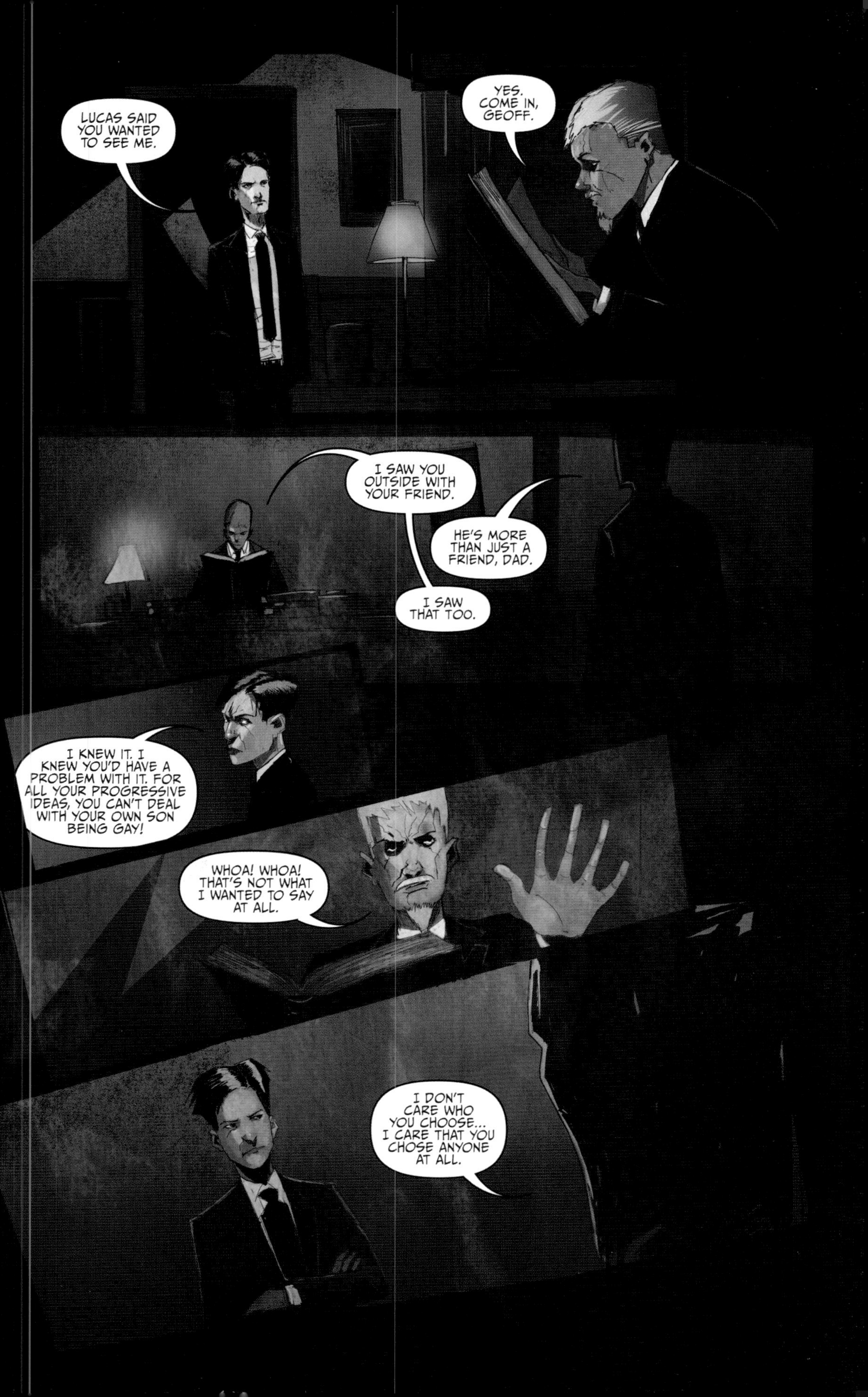
LUCAS SAID YOU WANTED TO SEE ME.
YES. COME IN, GEOFF.
I SAW YOU OUTSIDE WITH YOUR FRIEND.
HE'S MORE THAN JUST A FRIEND, DAD.
I SAW THAT TOO.
I KNEW IT. I KNEW YOU'D HAVE A PROBLEM WITH IT. FOR ALL YOUR PROGRESSIVE IDEAS, YOU CAN'T DEAL WITH YOUR OWN SON BEING GAY!
WHOA! WHOA! THAT'S NOT WHAT I WANTED TO SAY AT ALL.
I DON'T CARE WHO YOU CHOOSE... I CARE THAT YOU CHOSE ANYONE AT ALL.

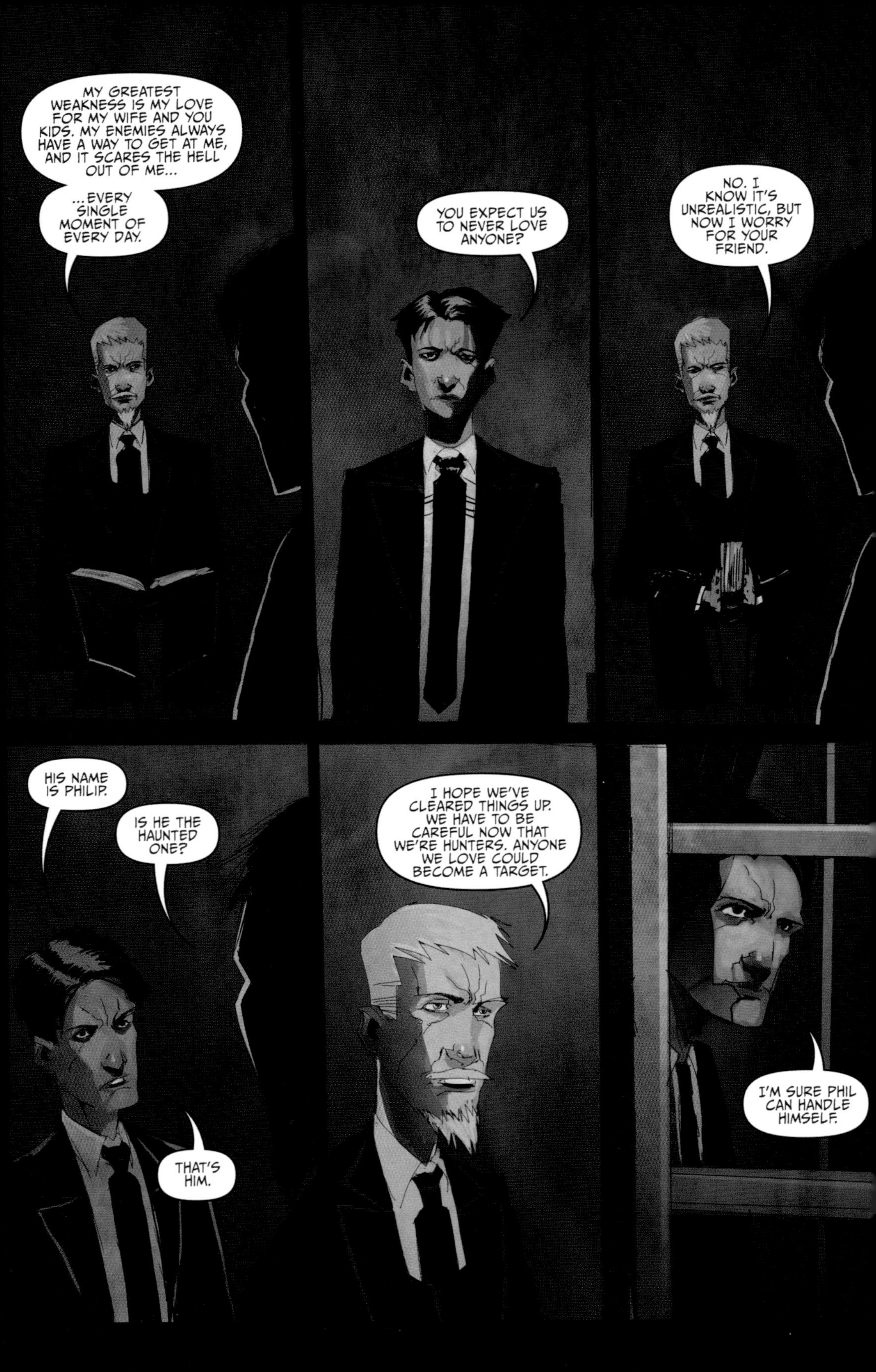
MY GREATEST WEAKNESS IS MY LOVE FOR MY WIFE AND YOU KIDS. MY ENEMIES ALWAYS HAVE A WAY TO GET AT ME, AND IT SCARES THE HELL OUT OF ME...
...EVERY SINGLE MOMENT OF EVERY DAY.
YOU EXPECT US TO NEVER LOVE ANYONE?
NO. I KNOW IT'S UNREALISTIC, BUT NOW I WORRY FOR YOUR FRIEND.
HIS NAME IS PHILIP.
IS HE THE HAUNTED ONE?
THAT'S HIM.
I HOPE WE'VE CLEARED THINGS UP. WE HAVE TO BE CAREFUL NOW THAT WE'RE HUNTERS. ANYONE WE LOVE COULD BECOME A TARGET.
I'M SURE PHIL CAN HANDLE HIMSELF.

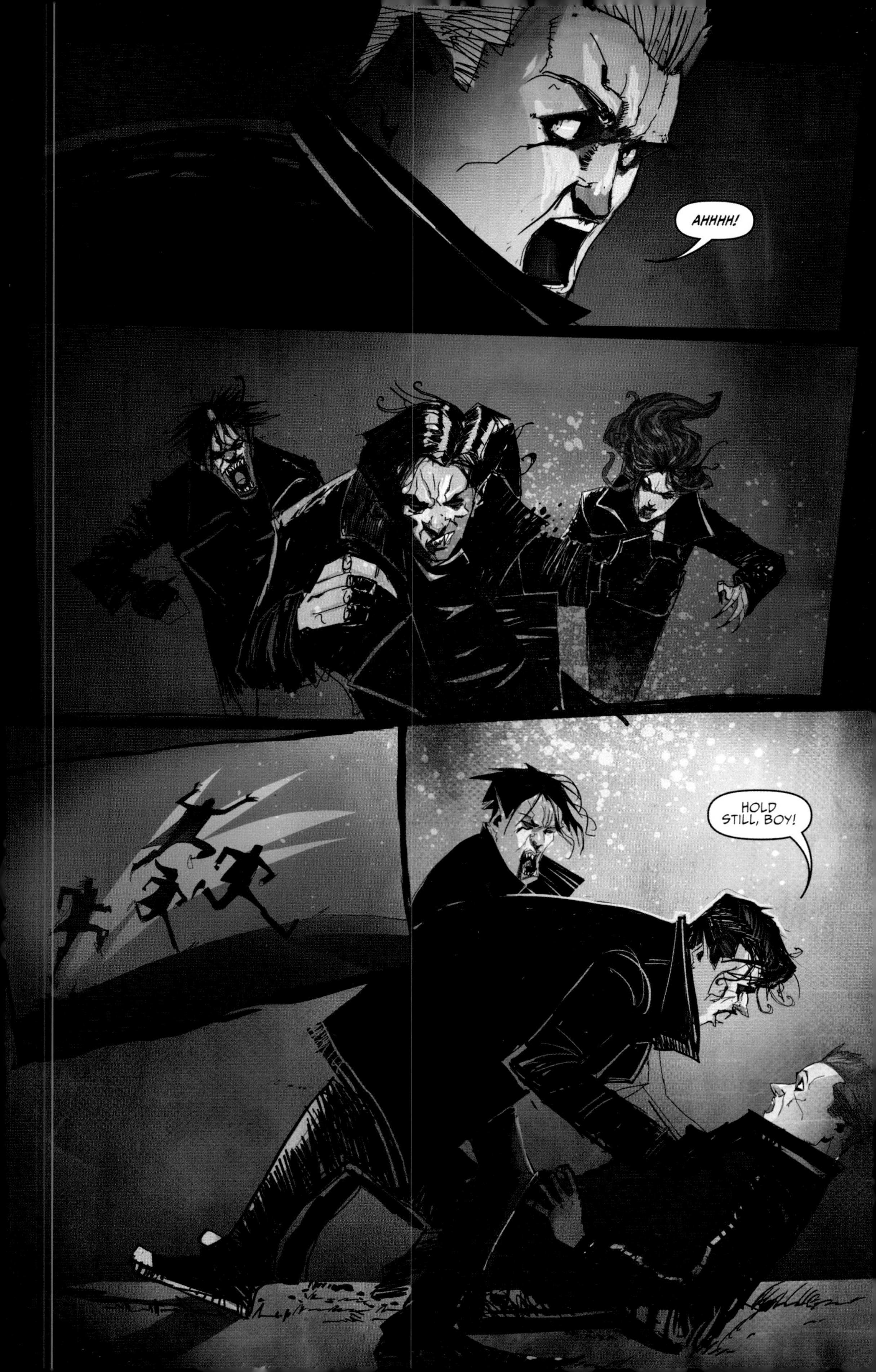
AHHHH!
HOLD STILL, BOY!

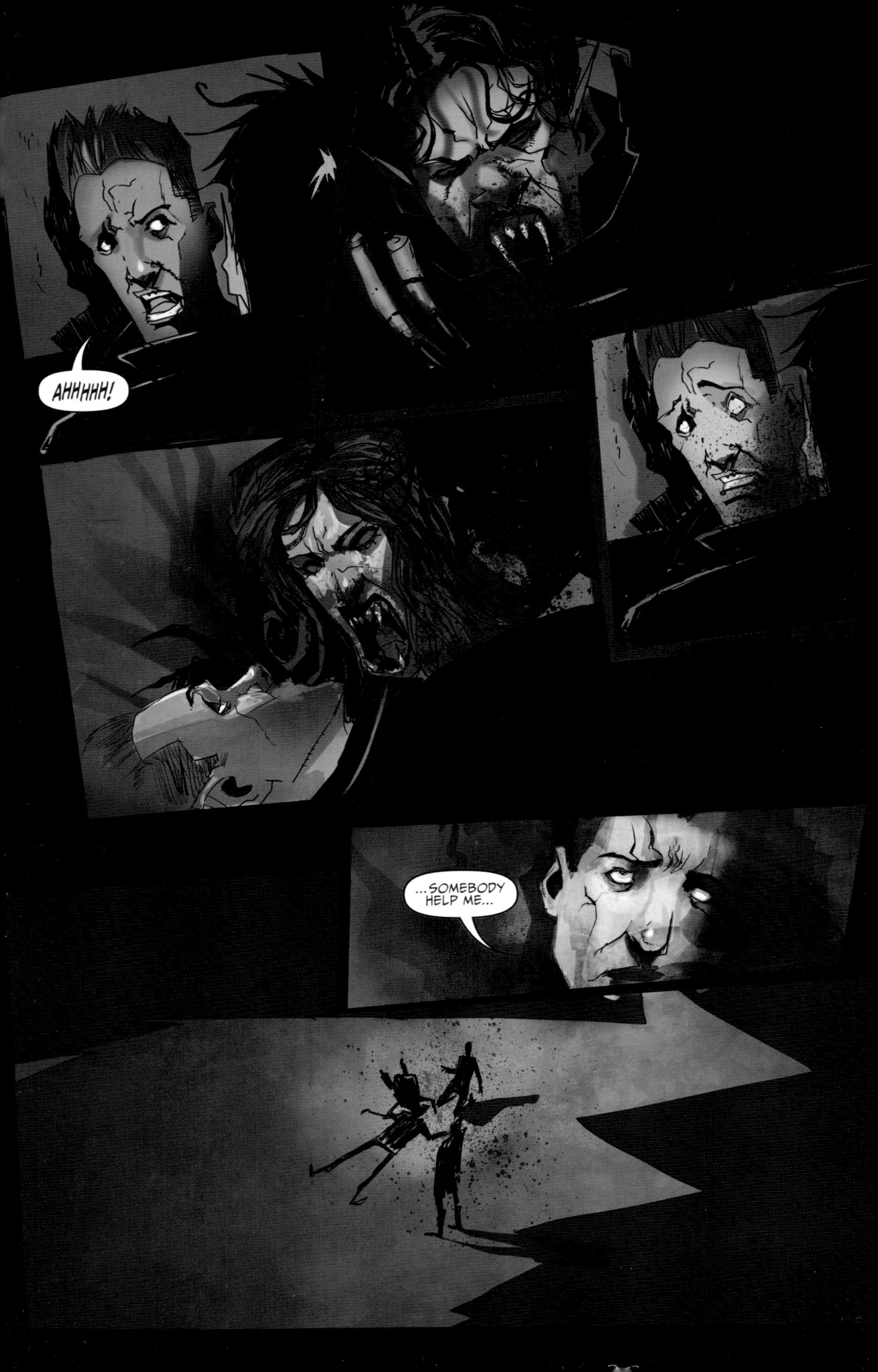
AHHHHH!
...SOMEBODY HELP ME...

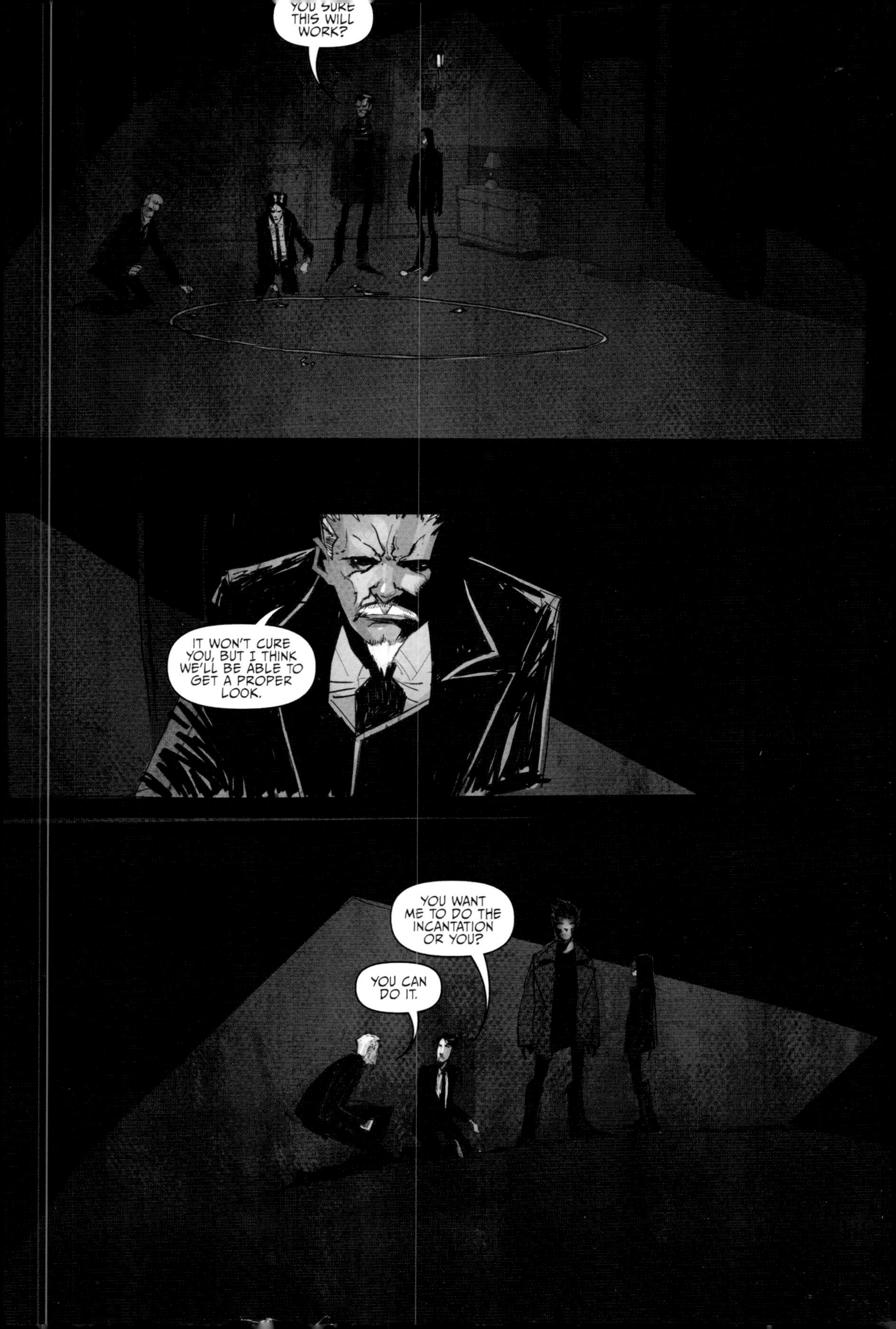
YOU SURE THIS WILL WORK?
IT WON'T CURE YOU, BUT I THINK WE'LL BE ABLE TO GET A PROPER LOOK.
YOU WANT ME TO DO THE INCANTATION OR YOU?
YOU CAN DO IT.

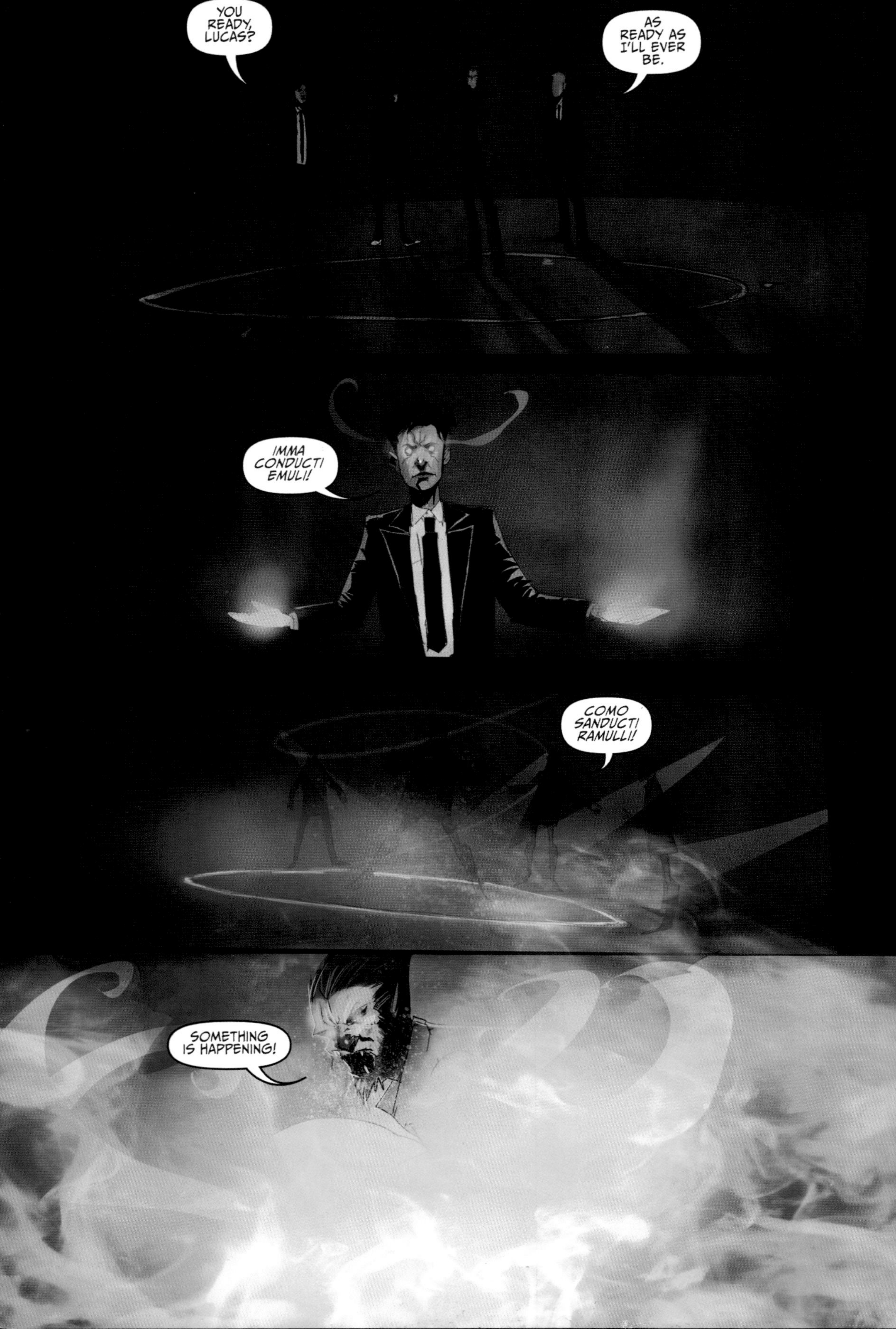
YOU READY, LUCAS?
AS READY AS I'LL EVER BE.
IMMA CONDUCTI EMULI!
COMO SANDUCTI RAMULLI!
SOMETHING IS HAPPENING!

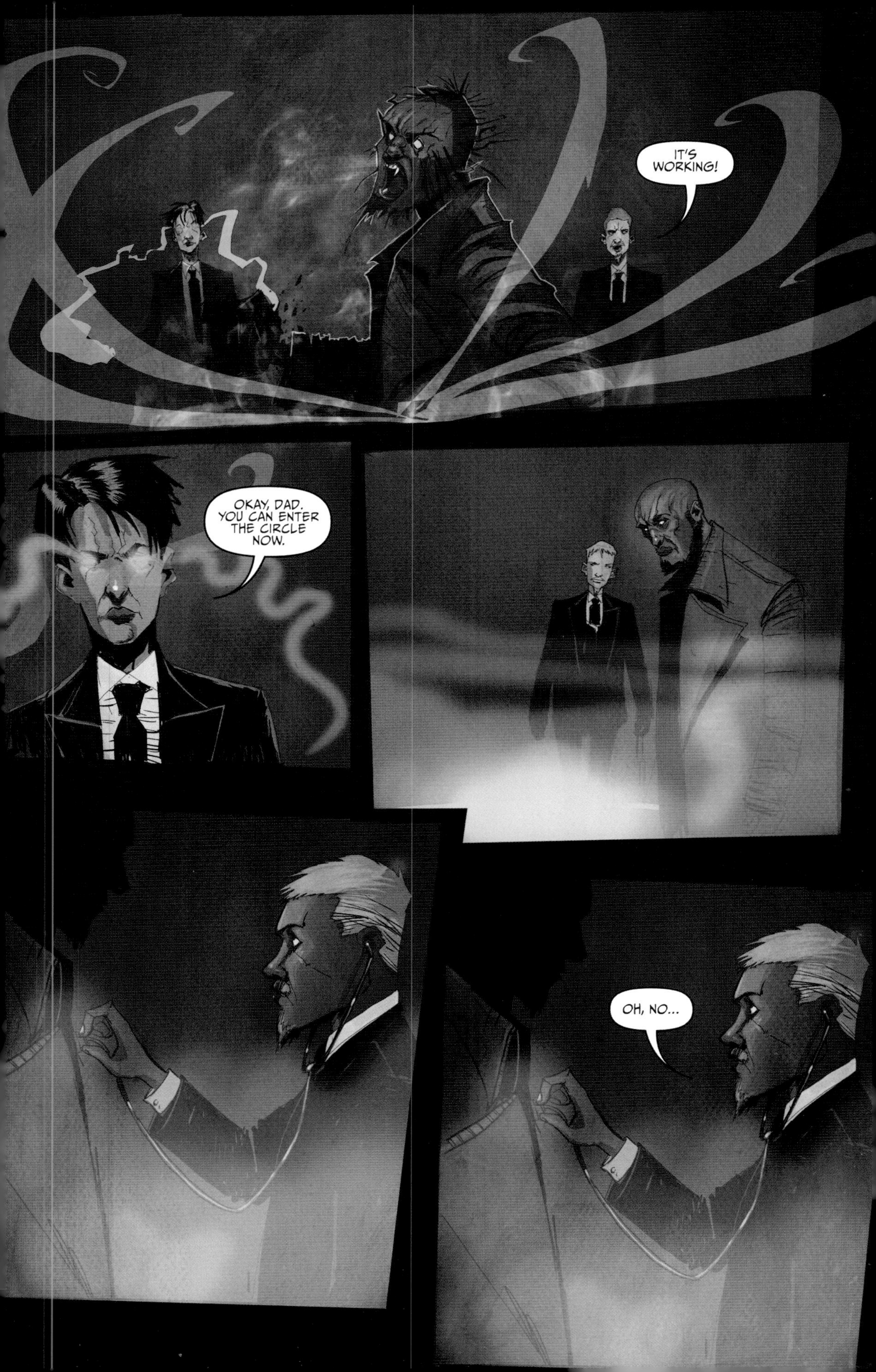
IT'S WORKING!
OKAY, DAD. YOU CAN ENTER THE CIRCLE NOW.
OH, NO...

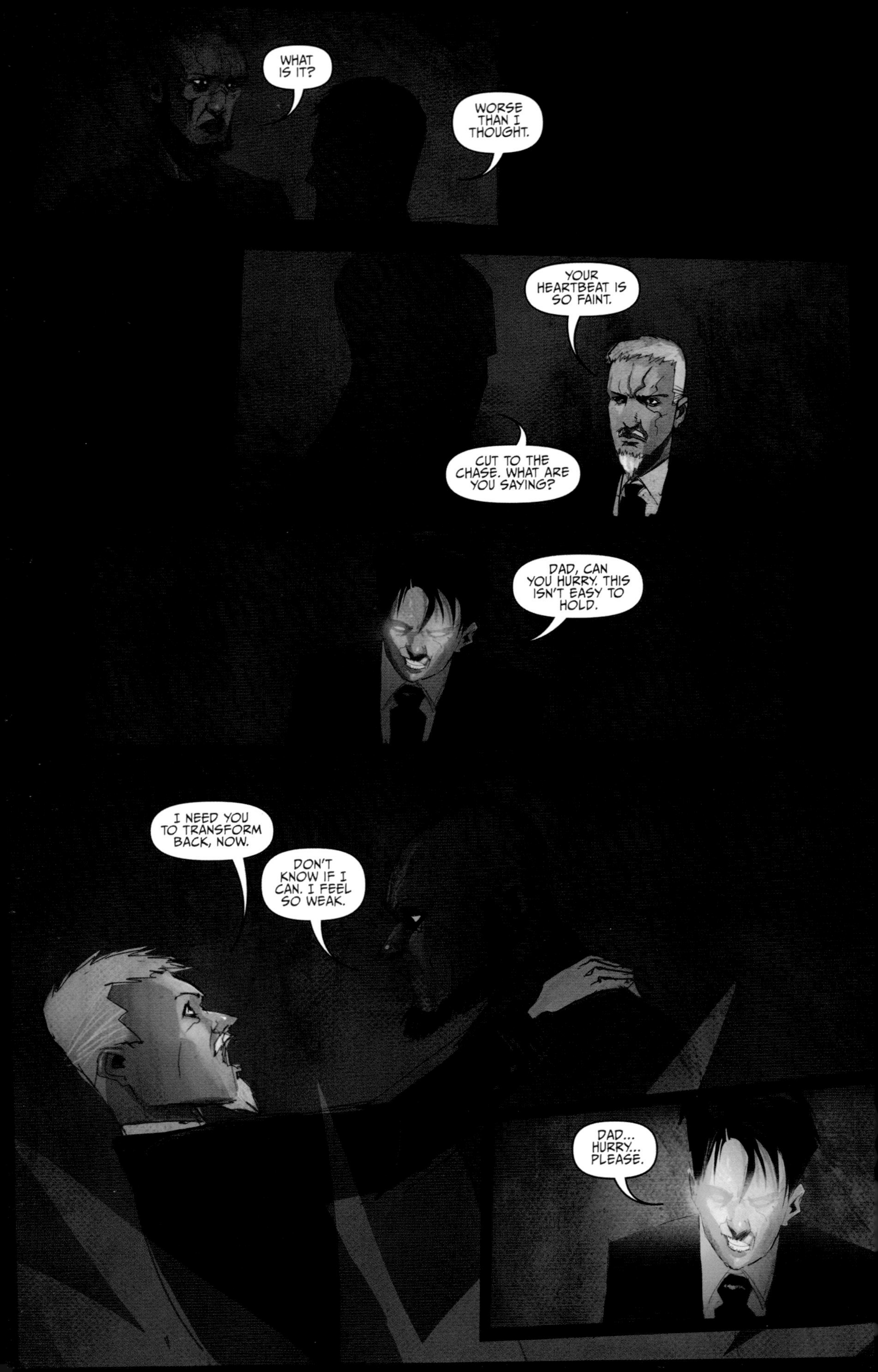
WHAT IS IT?
WORSE THAN I THOUGHT.
YOUR HEARTBEAT IS SO FAINT.
CUT TO THE CHASE. WHAT ARE YOU SAYING?
DAD, CAN YOU HURRY. THIS ISN'T EASY TO HOLD.
I NEED YOU TO TRANSFORM BACK, NOW.
DON'T KNOW IF I CAN. I FEEL SO WEAK.
DAD... HURRY... PLEASE.

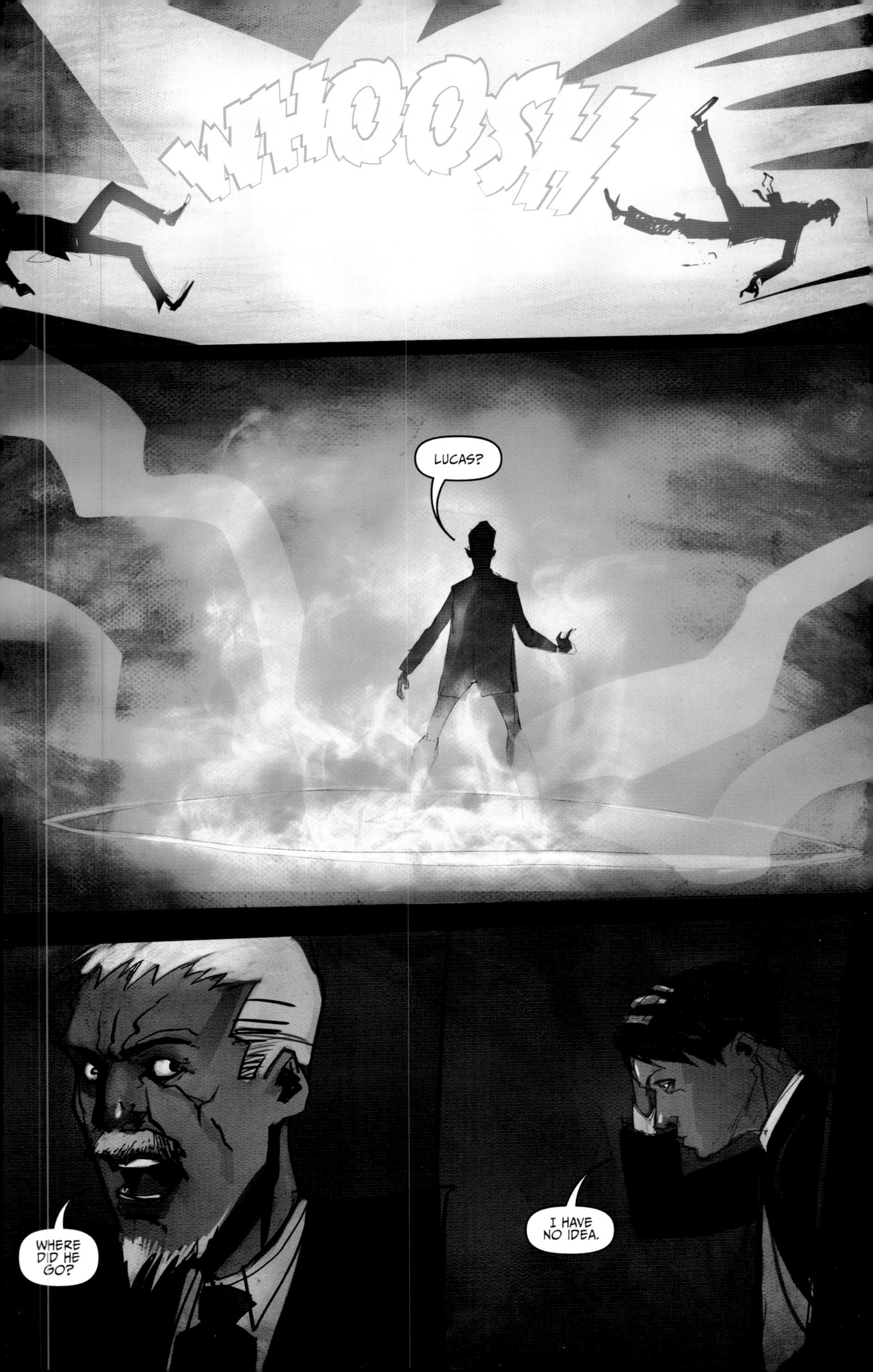
WHOOSH
LUCAS?
WHERE DID HE GO?
I HAVE NO IDEA.

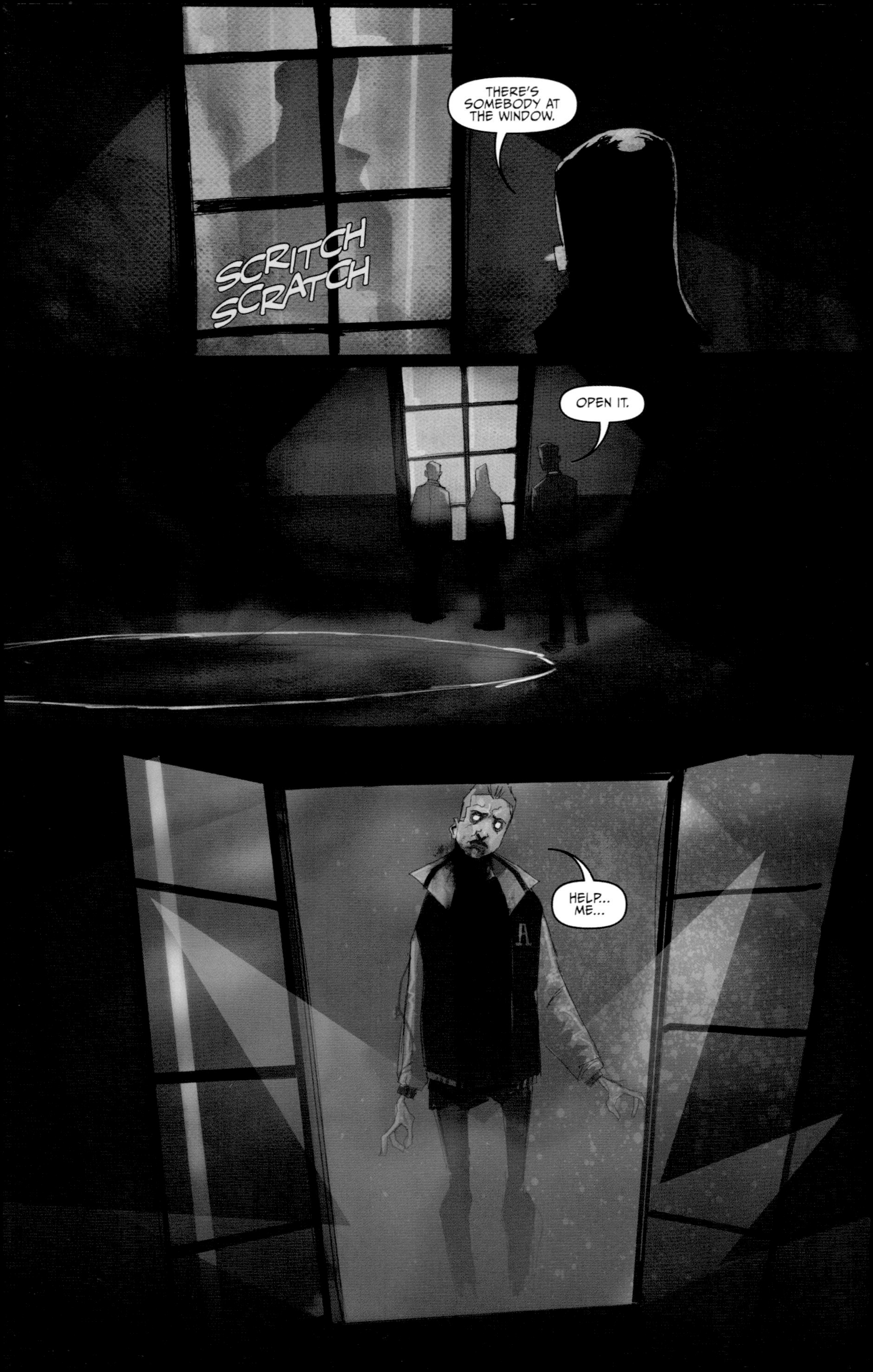
THERE'S SOMEBODY AT THE WINDOW.
SCRITCH SCRATCH
OPEN IT.
HELP... ME...

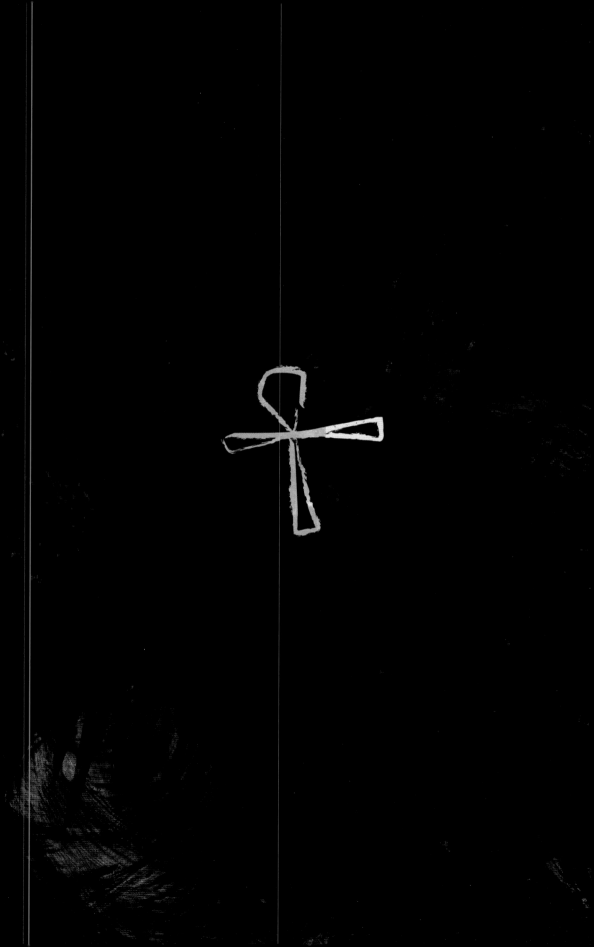

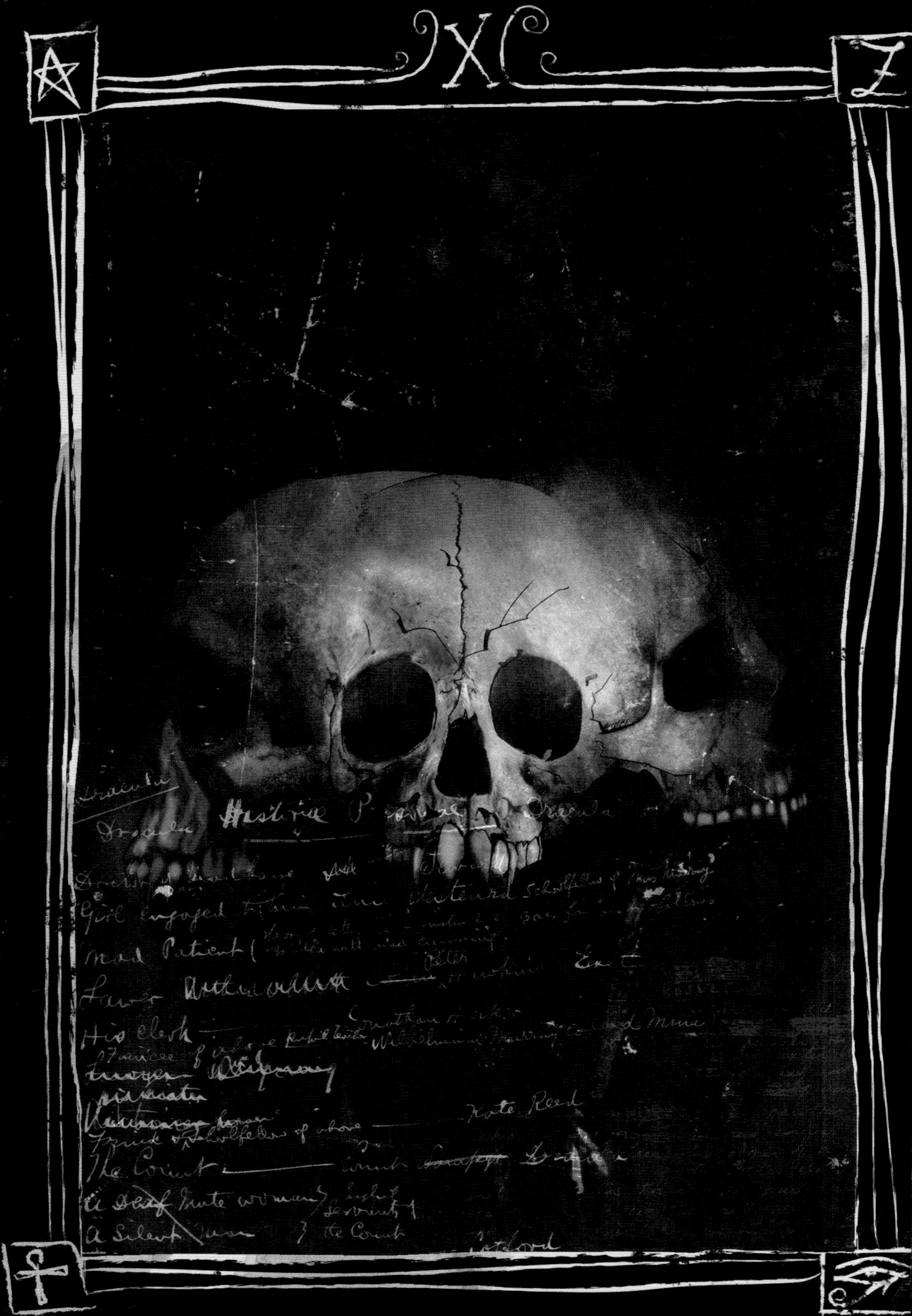

X

Dracula

Dr. Seward   Historia Personae? Dracula

Girl engaged to him   ...   ... schoolfellows of Miss ...
Mad Patient (...   ...   ...
Lawyer ...   Peter   ... Esq.
His clerk   Jonathan ...   Wilhelmina Murray called Mina
Fiancée of above   ...
lawyer ...
...
...   Kate Reed
Frank ... schoolfellows of above
The Count   ...
A Deaf Mute woman   ...
A Silent Man   of the Count   ...

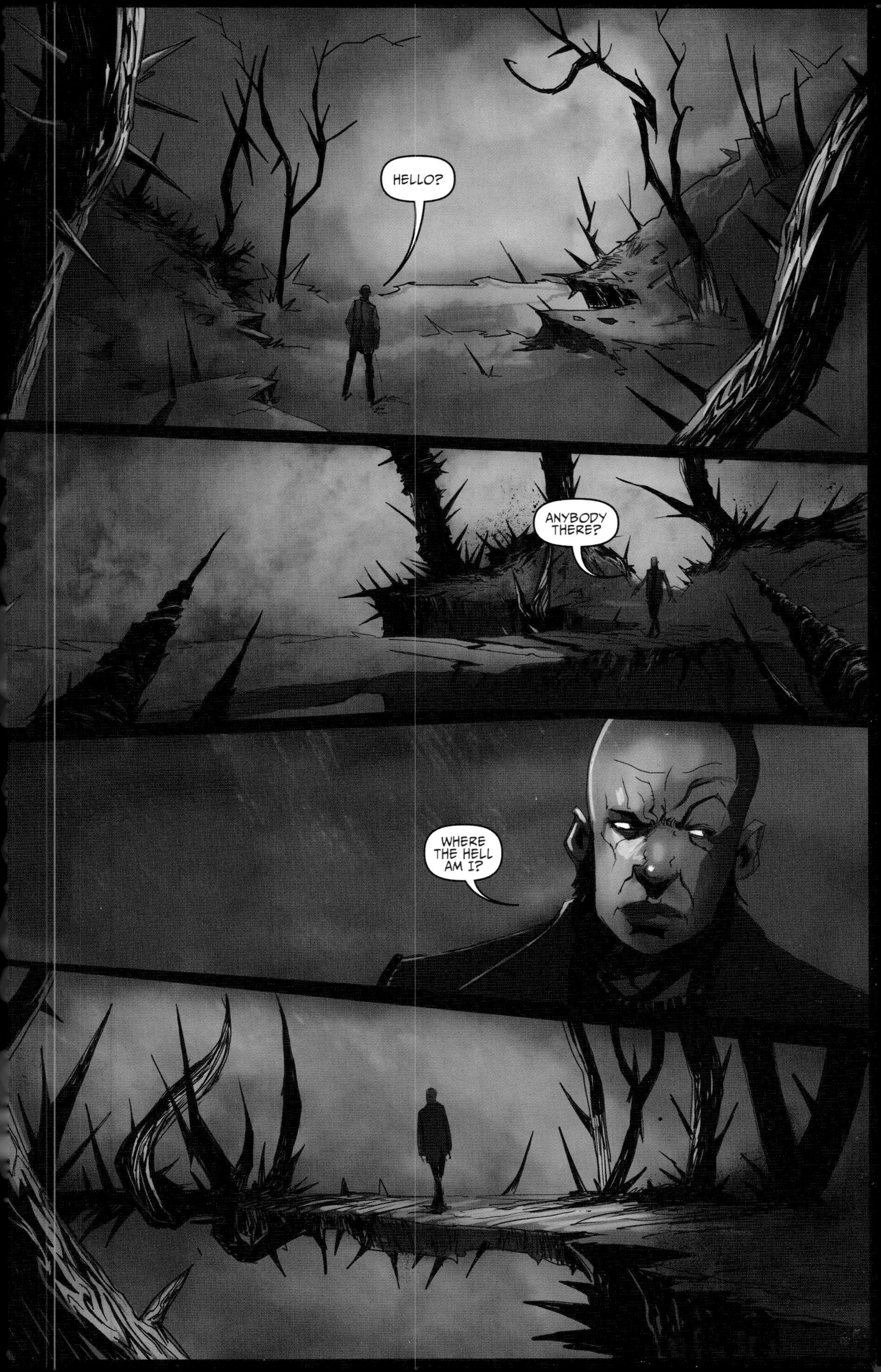
HELLO?
ANYBODY THERE?
WHERE THE HELL AM I?

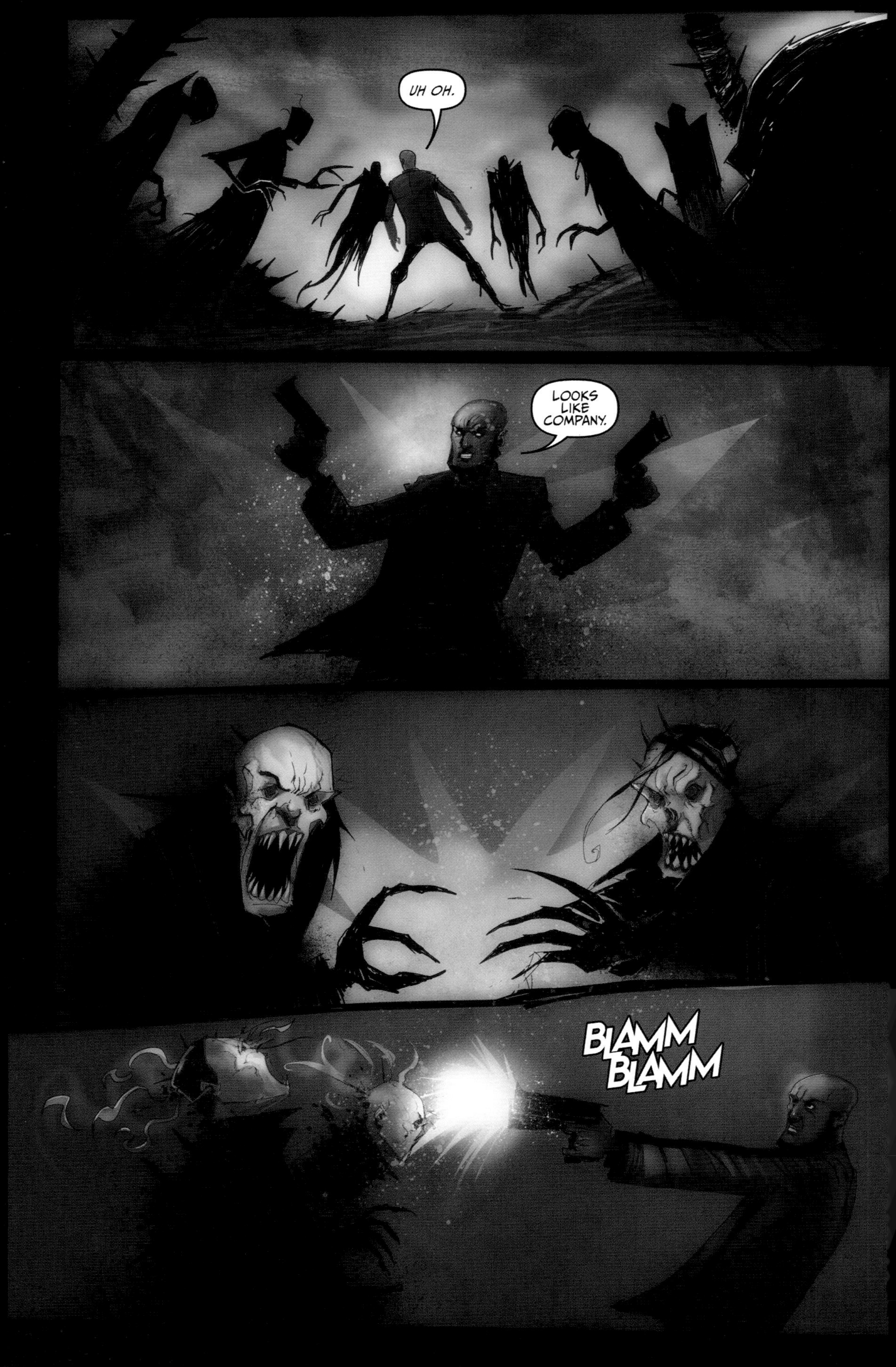
UH OH.
LOOKS LIKE COMPANY.
BLAMM BLAMM

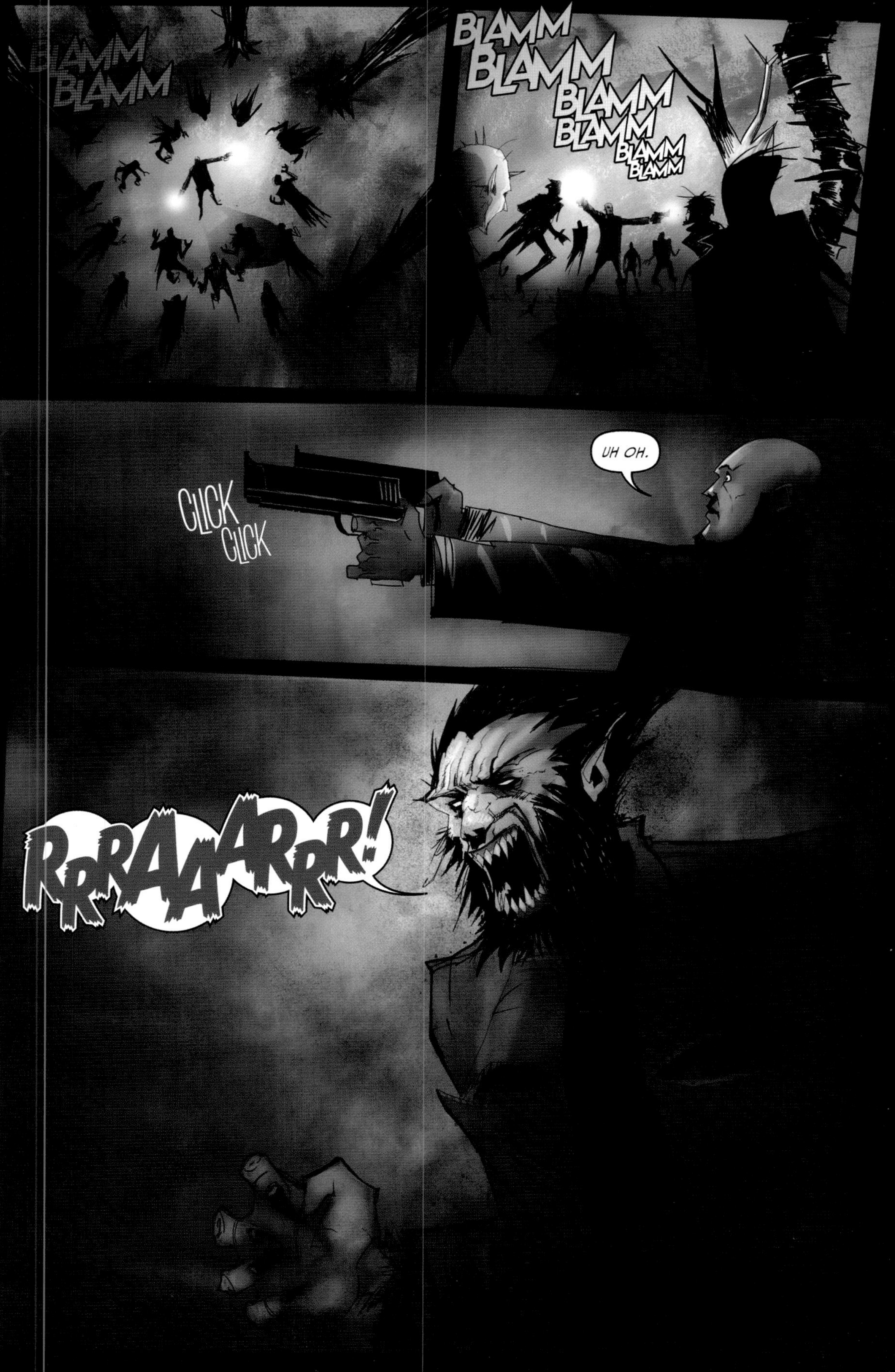
BLAMM
BLAMM
BLAMM
BLAMM
BLAMM
BLAMM
BLAMM
BLAMM
CLICK
CLICK
UH OH.
RRRAAARRR!

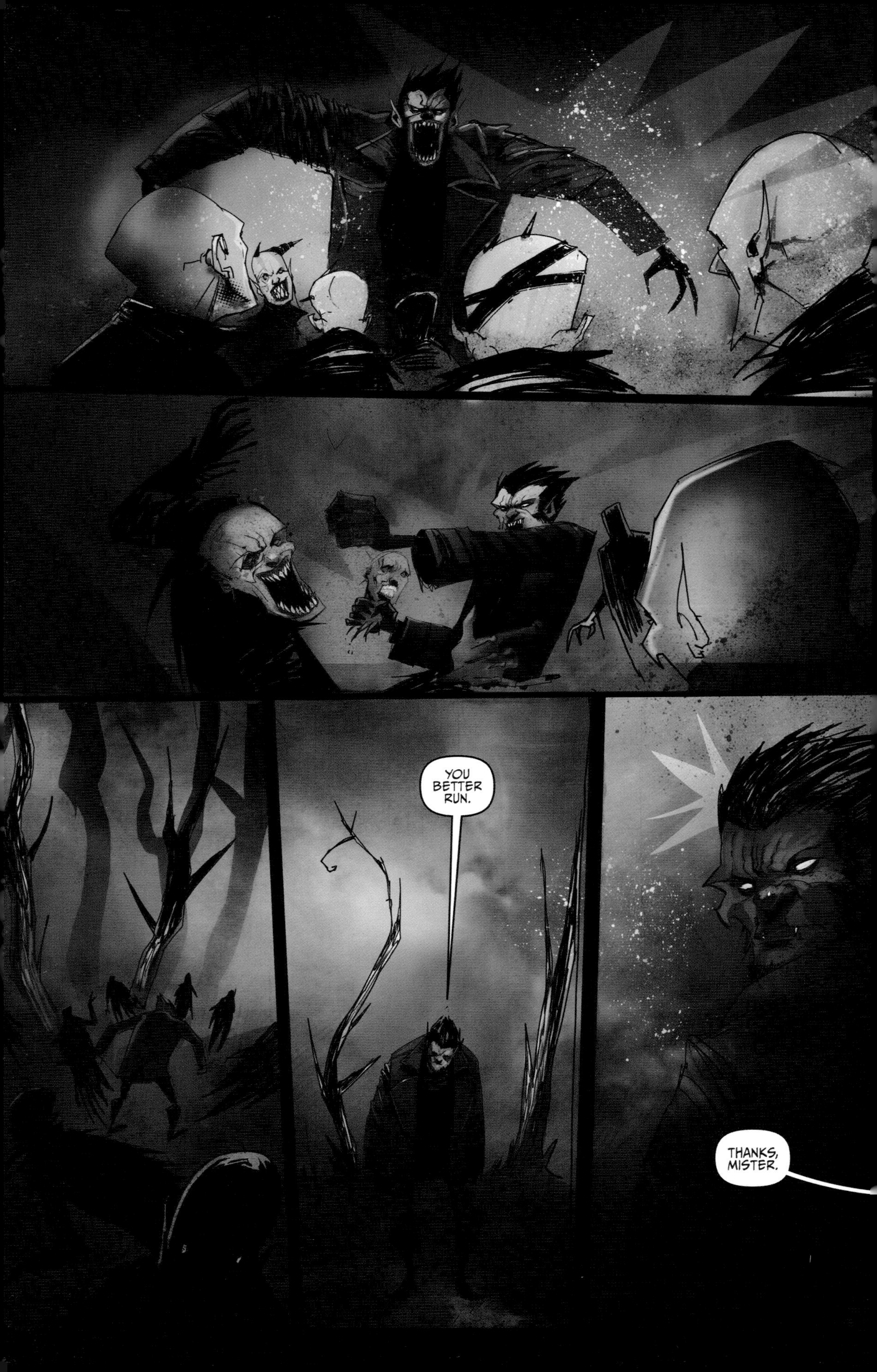
YOU BETTER RUN.
THANKS, MISTER.

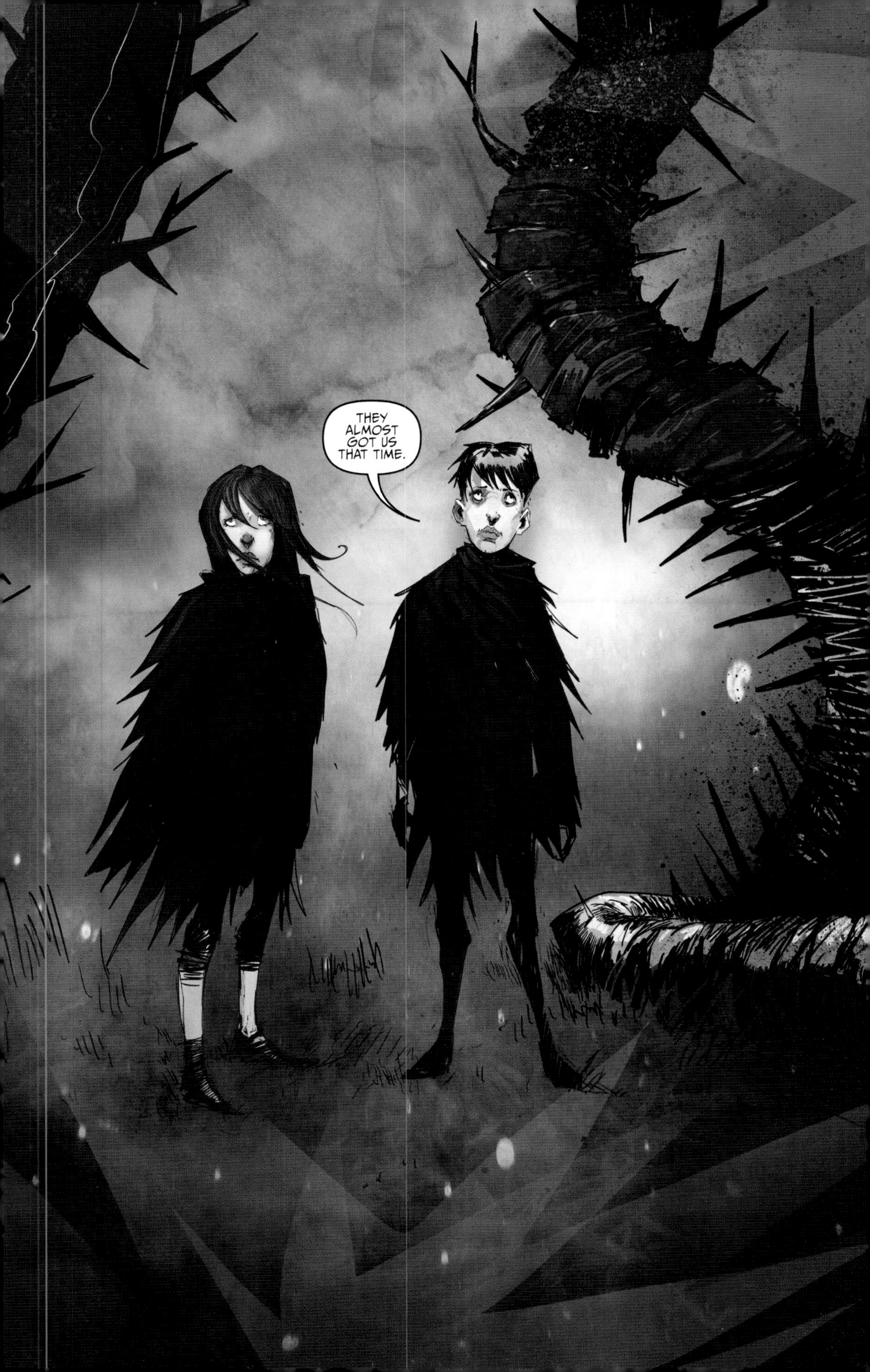
THEY ALMOST GOT US THAT TIME.

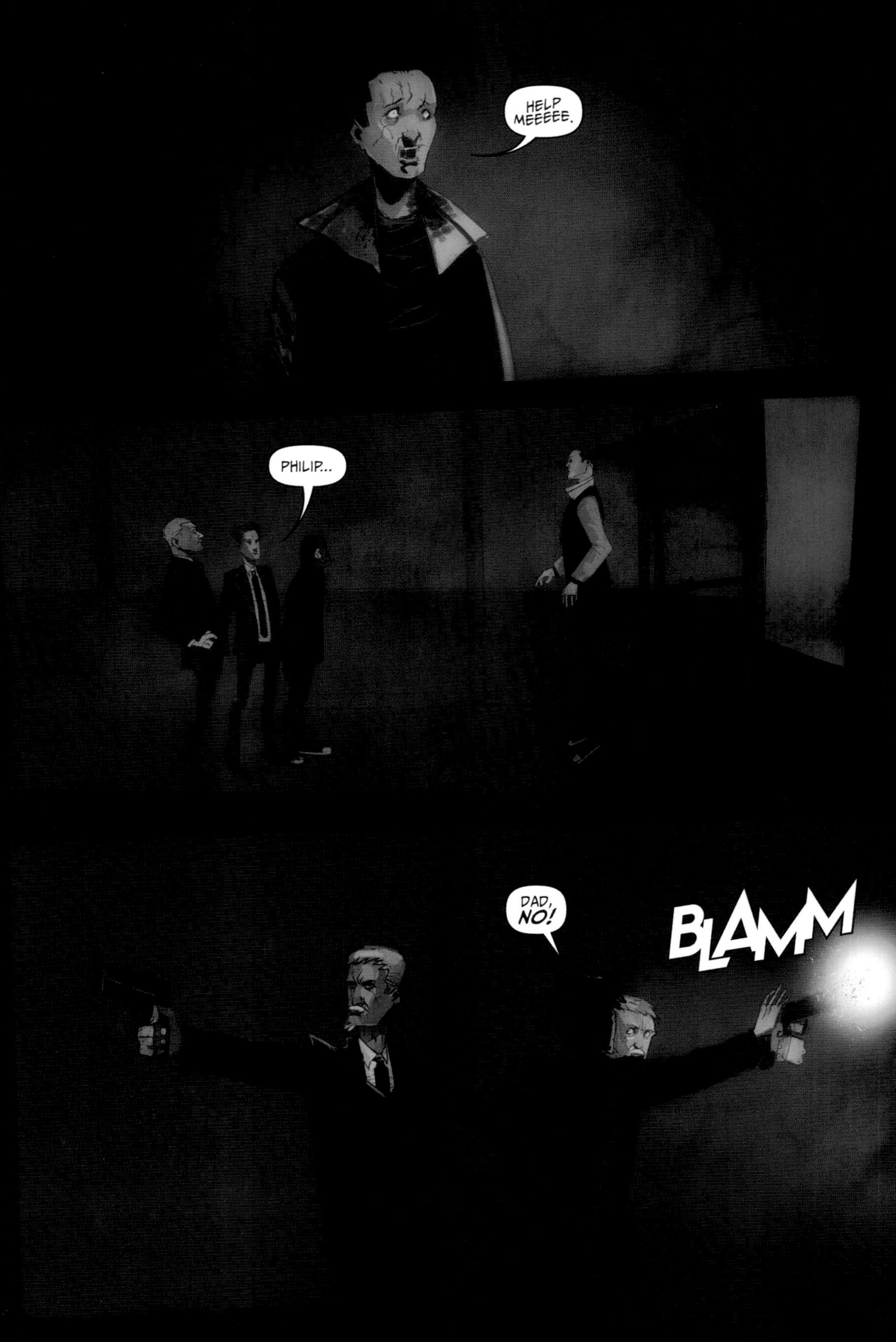
HELP MEEEEE.
PHILIP...
DAD, NO!
BLAMM

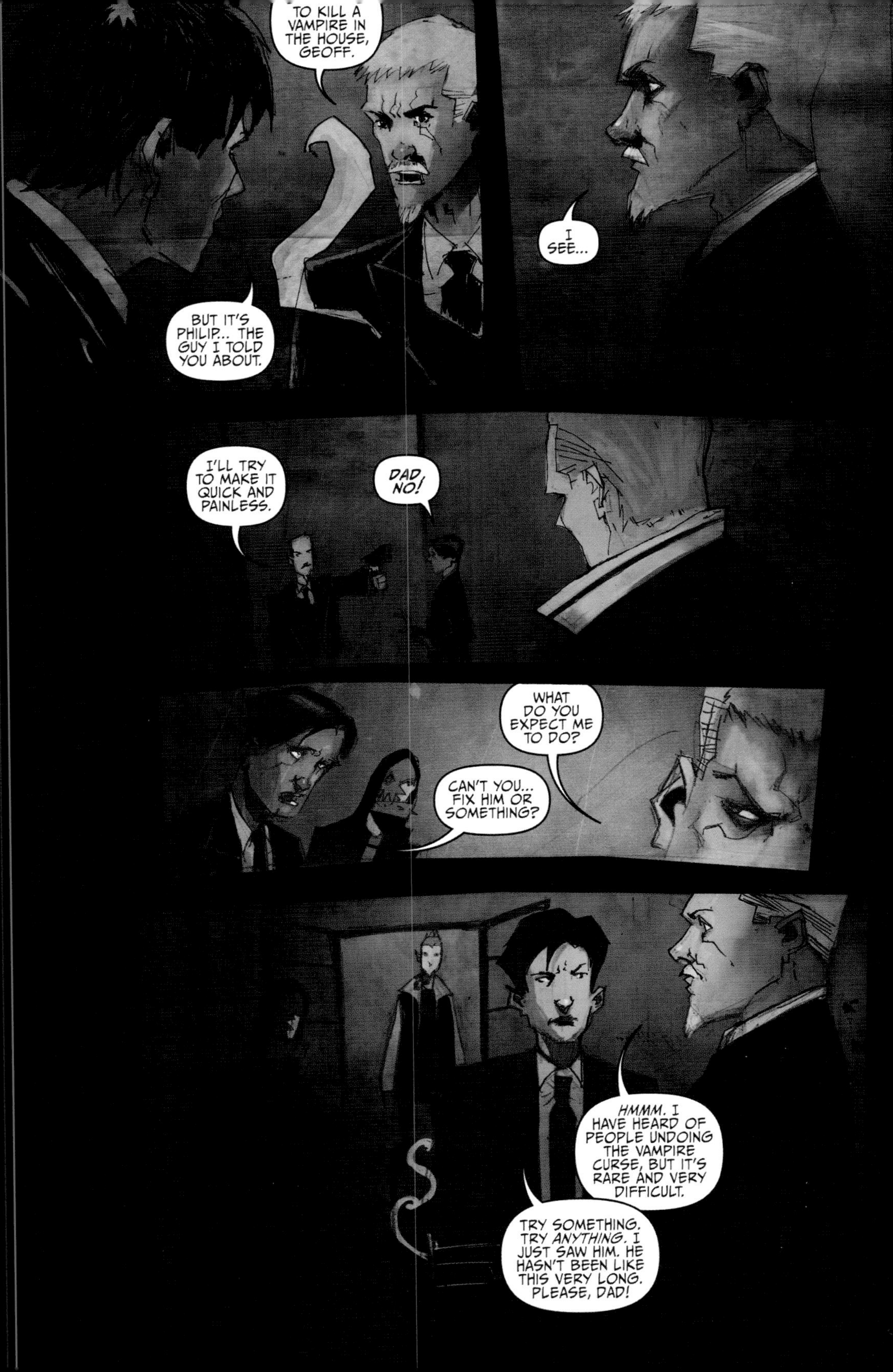
TO KILL A VAMPIRE IN THE HOUSE, GEOFF.
BUT IT'S PHILIP... THE GUY I TOLD YOU ABOUT.
I SEE...
I'LL TRY TO MAKE IT QUICK AND PAINLESS.
DAD, NO!
WHAT DO YOU EXPECT ME TO DO?
CAN'T YOU... FIX HIM OR SOMETHING?
HMMM. I HAVE HEARD OF PEOPLE UNDOING THE VAMPIRE CURSE, BUT IT'S RARE AND VERY DIFFICULT.
TRY SOMETHING. TRY *ANYTHING.* I JUST SAW HIM. HE HASN'T BEEN LIKE THIS VERY LONG. PLEASE, DAD!

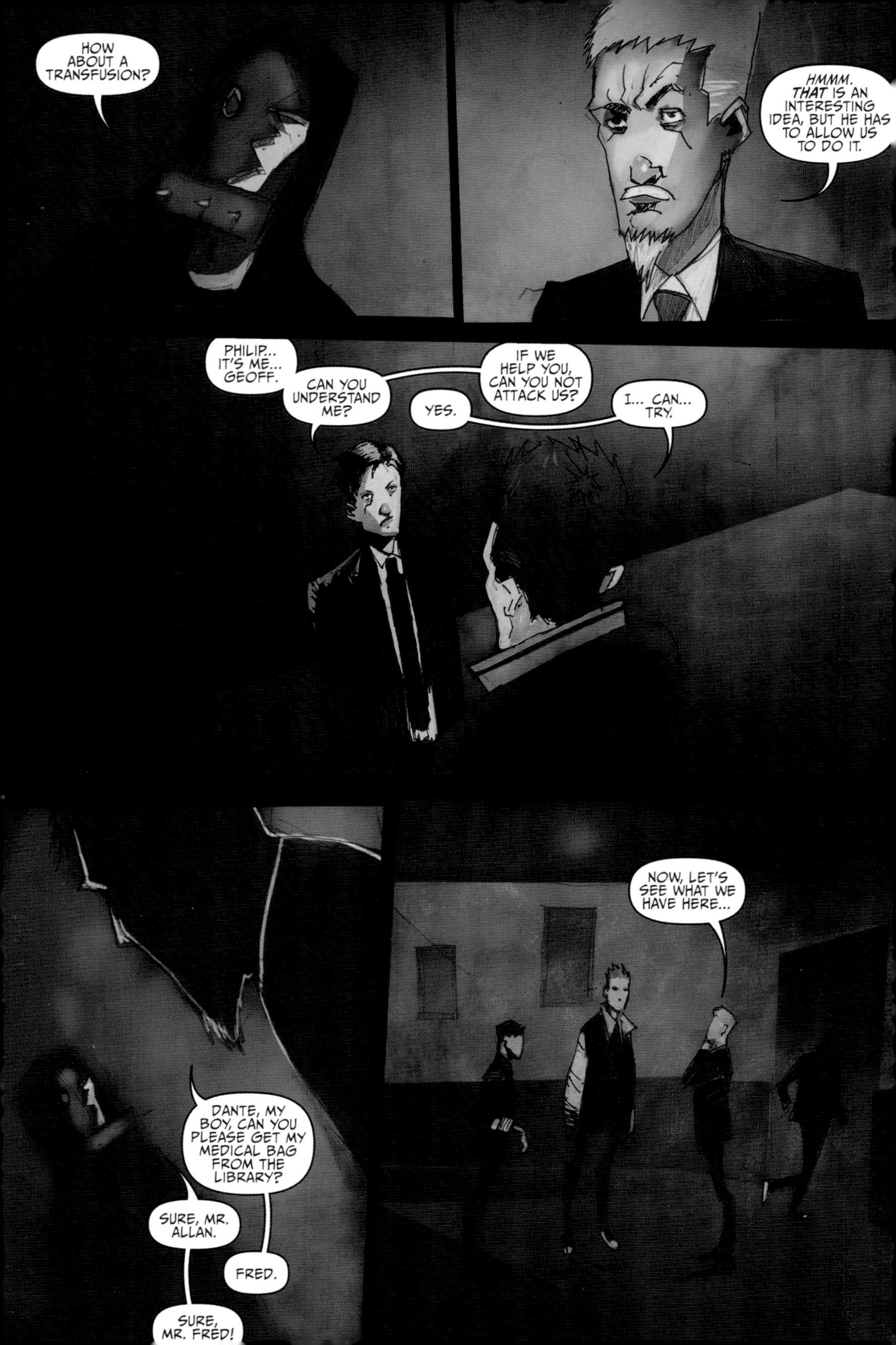
HOW ABOUT A TRANSFUSION?
HMMM. THAT IS AN INTERESTING IDEA, BUT HE HAS TO ALLOW US TO DO IT.
PHILIP... IT'S ME... GEOFF.
CAN YOU UNDERSTAND ME?
YES.
IF WE HELP YOU, CAN YOU NOT ATTACK US?
I... CAN... TRY.
DANTE, MY BOY, CAN YOU PLEASE GET MY MEDICAL BAG FROM THE LIBRARY?
SURE, MR. ALLAN.
FRED.
SURE, MR. FRED!
NOW, LET'S SEE WHAT WE HAVE HERE...

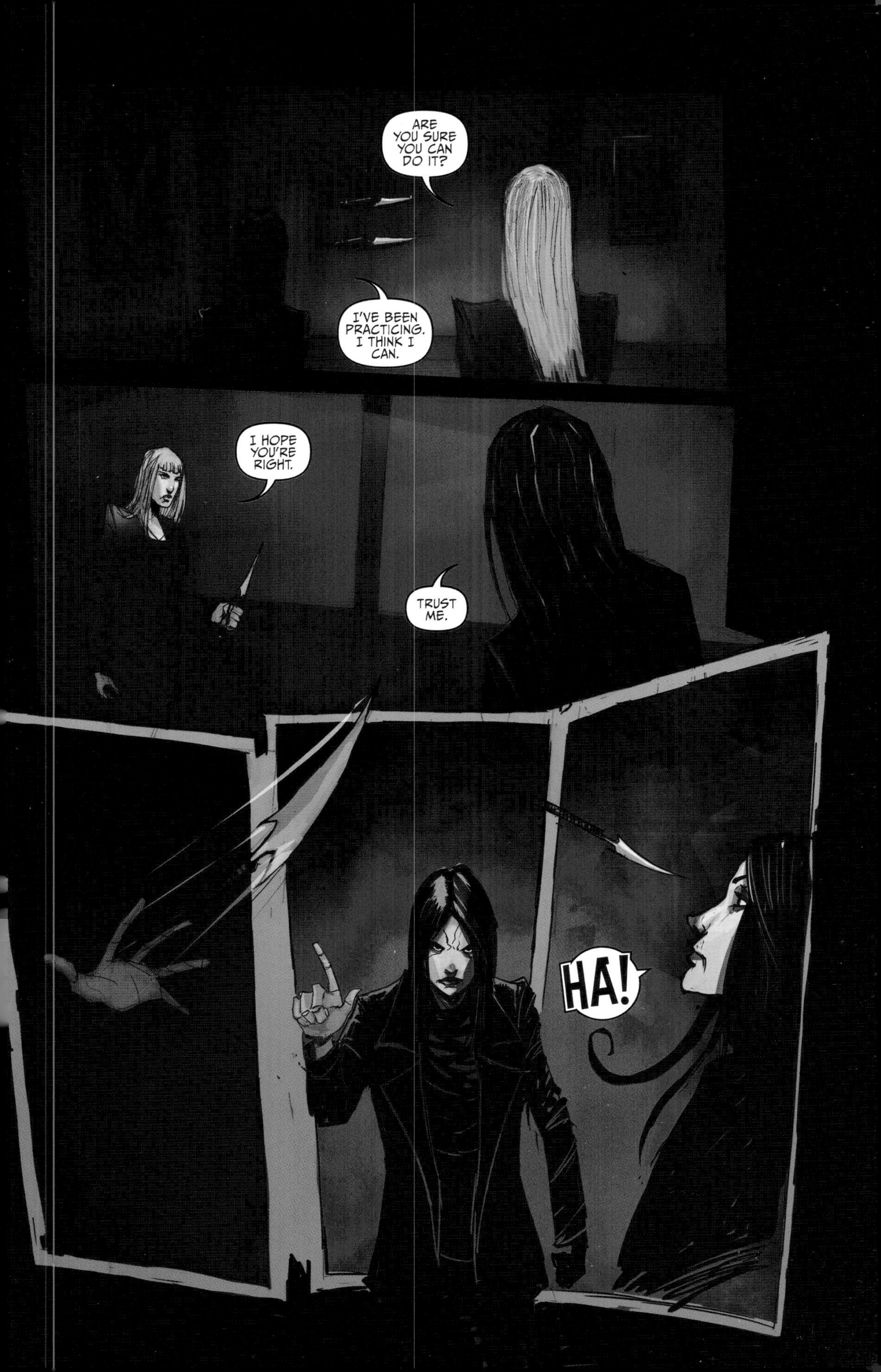
ARE YOU SURE YOU CAN DO IT?
I'VE BEEN PRACTICING. I THINK I CAN.
I HOPE YOU'RE RIGHT.
TRUST ME.
HA!

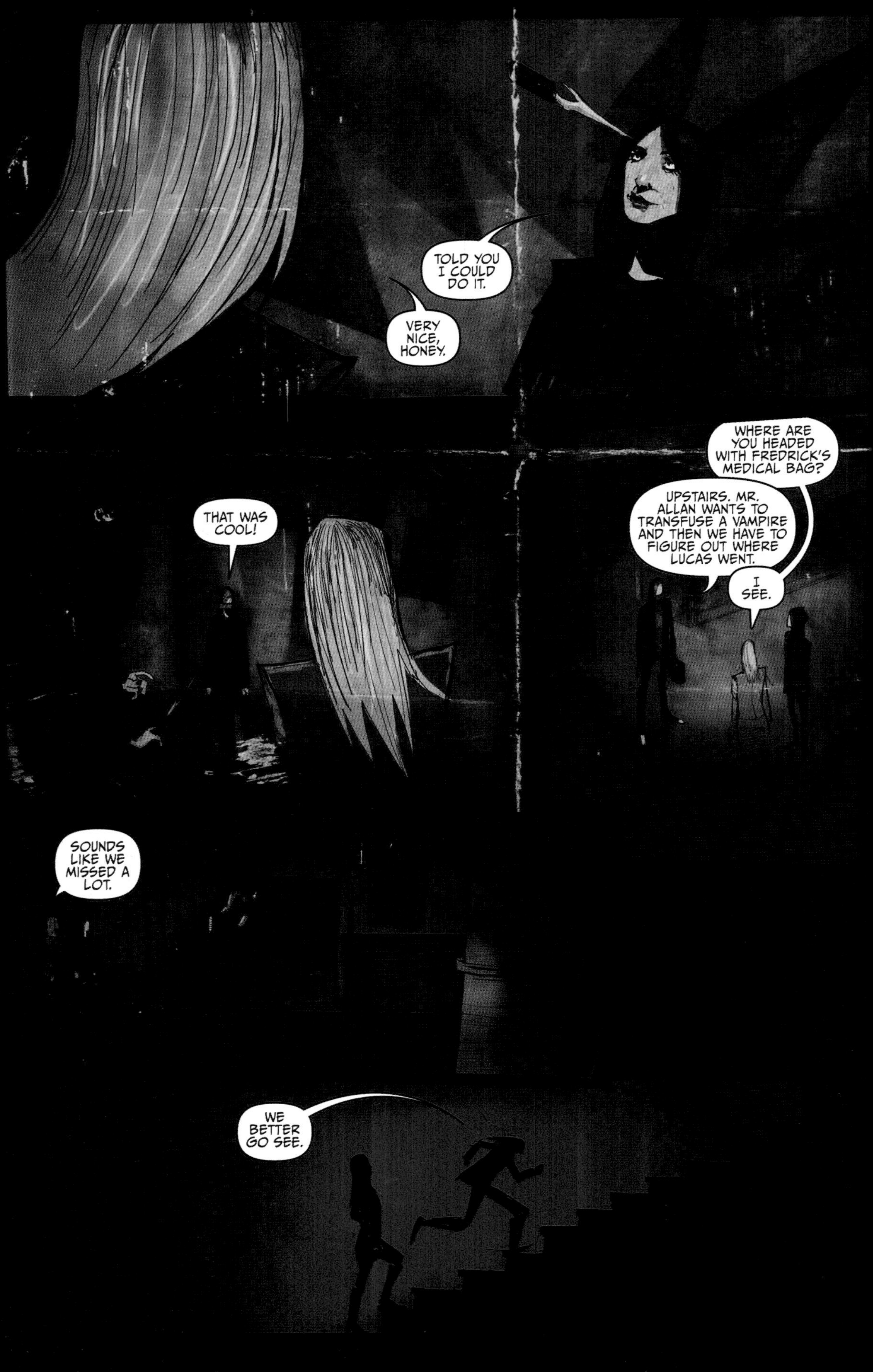
TOLD YOU I COULD DO IT.
VERY NICE, HONEY.
THAT WAS COOL!
WHERE ARE YOU HEADED WITH FREDRICK'S MEDICAL BAG?
UPSTAIRS. MR. ALLAN WANTS TO TRANSFUSE A VAMPIRE AND THEN WE HAVE TO FIGURE OUT WHERE LUCAS WENT.
I SEE.
SOUNDS LIKE WE MISSED A LOT.
WE BETTER GO SEE.

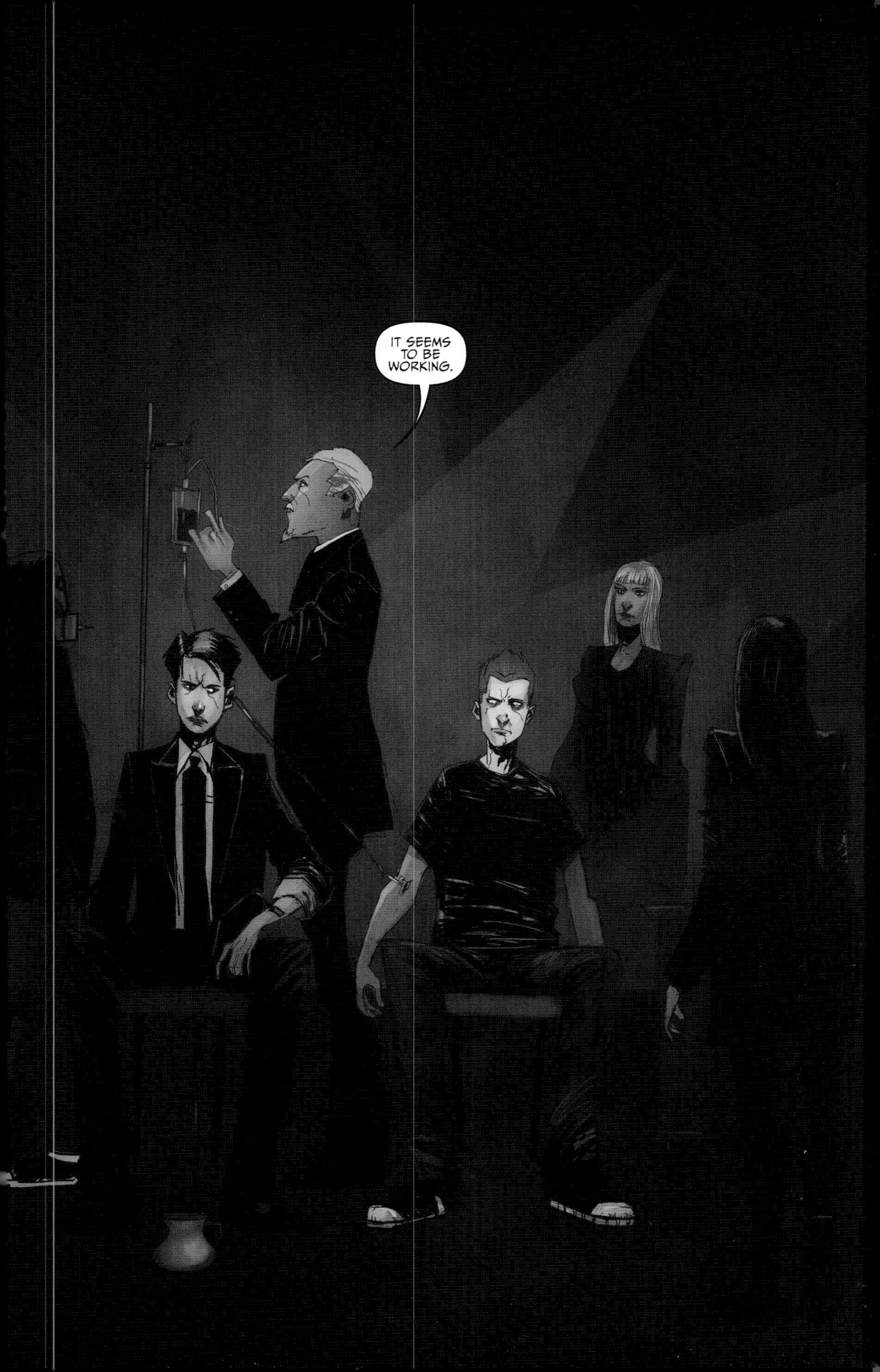
IT SEEMS TO BE WORKING.

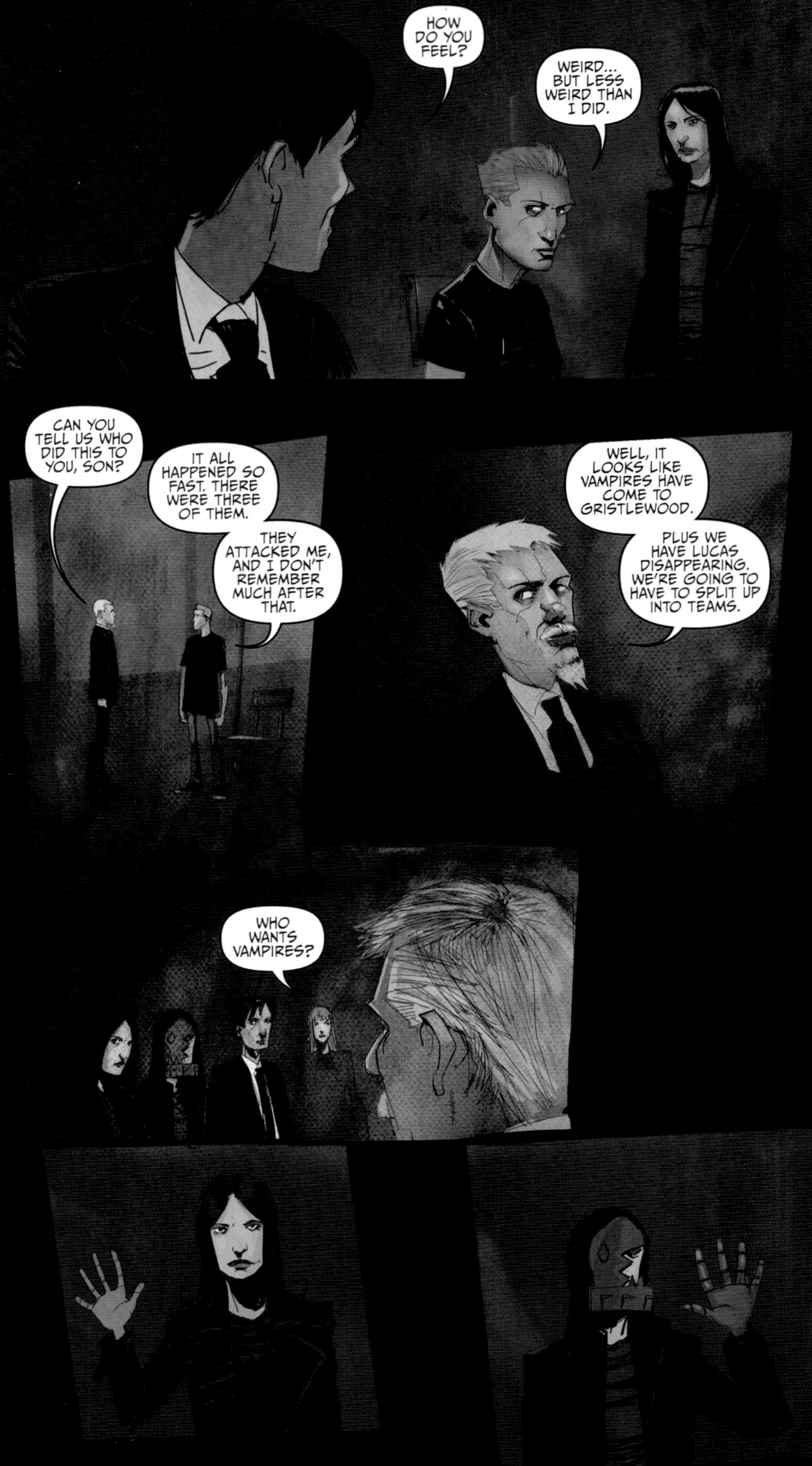
HOW DO YOU FEEL?
WEIRD... BUT LESS WEIRD THAN I DID.
CAN YOU TELL US WHO DID THIS TO YOU, SON?
IT ALL HAPPENED SO FAST. THERE WERE THREE OF THEM.
THEY ATTACKED ME, AND I DON'T REMEMBER MUCH AFTER THAT.
WELL, IT LOOKS LIKE VAMPIRES HAVE COME TO GRISTLEWOOD.
PLUS WE HAVE LUCAS DISAPPEARING. WE'RE GOING TO HAVE TO SPLIT UP INTO TEAMS.
WHO WANTS VAMPIRES?

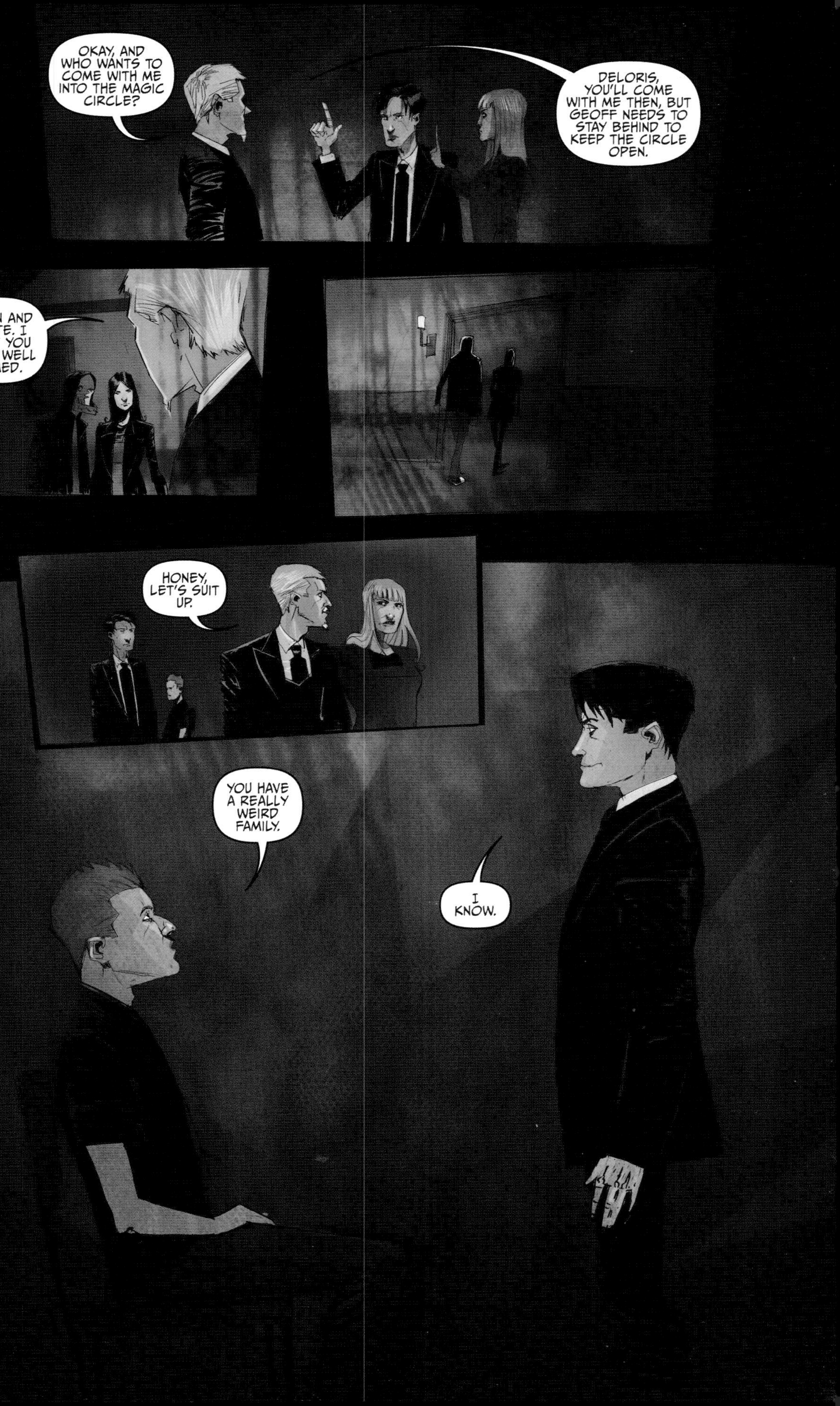
OKAY, AND WHO WANTS TO COME WITH ME INTO THE MAGIC CIRCLE?
DELORIS, YOU'LL COME WITH ME THEN, BUT GEOFF NEEDS TO STAY BEHIND TO KEEP THE CIRCLE OPEN.
VIVIAN AND DANTE. I WANT YOU BOTH WELL ARMED.
HONEY, LET'S SUIT UP.
YOU HAVE A REALLY WEIRD FAMILY.
I KNOW.

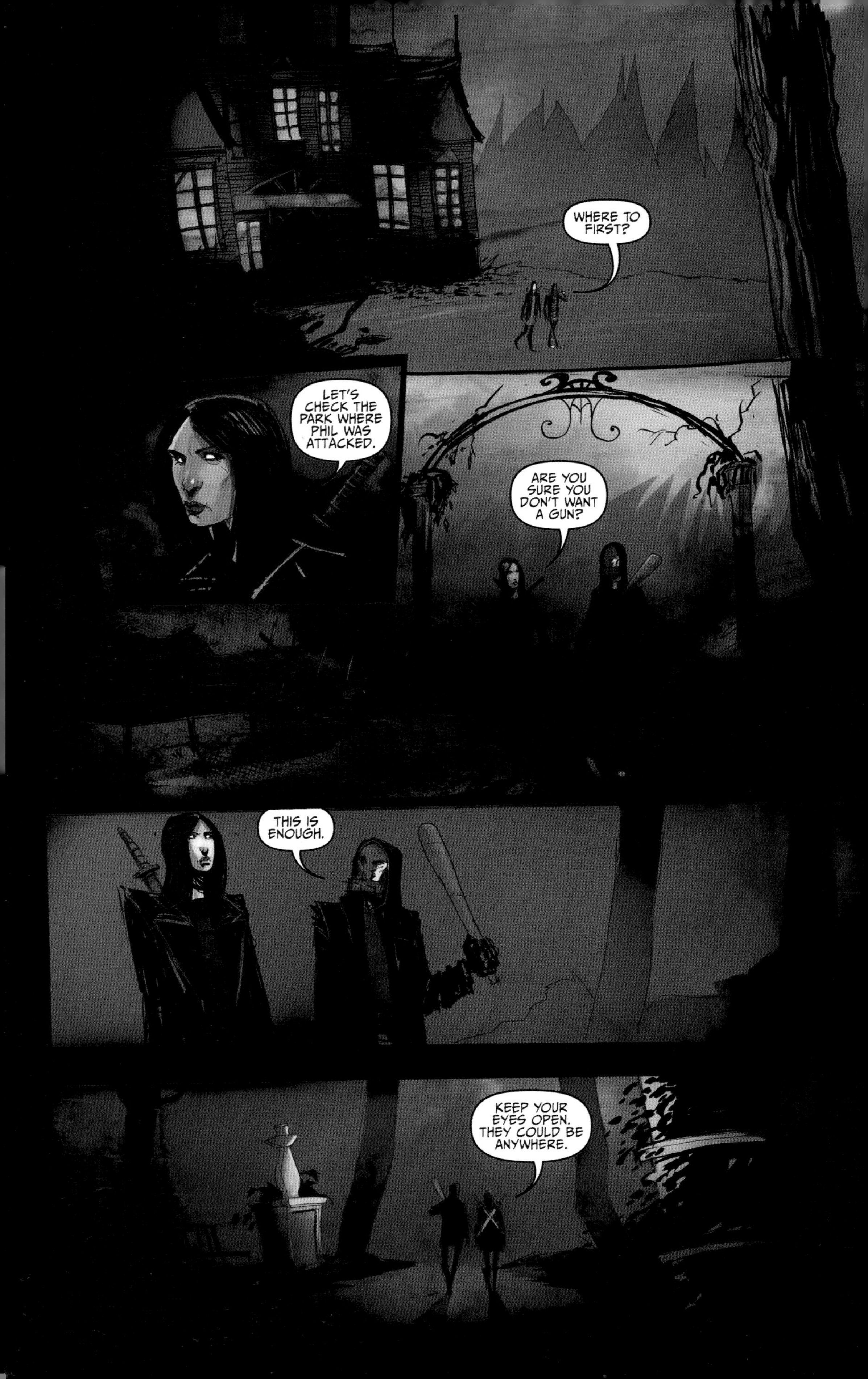
WHERE TO FIRST?
LET'S CHECK THE PARK WHERE PHIL WAS ATTACKED.
ARE YOU SURE YOU DON'T WANT A GUN?
THIS IS ENOUGH.
KEEP YOUR EYES OPEN. THEY COULD BE ANYWHERE.

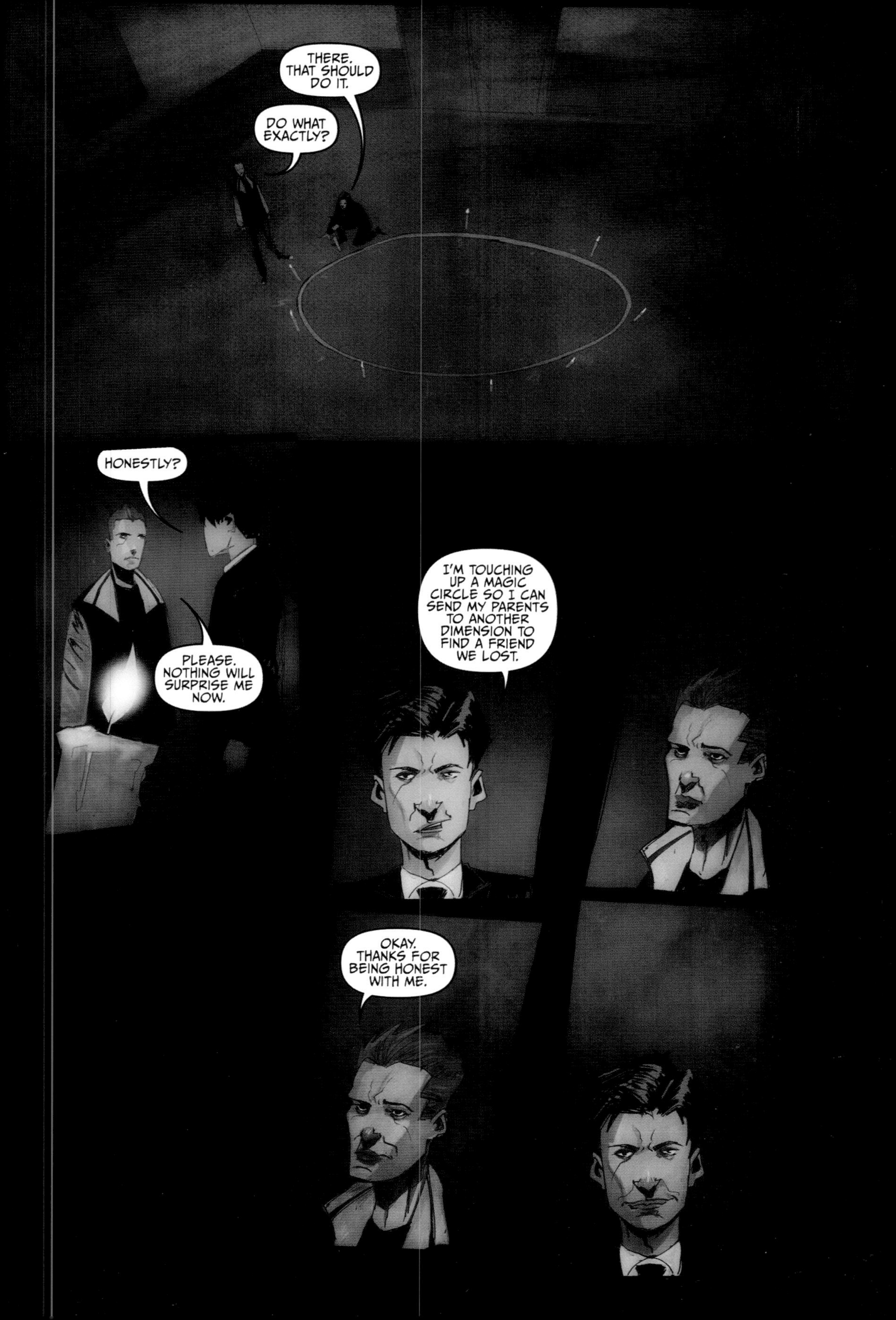
THERE. THAT SHOULD DO IT.
DO WHAT EXACTLY?
HONESTLY?
PLEASE. NOTHING WILL SURPRISE ME NOW.
I'M TOUCHING UP A MAGIC CIRCLE SO I CAN SEND MY PARENTS TO ANOTHER DIMENSION TO FIND A FRIEND WE LOST.
OKAY. THANKS FOR BEING HONEST WITH ME.

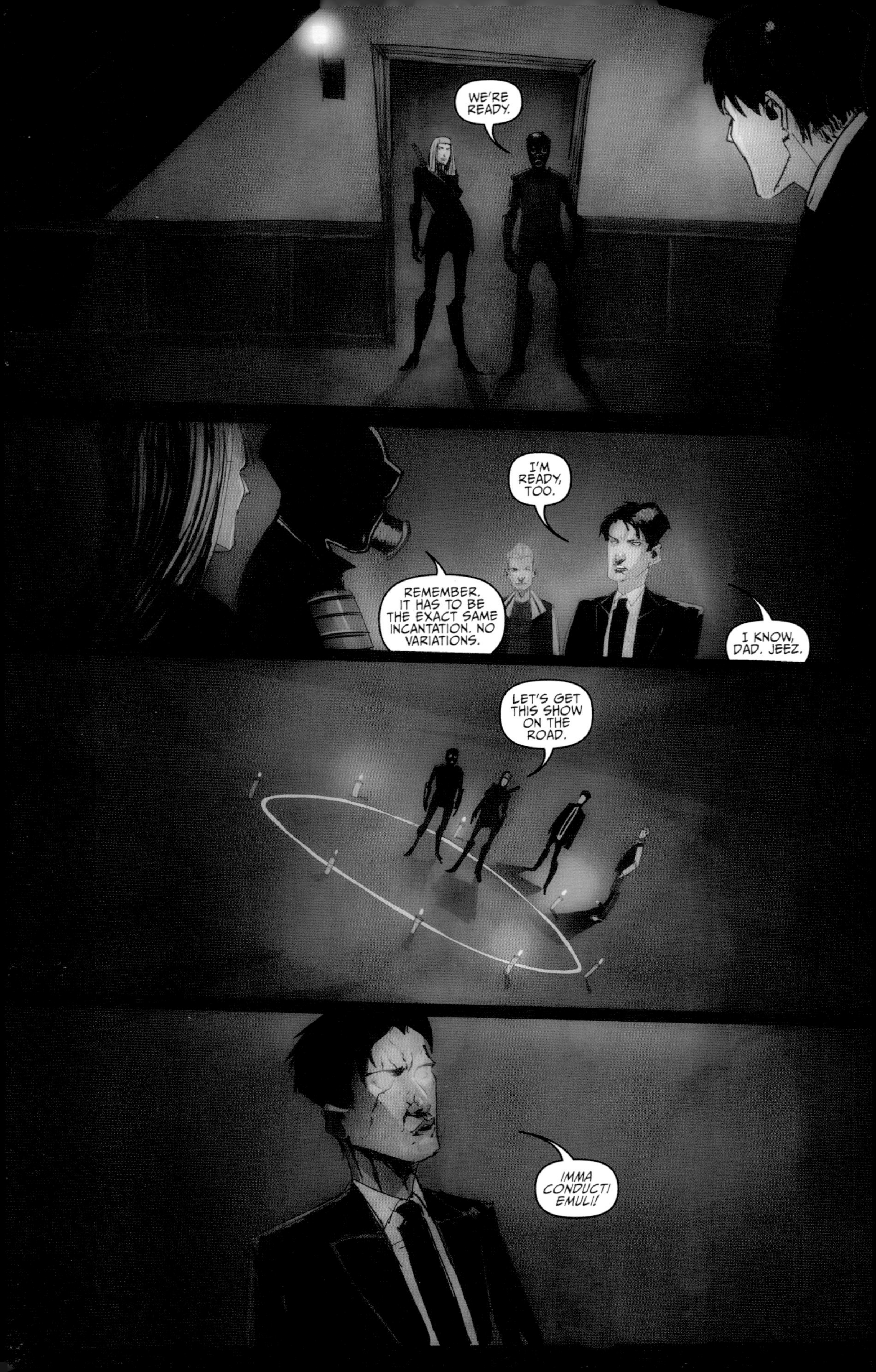
WE'RE READY.
I'M READY, TOO.
REMEMBER. IT HAS TO BE THE EXACT SAME INCANTATION. NO VARIATIONS.
I KNOW, DAD. JEEZ.
LET'S GET THIS SHOW ON THE ROAD.
IMMA CONDUCTI EMULI!

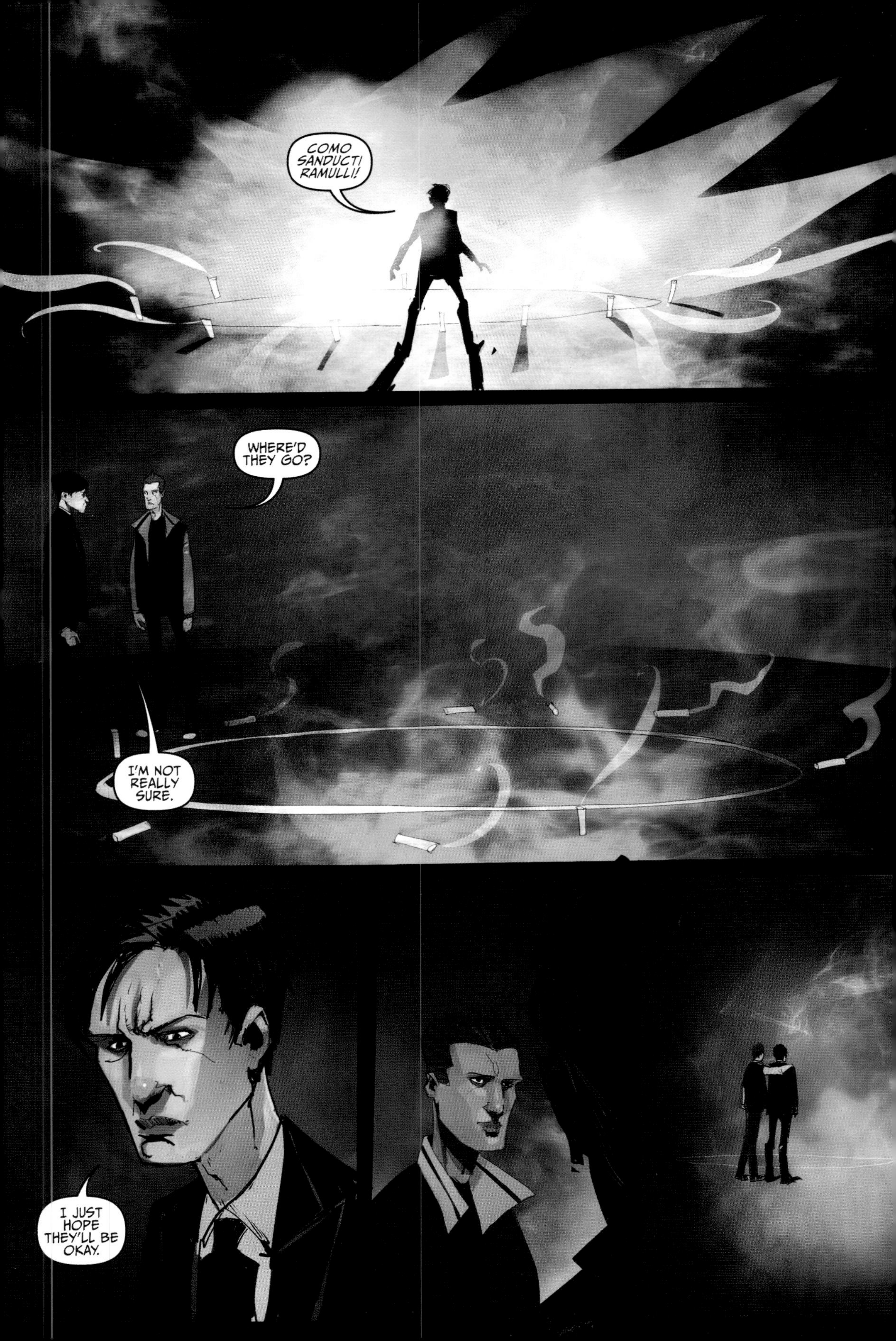
COMO SANDUCTI RAMULLI!
WHERE'D THEY GO?
I'M NOT REALLY SURE.
I JUST HOPE THEY'LL BE OKAY.

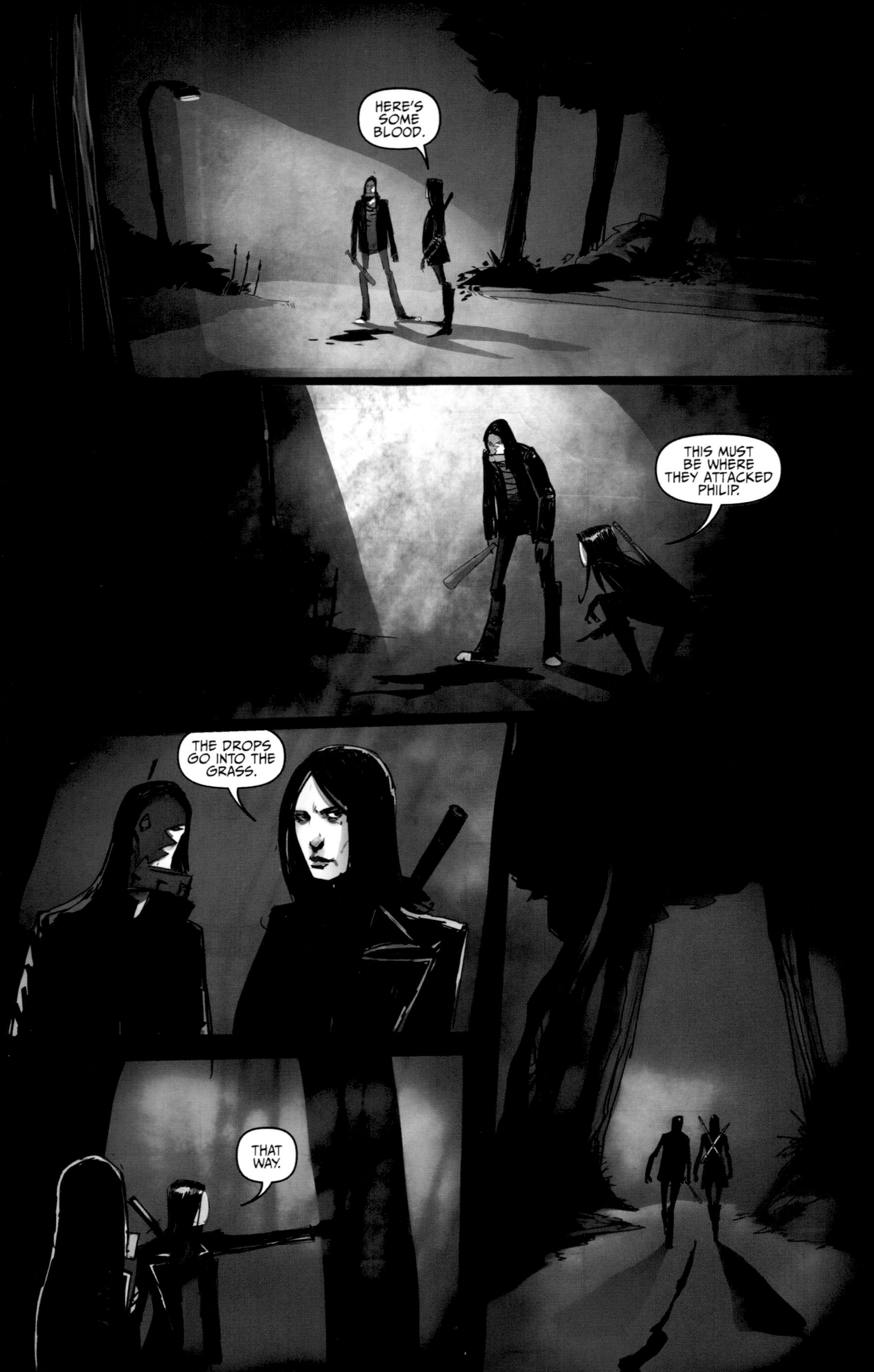
HERE'S SOME BLOOD.
THIS MUST BE WHERE THEY ATTACKED PHILIP.
THE DROPS GO INTO THE GRASS.
THAT WAY.

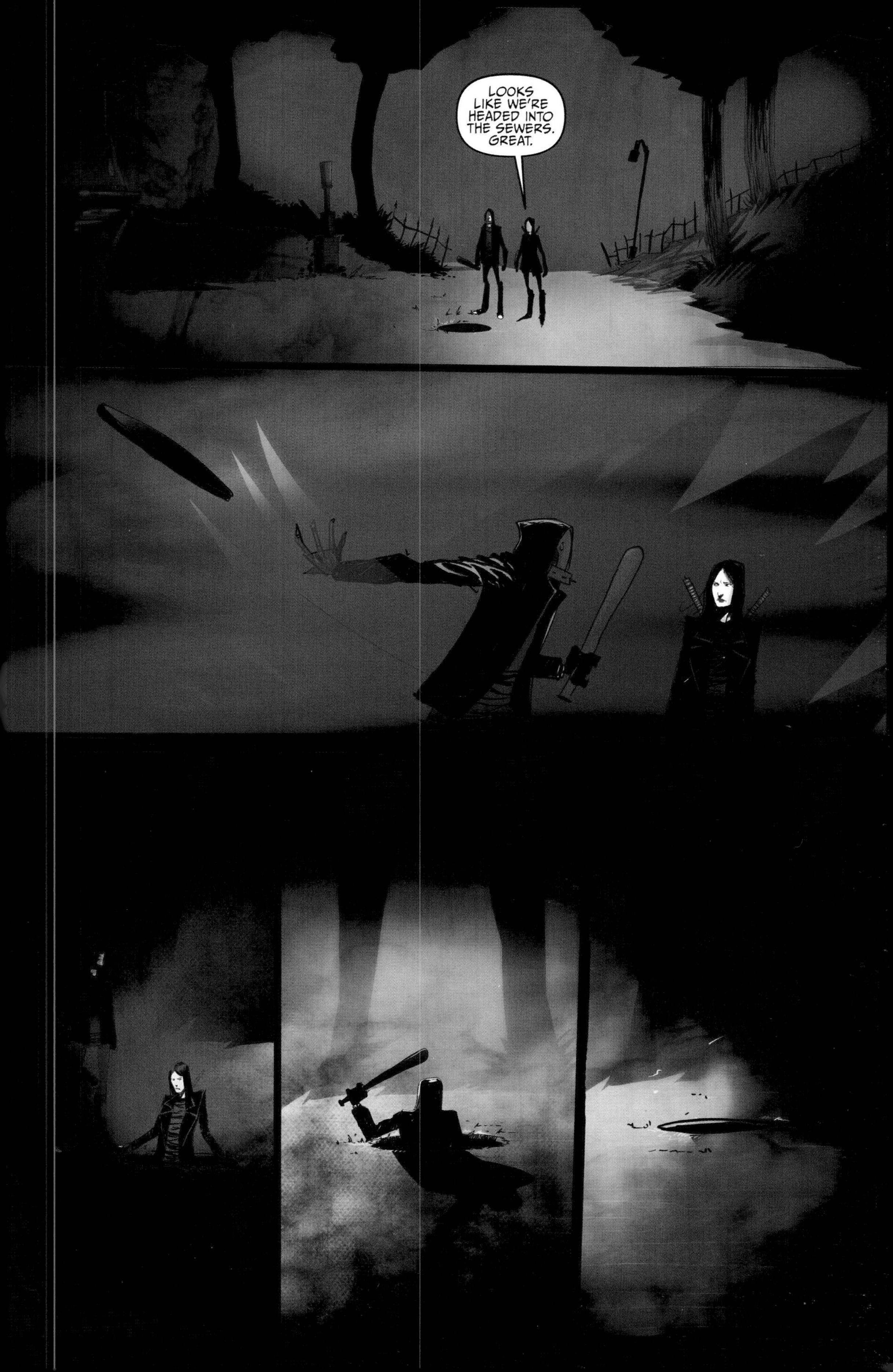
LOOKS LIKE WE'RE HEADED INTO THE SEWERS. GREAT.

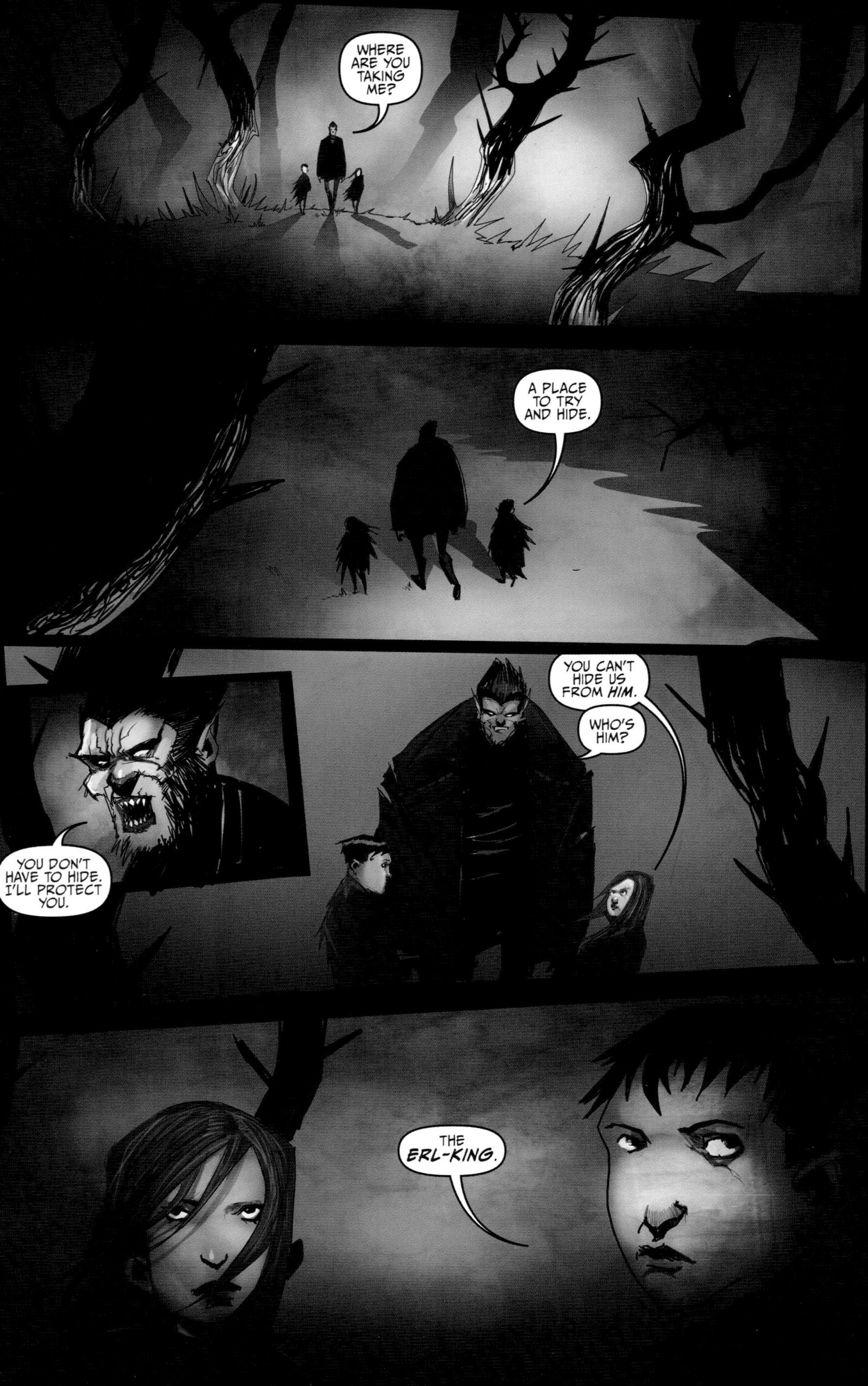

WHERE ARE YOU TAKING ME?
A PLACE TO TRY AND HIDE.
YOU CAN'T HIDE US FROM *HIM*.
WHO'S HIM?
YOU DON'T HAVE TO HIDE. I'LL PROTECT YOU.
THE *ERL-KING*.

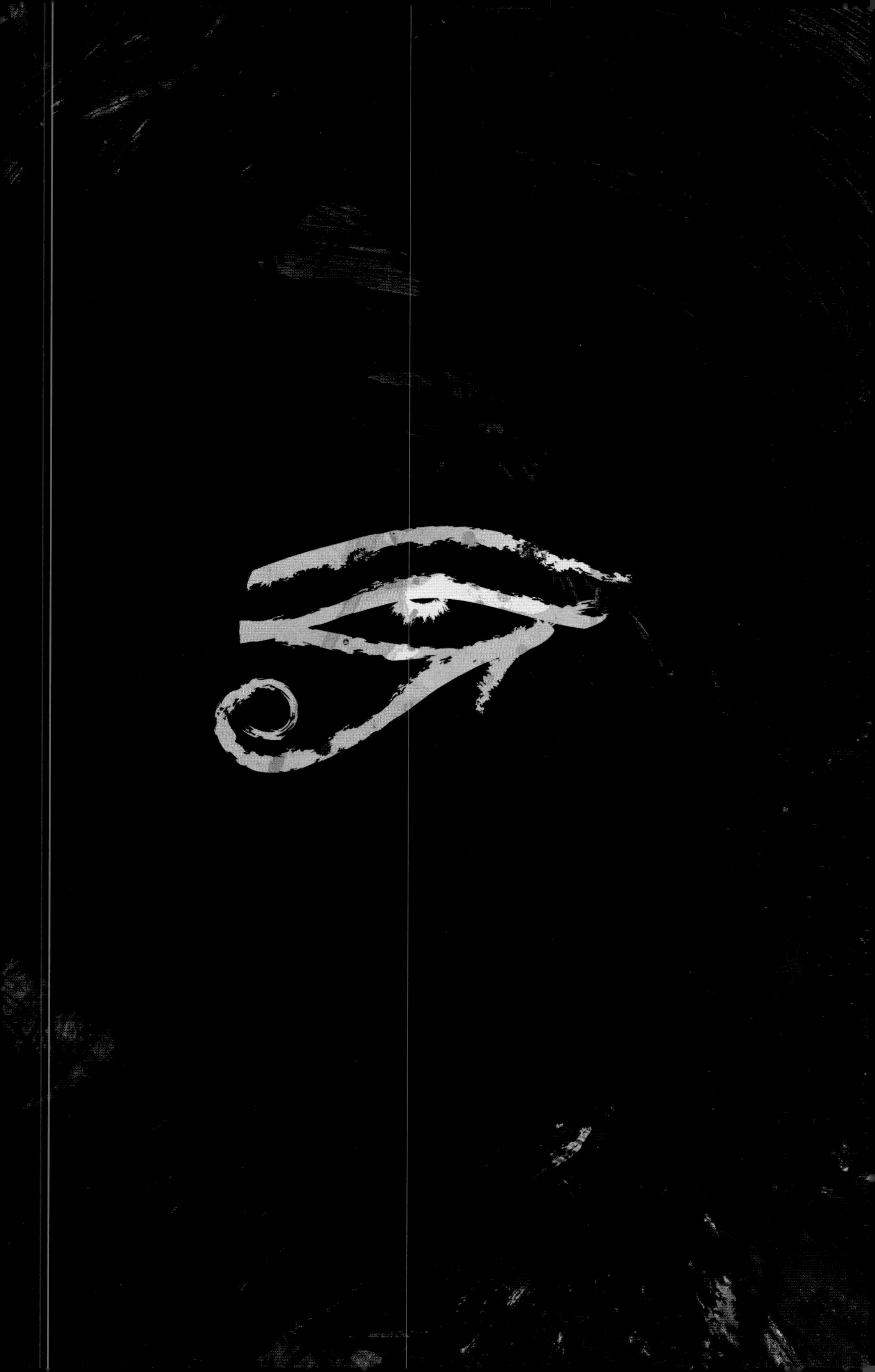

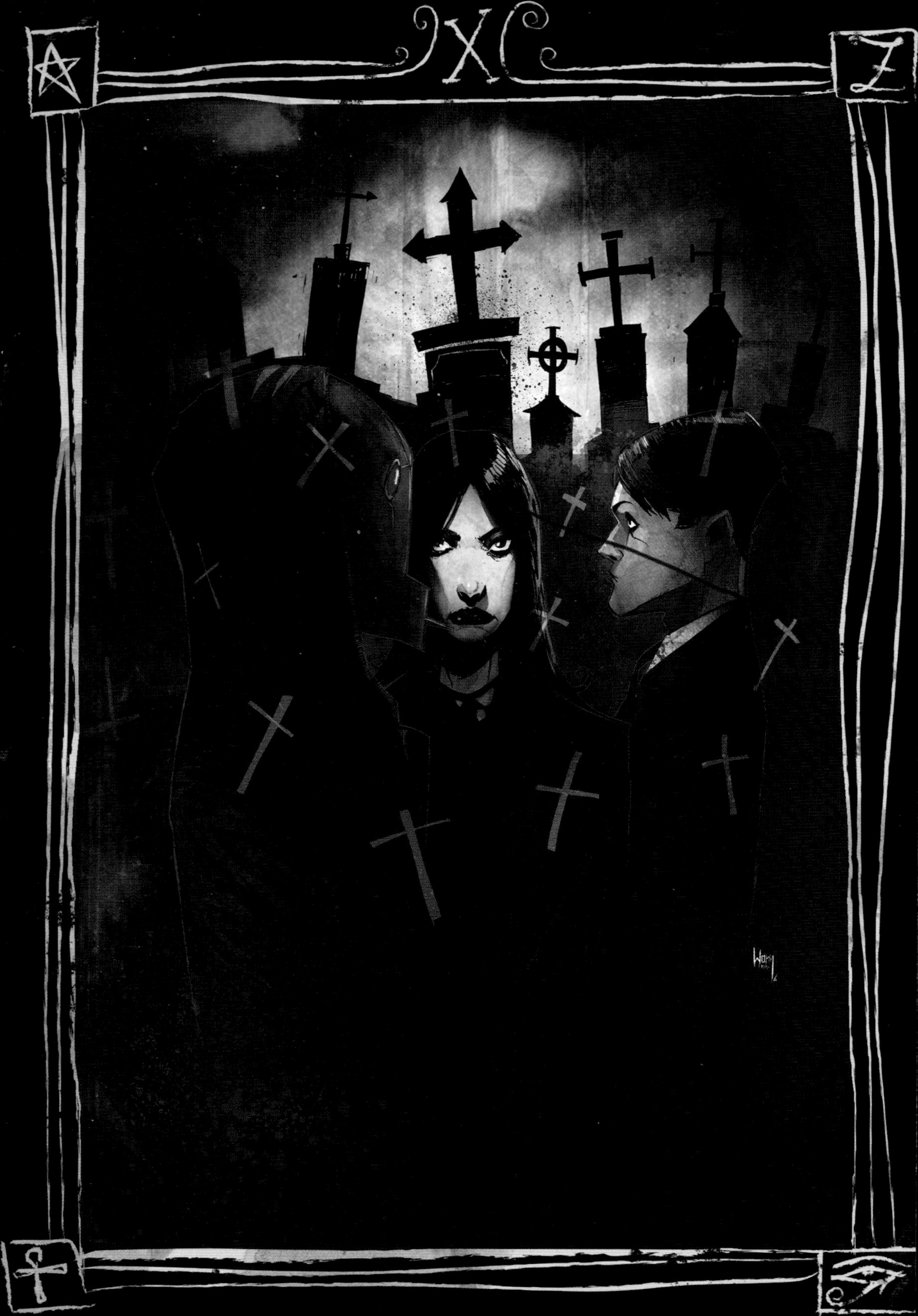
X

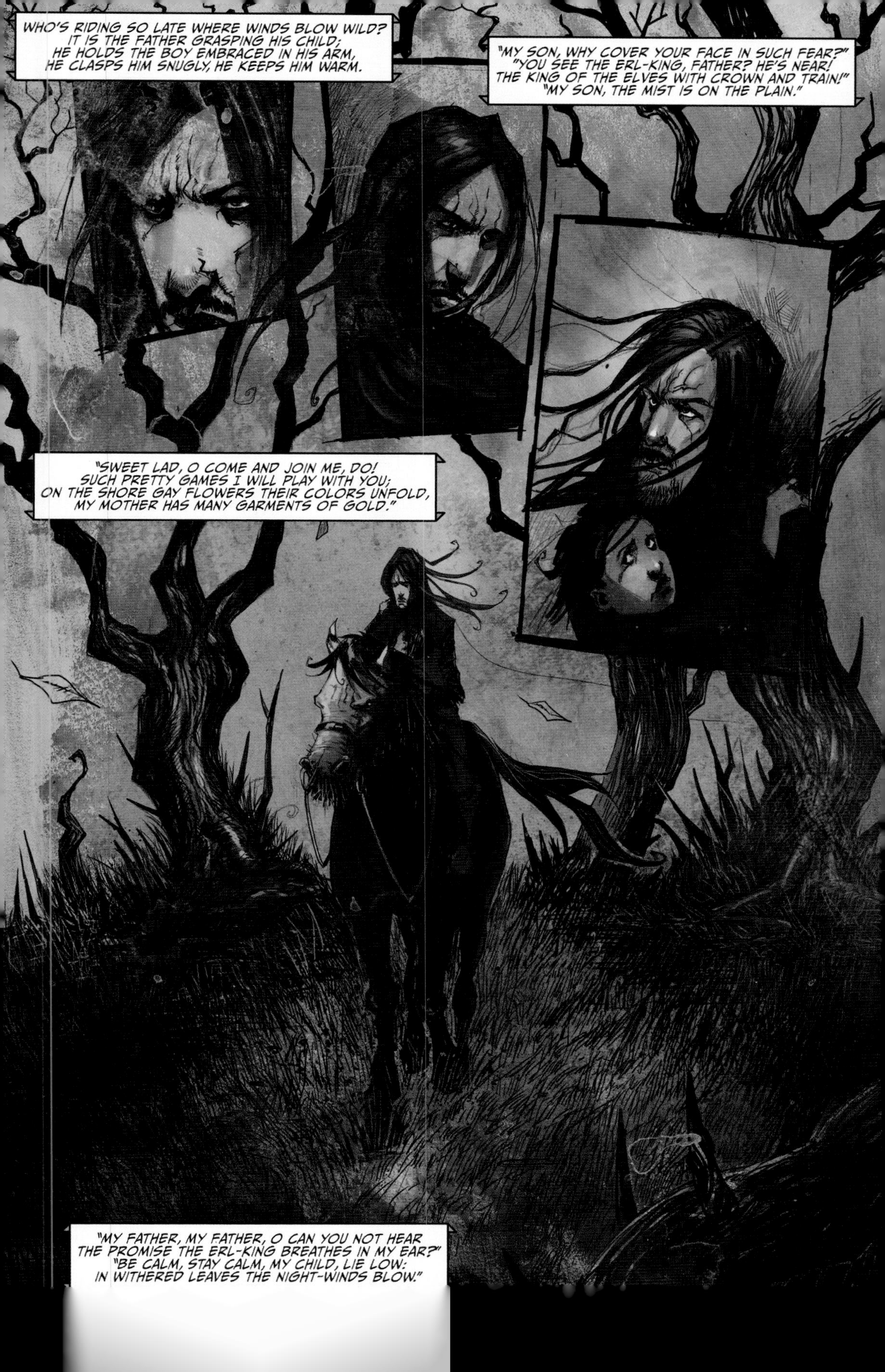
WHO'S RIDING SO LATE WHERE WINDS BLOW WILD? IT IS THE FATHER GRASPING HIS CHILD; HE HOLDS THE BOY EMBRACED IN HIS ARM, HE CLASPS HIM SNUGLY, HE KEEPS HIM WARM.
"MY SON, WHY COVER YOUR FACE IN SUCH FEAR?" "YOU SEE THE ERL-KING, FATHER? HE'S NEAR! THE KING OF THE ELVES WITH CROWN AND TRAIN!" "MY SON, THE MIST IS ON THE PLAIN."
"SWEET LAD, O COME AND JOIN ME, DO! SUCH PRETTY GAMES I WILL PLAY WITH YOU; ON THE SHORE GAY FLOWERS THEIR COLORS UNFOLD, MY MOTHER HAS MANY GARMENTS OF GOLD."
"MY FATHER, MY FATHER, O CAN YOU NOT HEAR THE PROMISE THE ERL-KING BREATHES IN MY EAR?" "BE CALM, STAY CALM, MY CHILD, LIE LOW: IN WITHERED LEAVES THE NIGHT-WINDS BLOW."

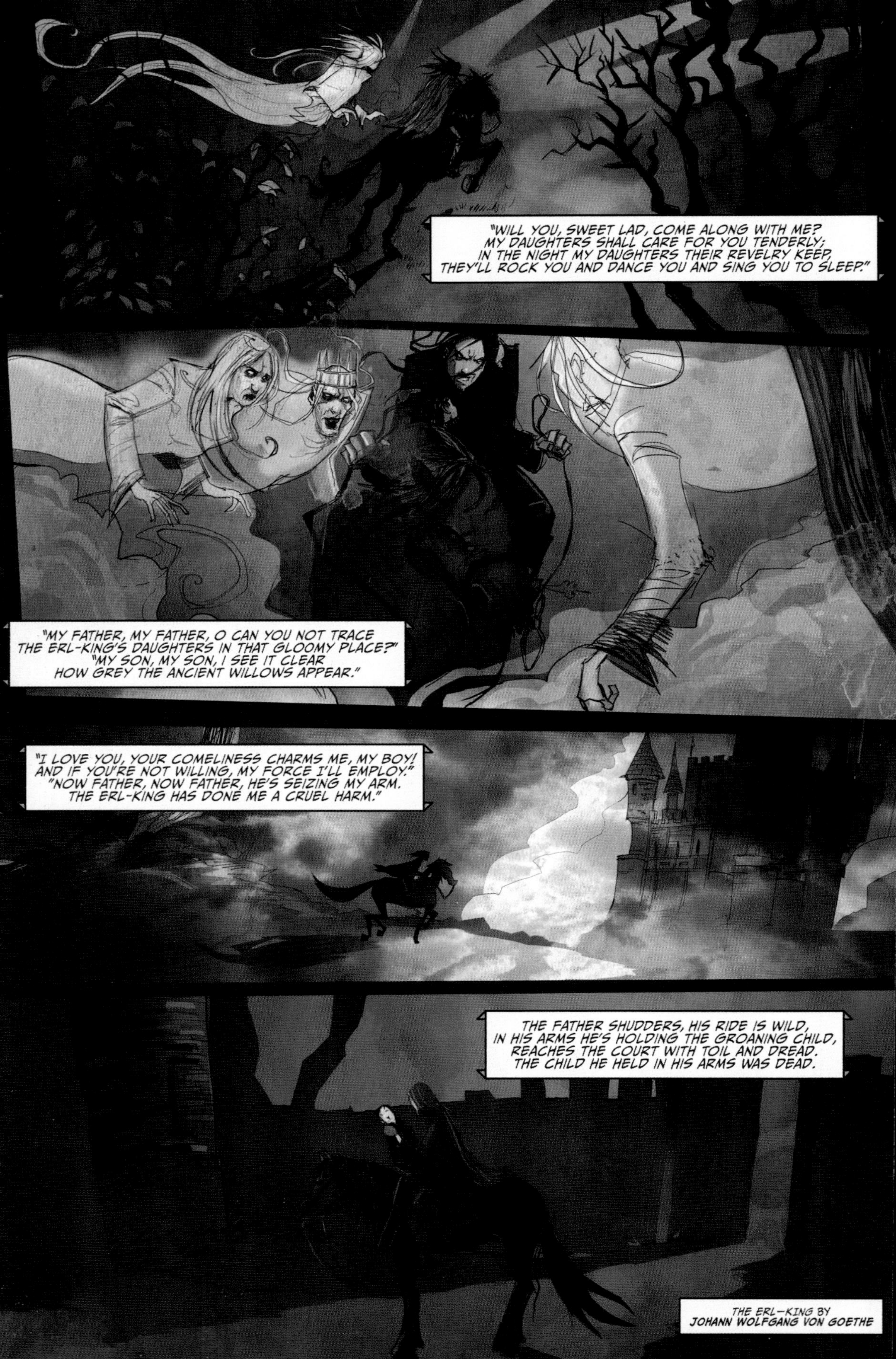
"WILL YOU, SWEET LAD, COME ALONG WITH ME? MY DAUGHTERS SHALL CARE FOR YOU TENDERLY; IN THE NIGHT MY DAUGHTERS THEIR REVELRY KEEP, THEY'LL ROCK YOU AND DANCE YOU AND SING YOU TO SLEEP."
"MY FATHER, MY FATHER, O CAN YOU NOT TRACE THE ERL-KING'S DAUGHTERS IN THAT GLOOMY PLACE?" "MY SON, MY SON, I SEE IT CLEAR HOW GREY THE ANCIENT WILLOWS APPEAR."
"I LOVE YOU, YOUR COMELINESS CHARMS ME, MY BOY! AND IF YOU'RE NOT WILLING, MY FORCE I'LL EMPLOY." "NOW FATHER, NOW FATHER, HE'S SEIZING MY ARM. THE ERL-KING HAS DONE ME A CRUEL HARM."
THE FATHER SHUDDERS, HIS RIDE IS WILD, IN HIS ARMS HE'S HOLDING THE GROANING CHILD, REACHES THE COURT WITH TOIL AND DREAD. THE CHILD HE HELD IN HIS ARMS WAS DEAD.
THE ERL-KING BY JOHANN WOLFGANG VON GOETHE

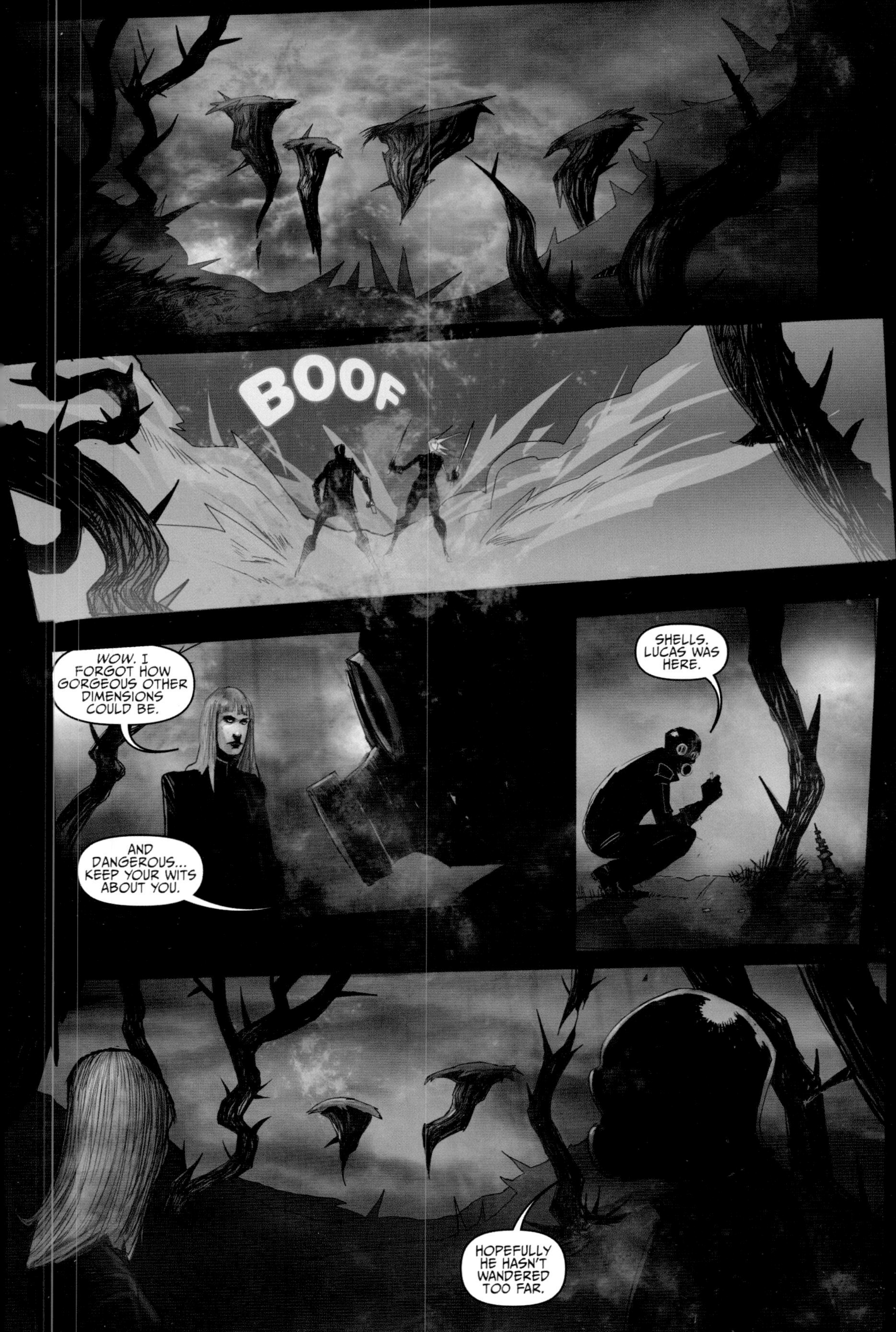
BOOF
WOW. I FORGOT HOW GORGEOUS OTHER DIMENSIONS COULD BE.
AND DANGEROUS... KEEP YOUR WITS ABOUT YOU.
SHELLS. LUCAS WAS HERE.
HOPEFULLY HE HASN'T WANDERED TOO FAR.

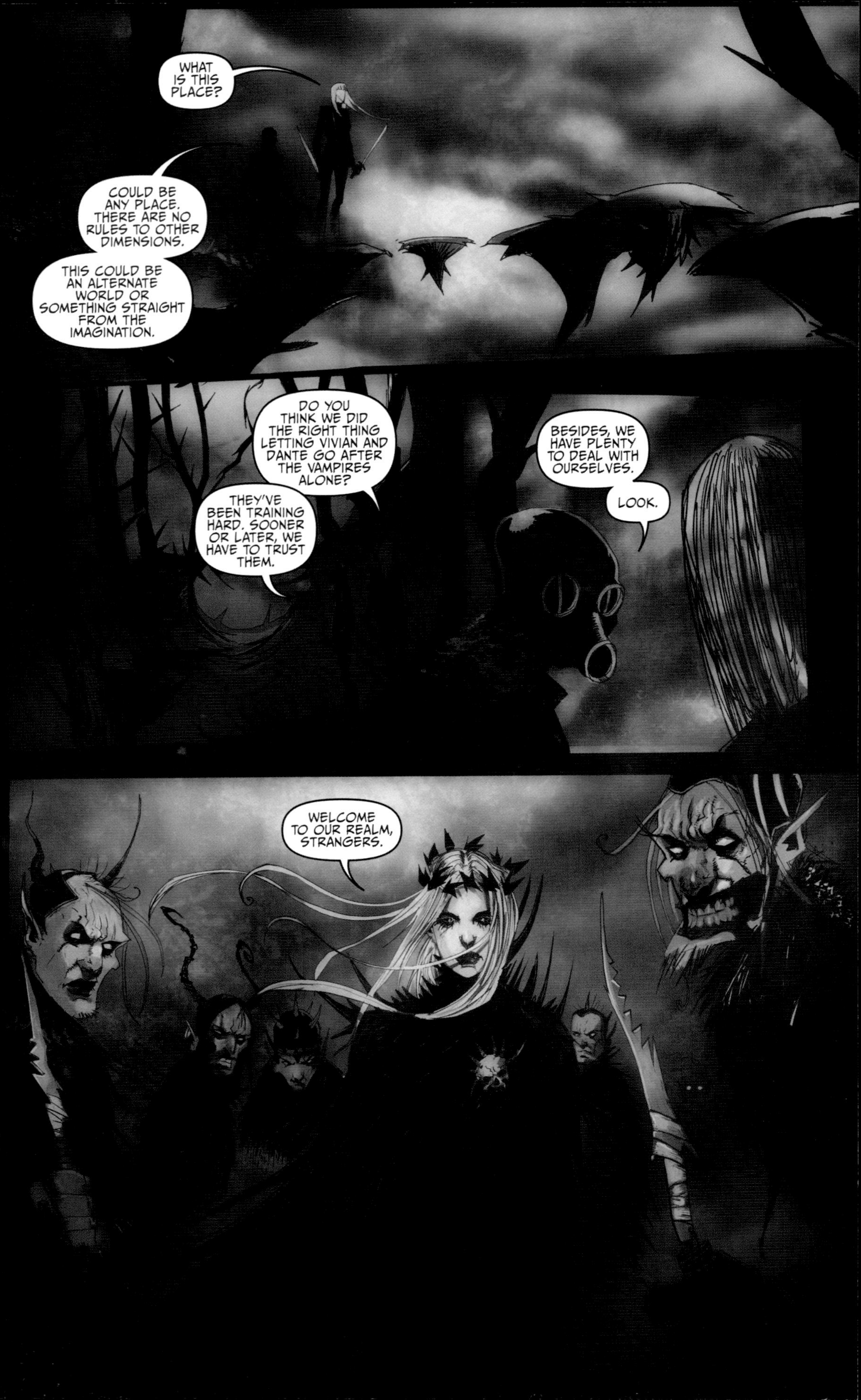
WHAT IS THIS PLACE?
COULD BE ANY PLACE. THERE ARE NO RULES TO OTHER DIMENSIONS.
THIS COULD BE AN ALTERNATE WORLD OR SOMETHING STRAIGHT FROM THE IMAGINATION.
DO YOU THINK WE DID THE RIGHT THING LETTING VIVIAN AND DANTE GO AFTER THE VAMPIRES ALONE?
THEY'VE BEEN TRAINING HARD. SOONER OR LATER, WE HAVE TO TRUST THEM.
BESIDES, WE HAVE PLENTY TO DEAL WITH OURSELVES.
LOOK.
WELCOME TO OUR REALM, STRANGERS.

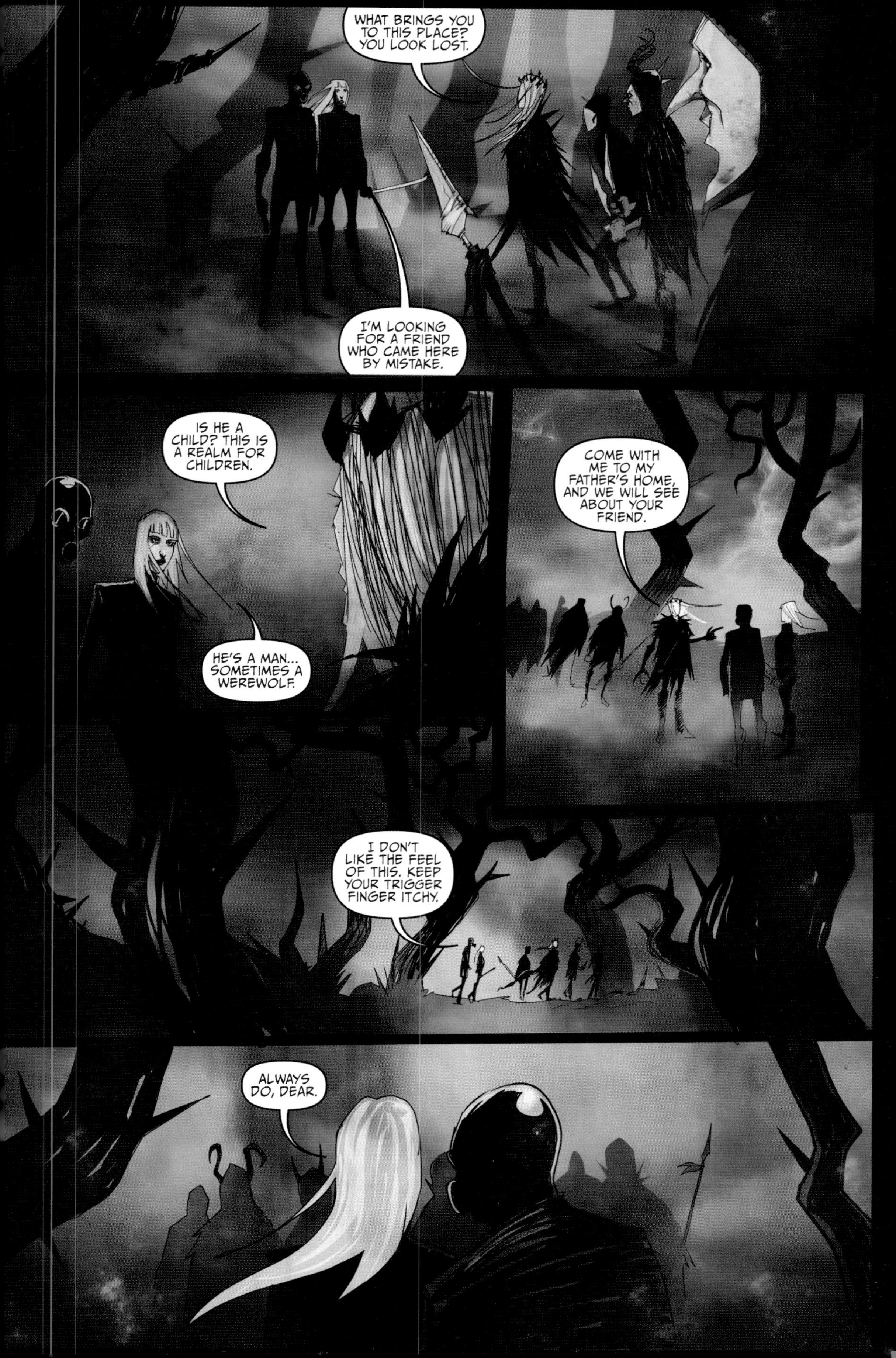
WHAT BRINGS YOU TO THIS PLACE? YOU LOOK LOST.
I'M LOOKING FOR A FRIEND WHO CAME HERE BY MISTAKE.
IS HE A CHILD? THIS IS A REALM FOR CHILDREN.
HE'S A MAN... SOMETIMES A WEREWOLF.
COME WITH ME TO MY FATHER'S HOME, AND WE WILL SEE ABOUT YOUR FRIEND.
I DON'T LIKE THE FEEL OF THIS. KEEP YOUR TRIGGER FINGER ITCHY.
ALWAYS DO, DEAR.

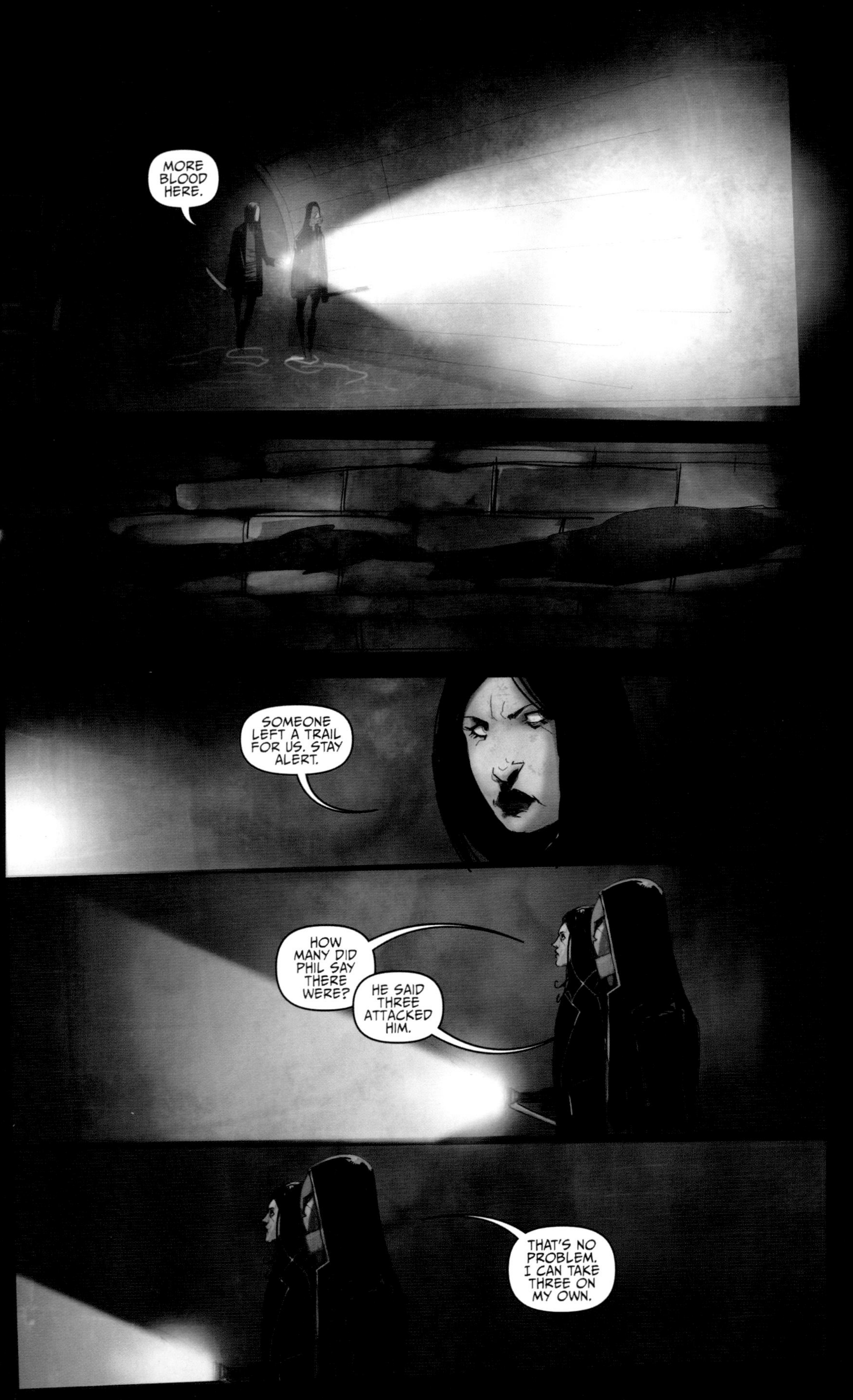
MORE BLOOD HERE.
SOMEONE LEFT A TRAIL FOR US. STAY ALERT.
HOW MANY DID PHIL SAY THERE WERE?
HE SAID THREE ATTACKED HIM.
THAT'S NO PROBLEM. I CAN TAKE THREE ON MY OWN.

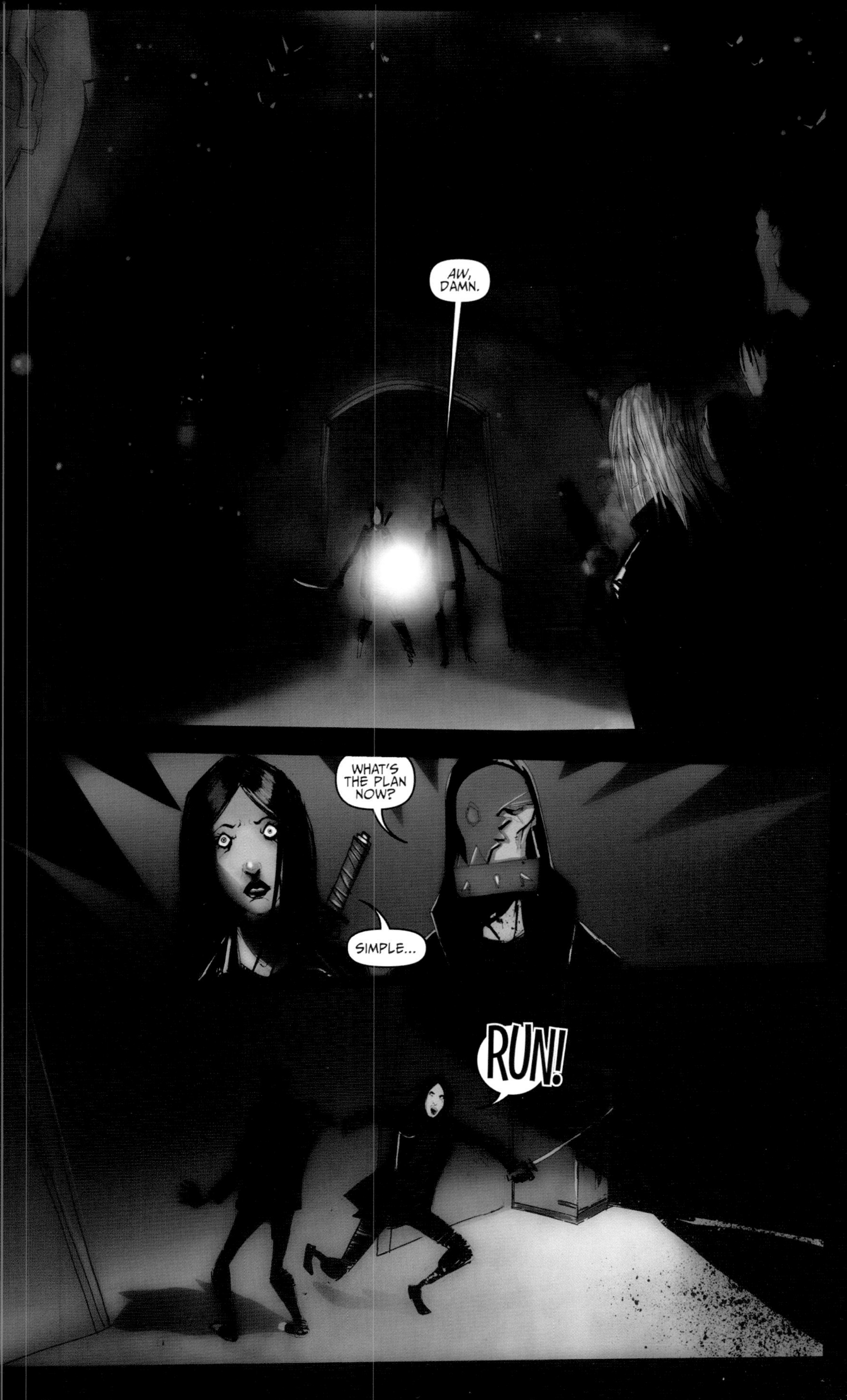
AW, DAMN.
WHAT'S THE PLAN NOW?
SIMPLE...
RUN!

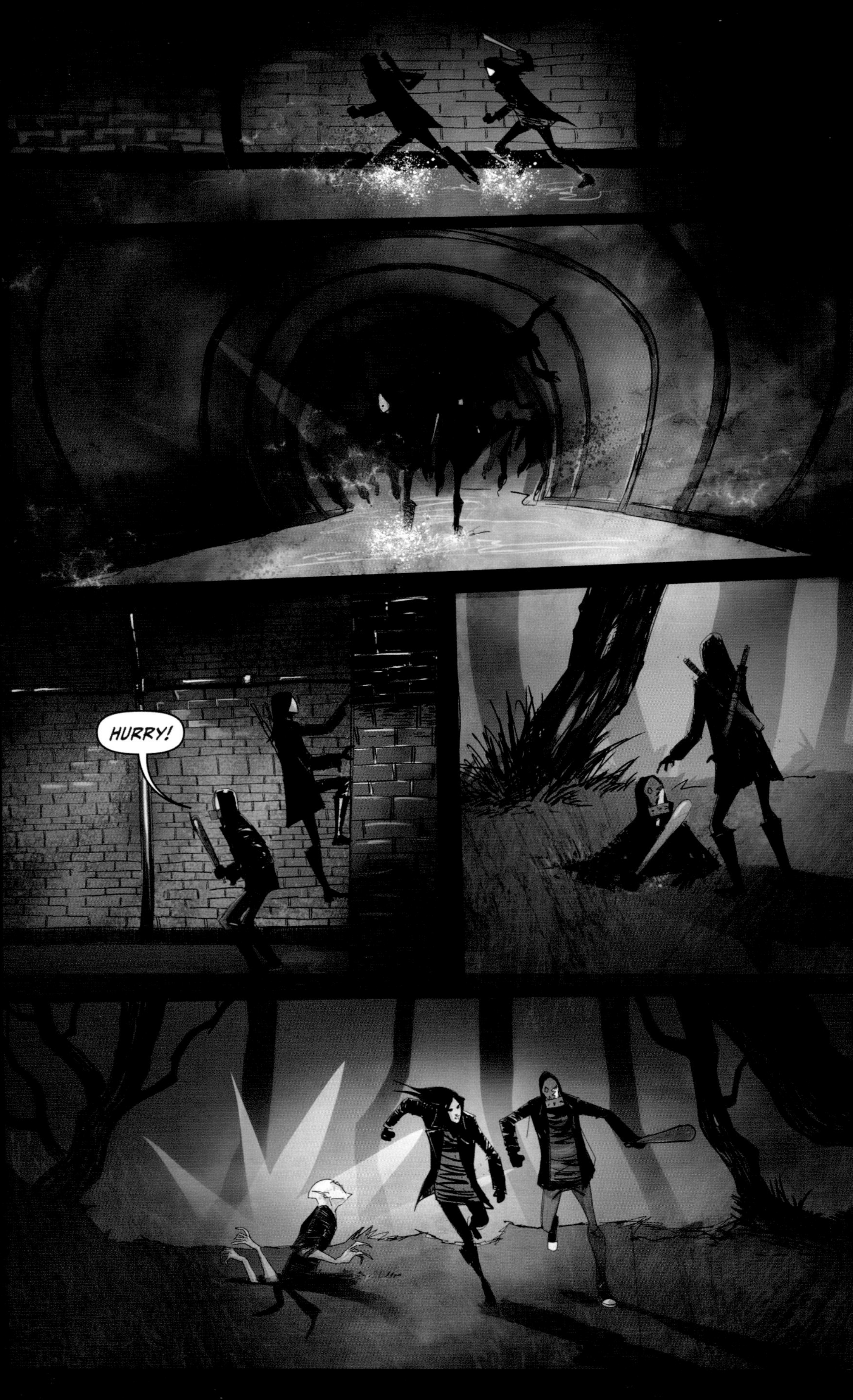
HURRY!

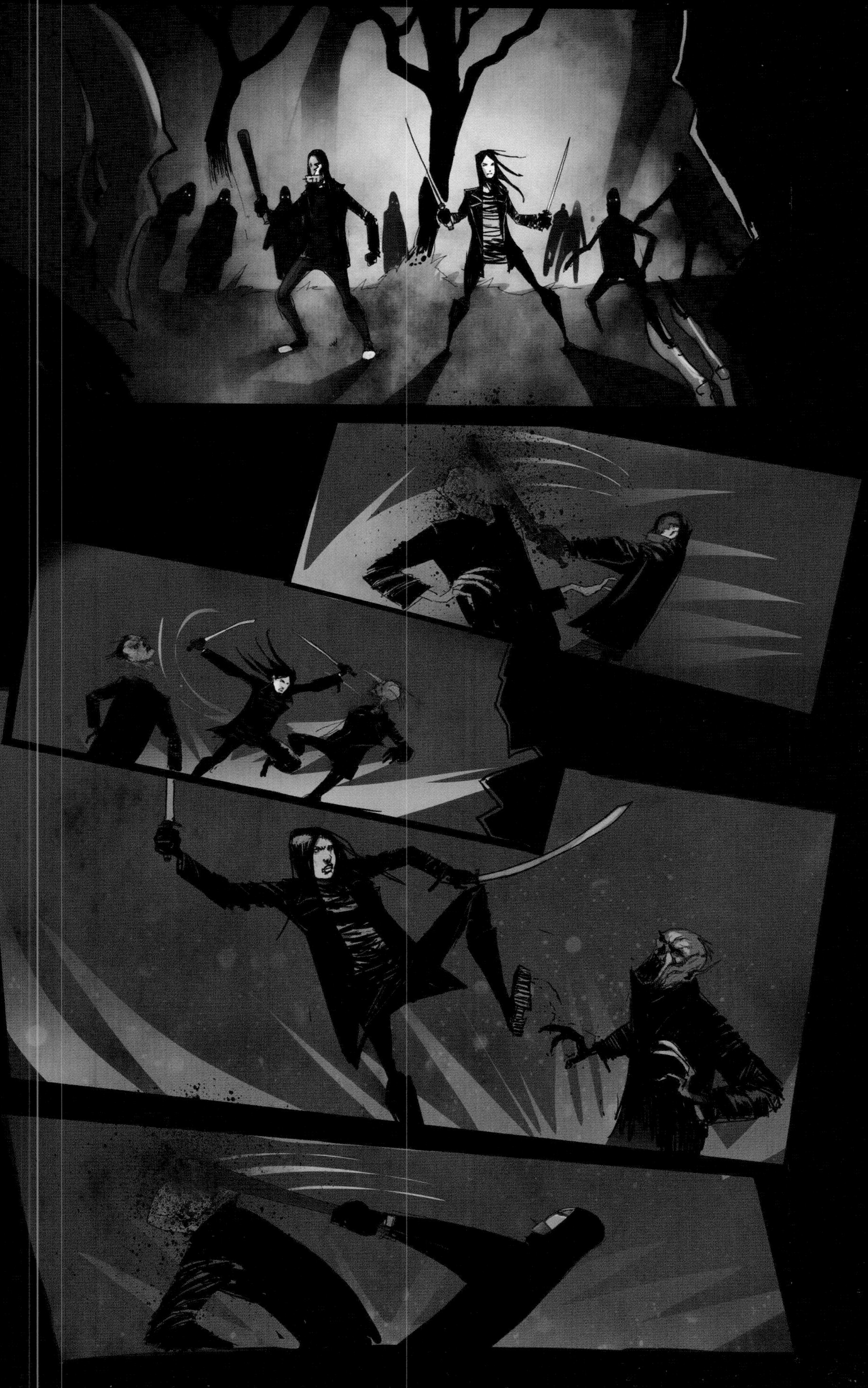

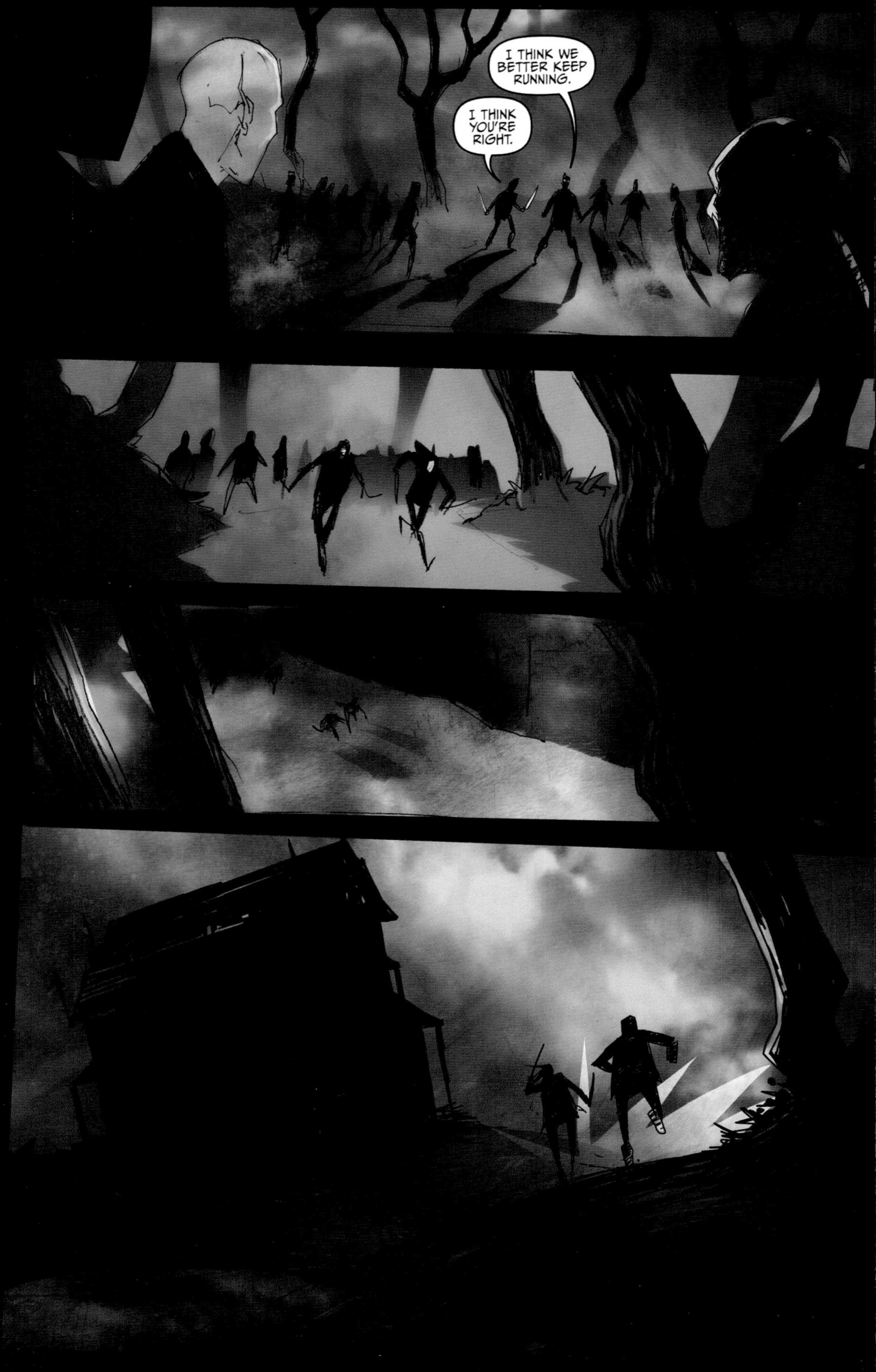
I THINK WE BETTER KEEP RUNNING.
I THINK YOU'RE RIGHT.

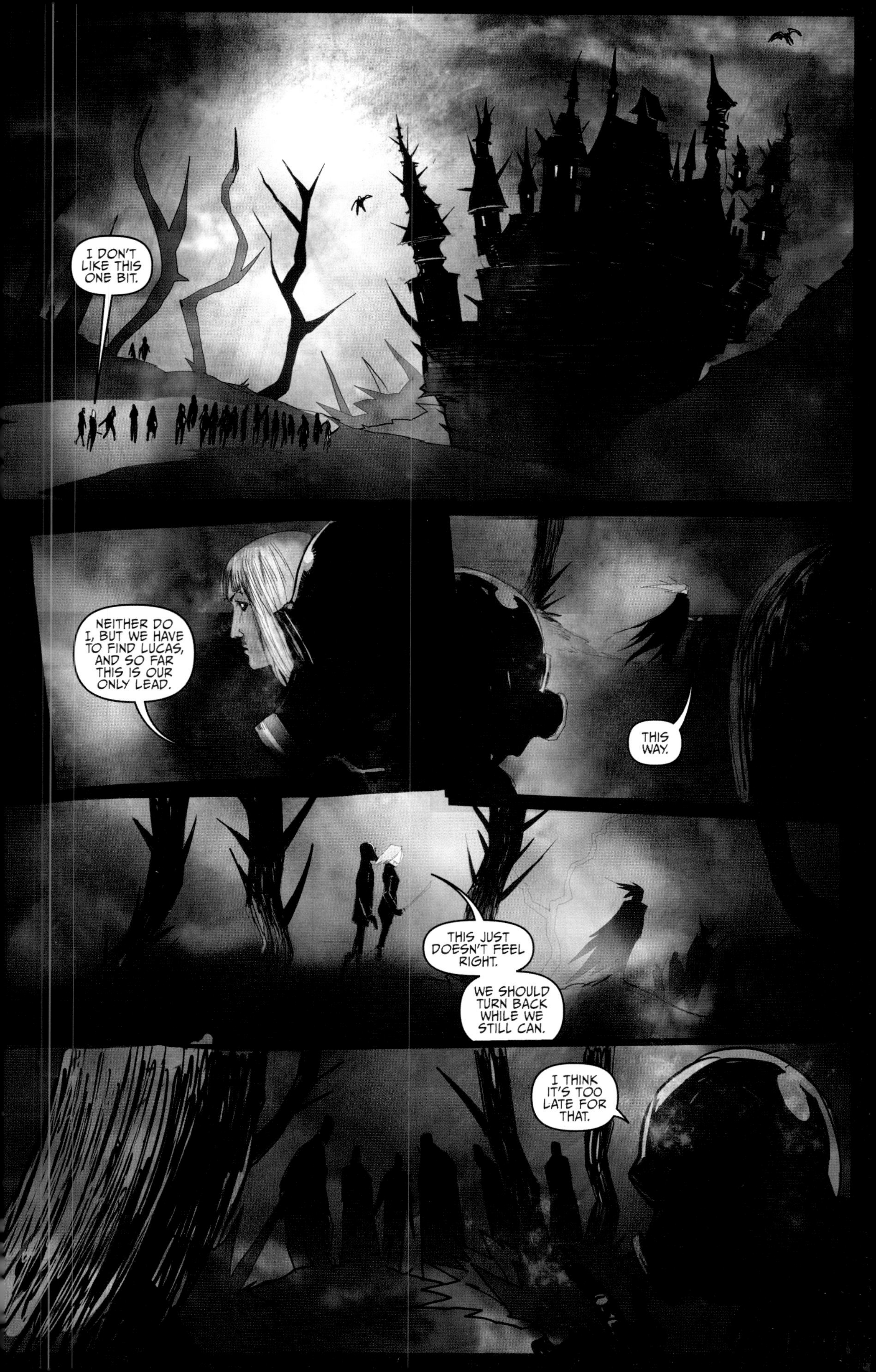
I DON'T LIKE THIS ONE BIT.
NEITHER DO I, BUT WE HAVE TO FIND LUCAS, AND SO FAR THIS IS OUR ONLY LEAD.
THIS WAY.
THIS JUST DOESN'T FEEL RIGHT.
WE SHOULD TURN BACK WHILE WE STILL CAN.
I THINK IT'S TOO LATE FOR THAT.

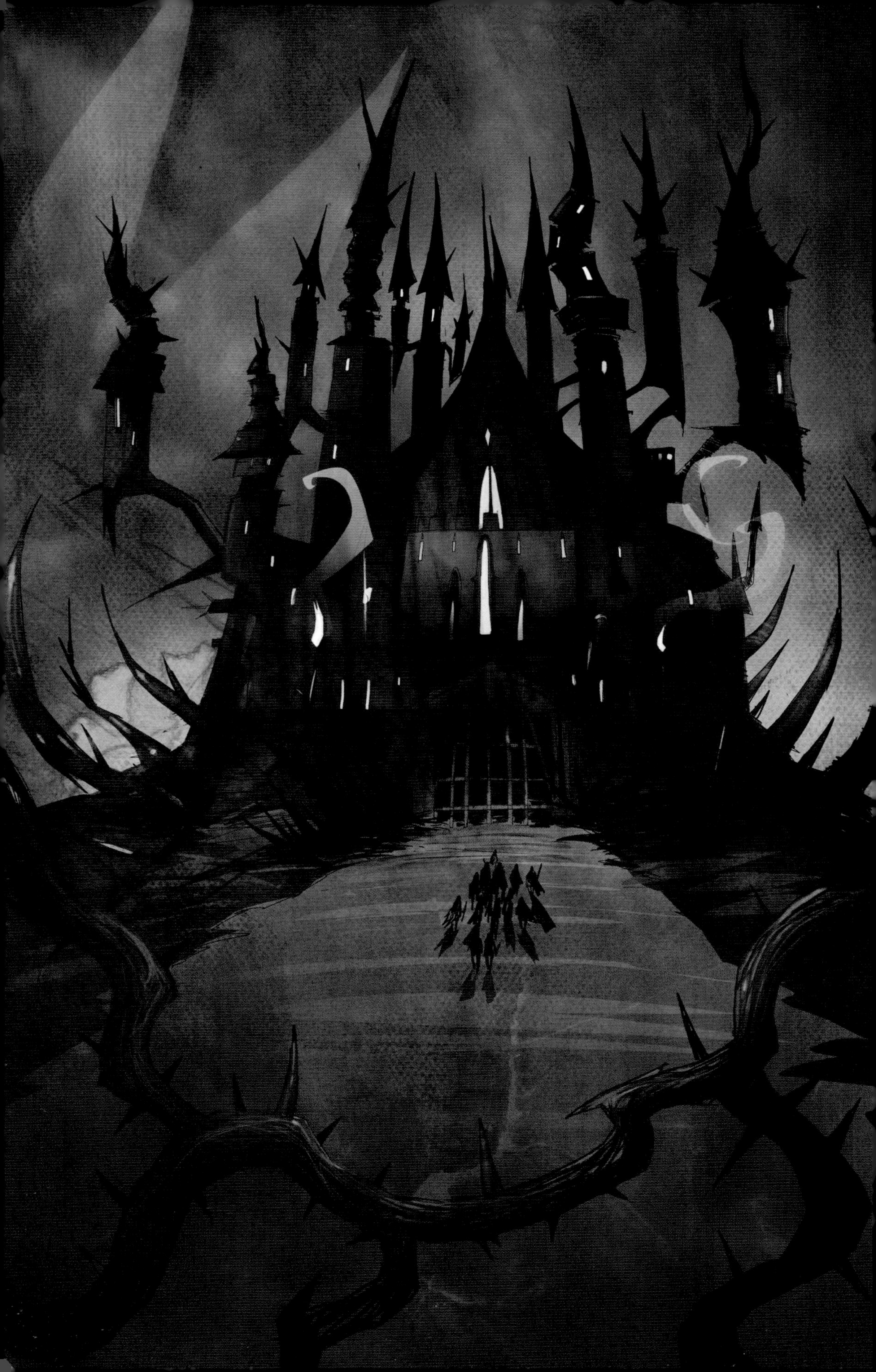

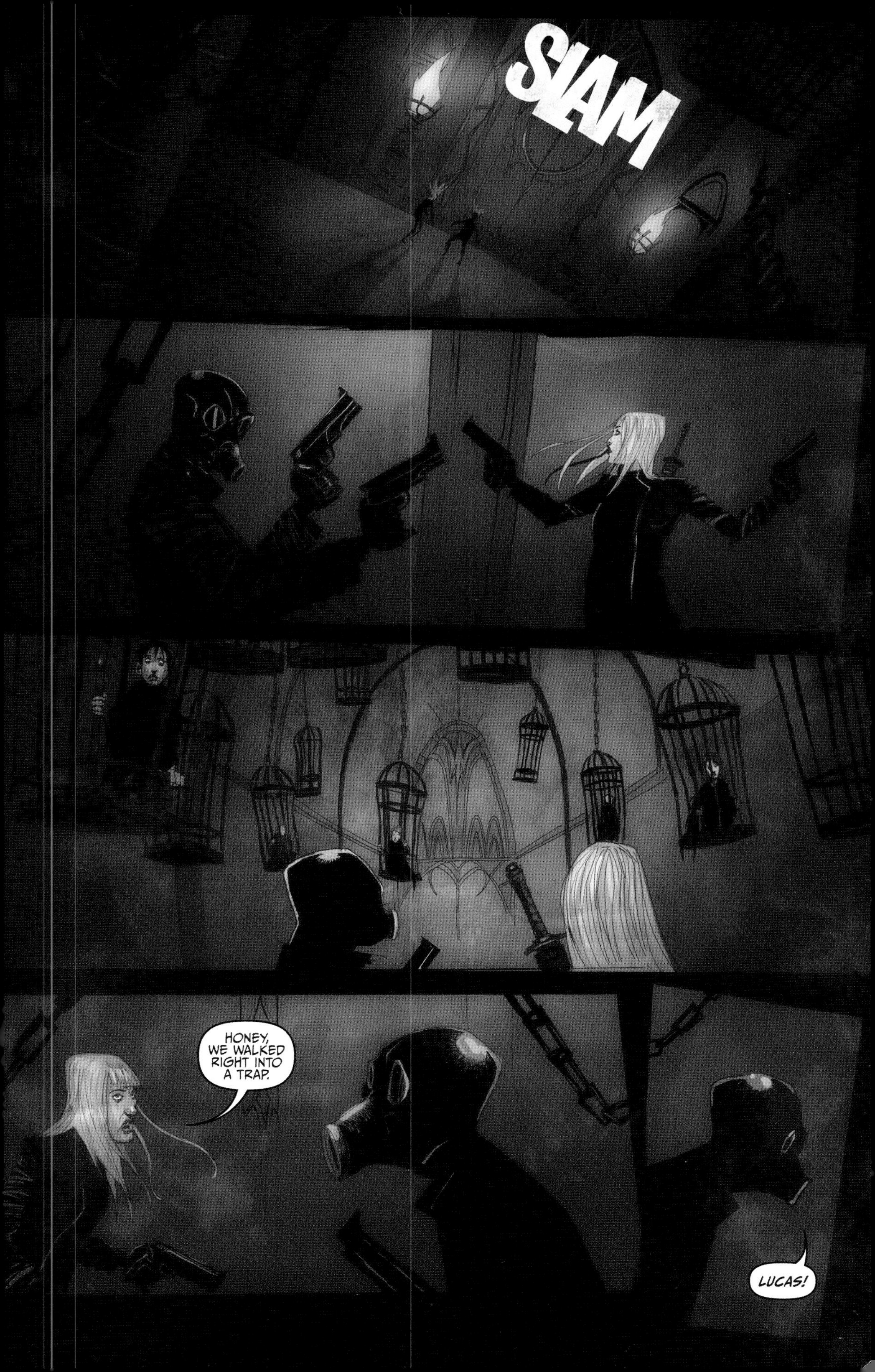
SLAM
HONEY, WE WALKED RIGHT INTO A TRAP.
LUCAS!

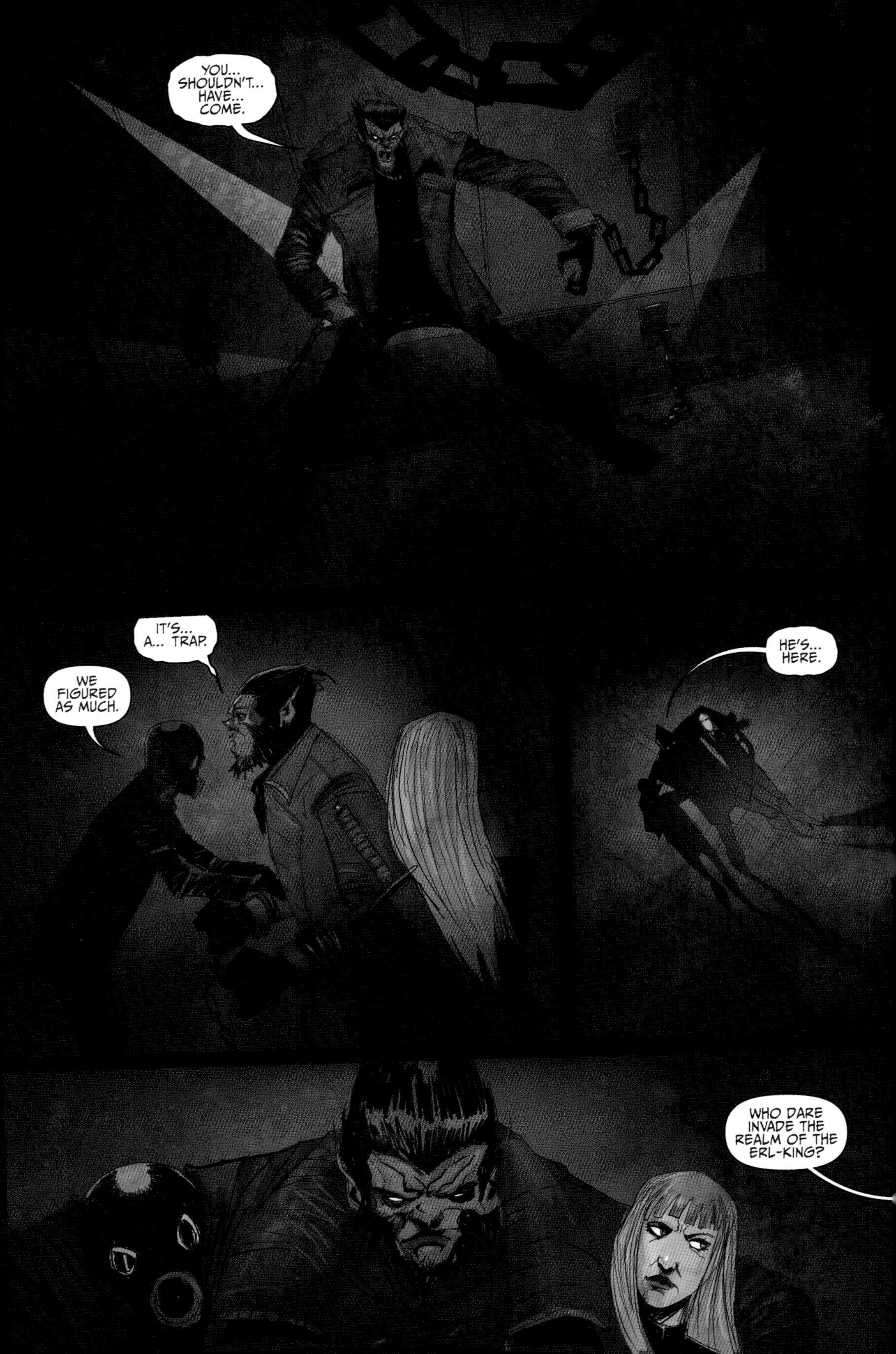
YOU... SHOULDN'T... HAVE... COME.
IT'S... A... TRAP.
WE FIGURED AS MUCH.
HE'S... HERE.
WHO DARE INVADE THE REALM OF THE ERL-KING?

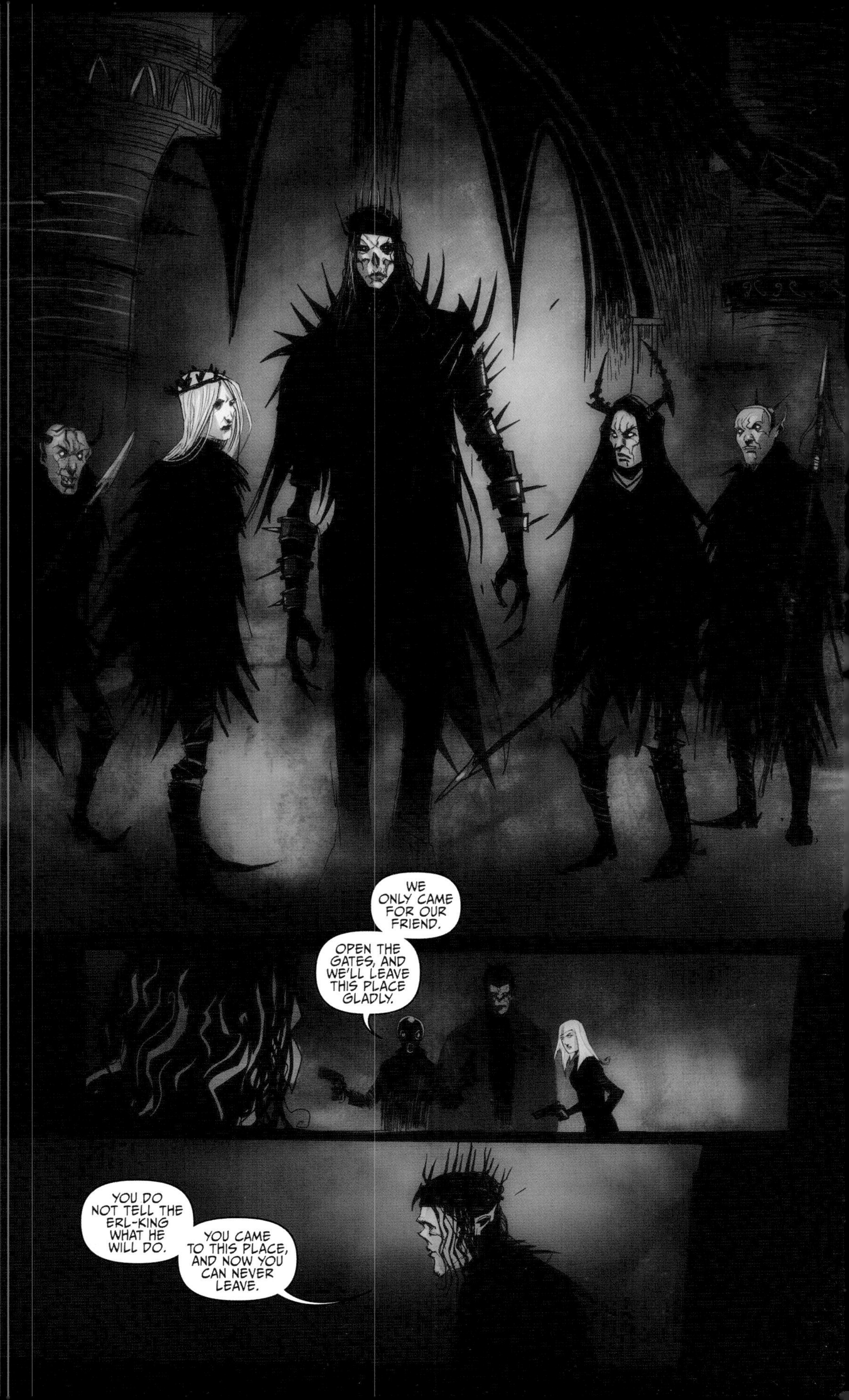

WE ONLY CAME FOR OUR FRIEND.
OPEN THE GATES, AND WE'LL LEAVE THIS PLACE GLADLY.
YOU DO NOT TELL THE ERL-KING WHAT HE WILL DO.
YOU CAME TO THIS PLACE, AND NOW YOU CAN NEVER LEAVE.

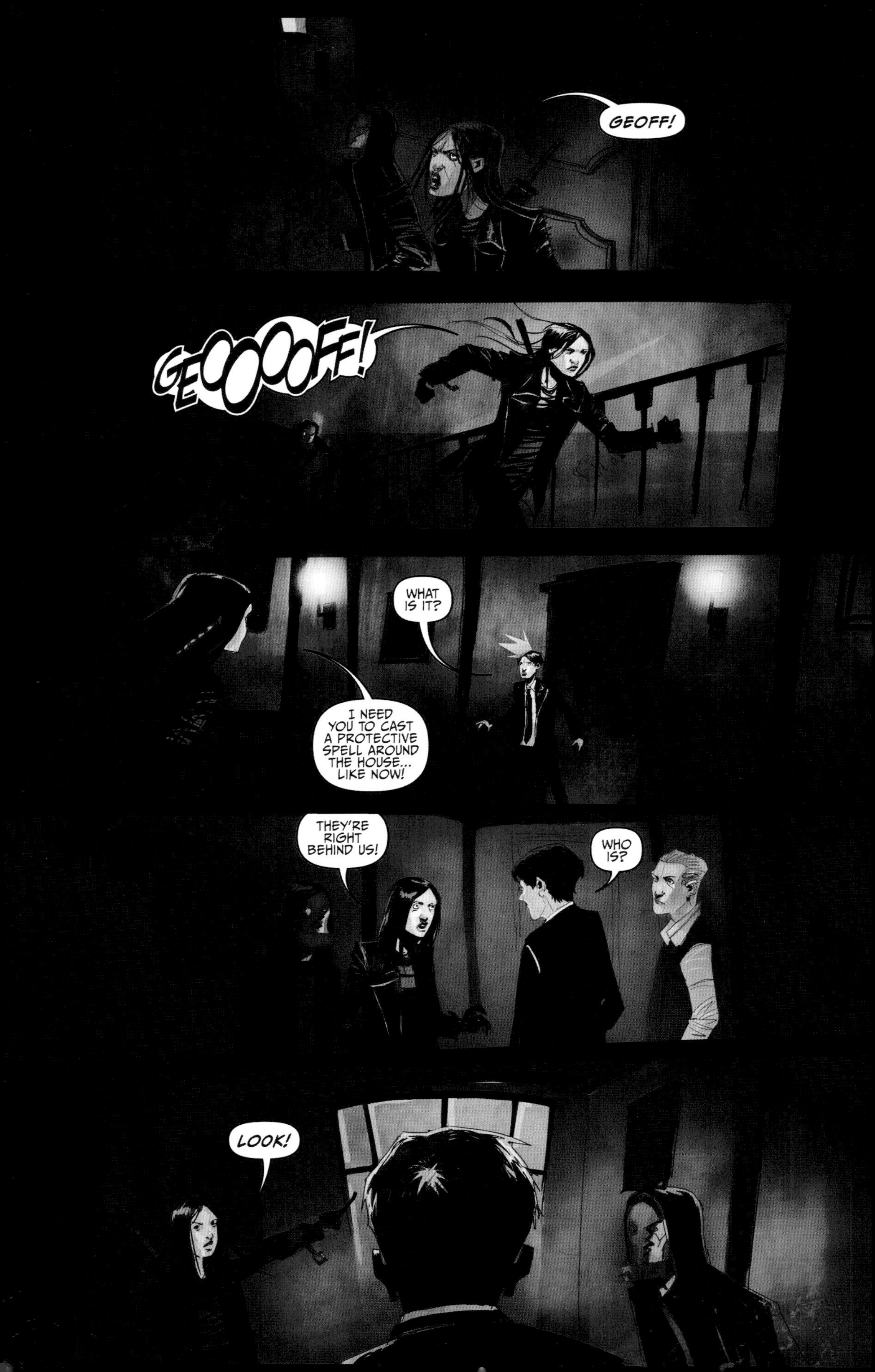
GEOFF!
GEOOOOFF!
WHAT IS IT?
I NEED YOU TO CAST A PROTECTIVE SPELL AROUND THE HOUSE... LIKE NOW!
THEY'RE RIGHT BEHIND US!
WHO IS?
LOOK!

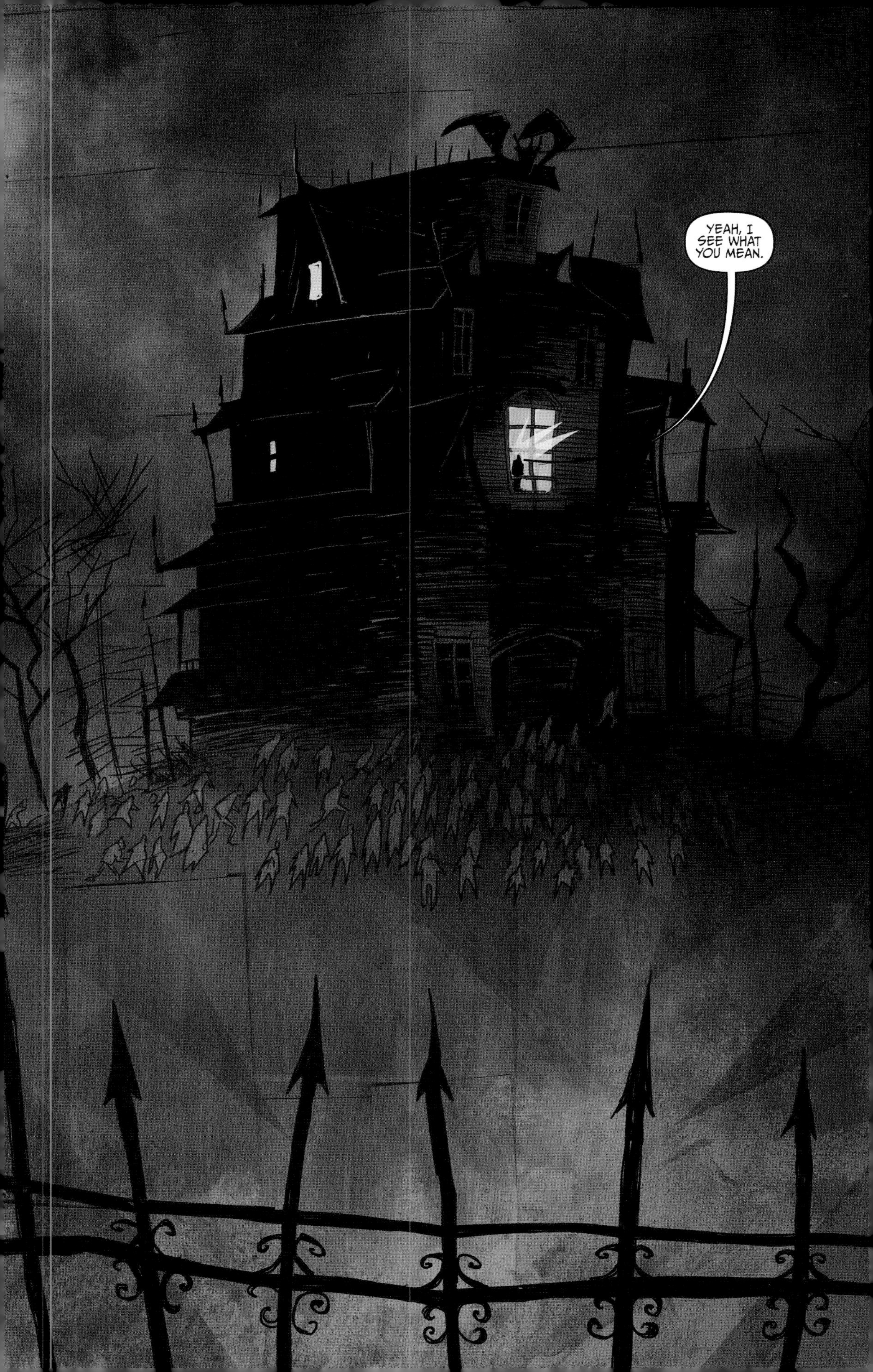
YEAH, I SEE WHAT YOU MEAN.

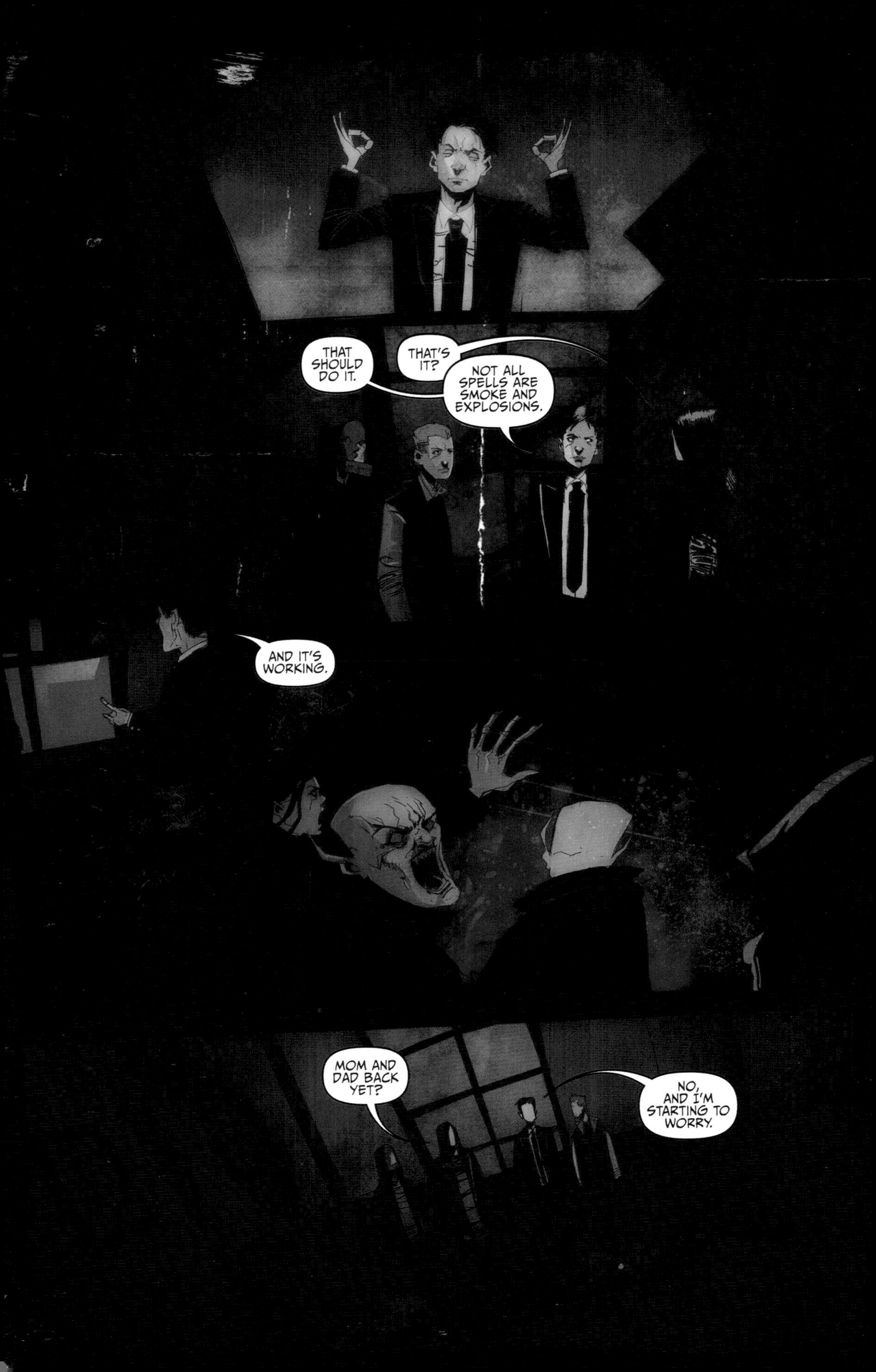
THAT SHOULD DO IT.
THAT'S IT?
NOT ALL SPELLS ARE SMOKE AND EXPLOSIONS.
AND IT'S WORKING.
MOM AND DAD BACK YET?
NO, AND I'M STARTING TO WORRY.

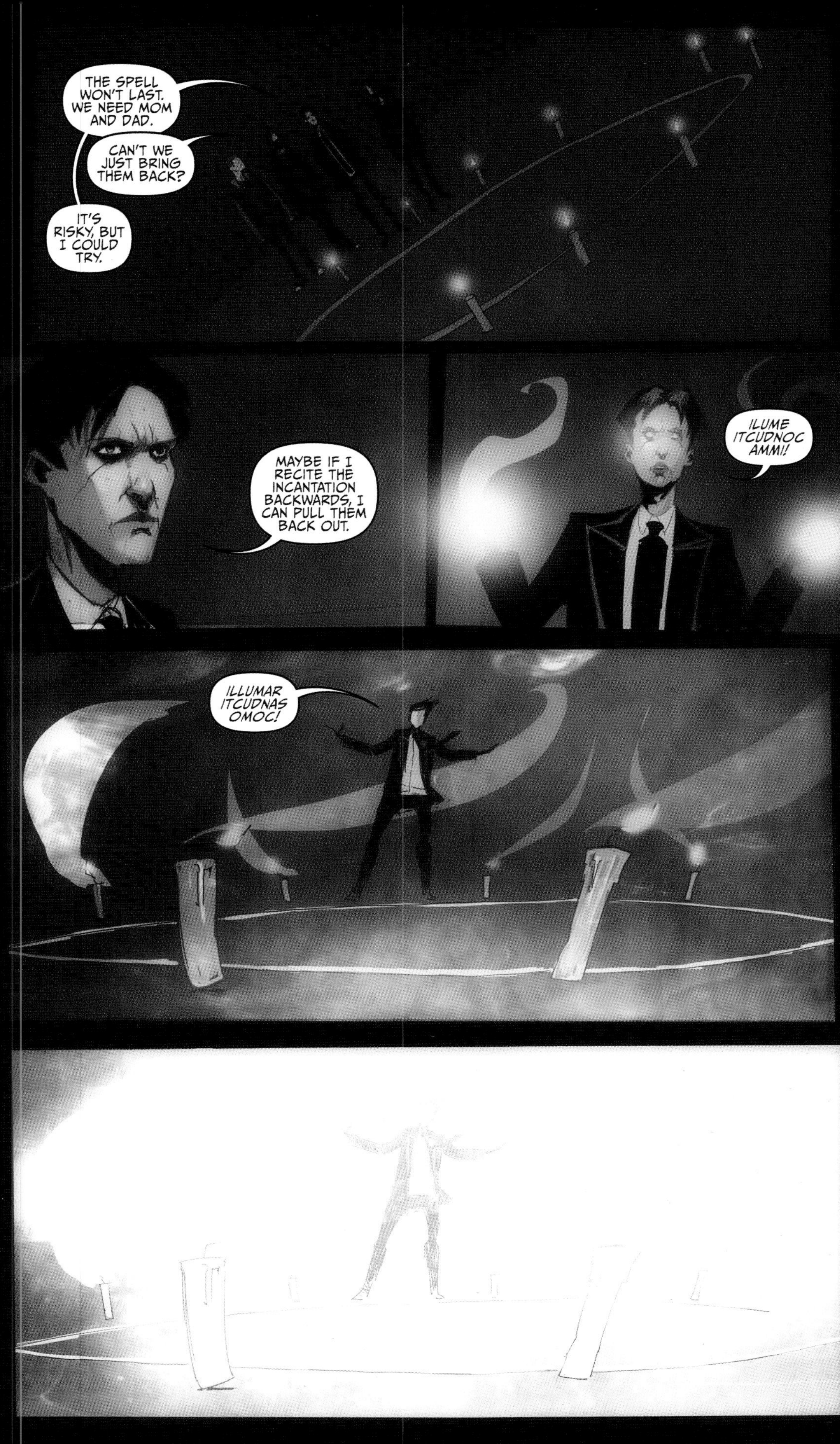
THE SPELL WON'T LAST. WE NEED MOM AND DAD.
CAN'T WE JUST BRING THEM BACK?
IT'S RISKY, BUT I COULD TRY.
MAYBE IF I RECITE THE INCANTATION BACKWARDS, I CAN PULL THEM BACK OUT.
ILUME ITCUDNOC AMMI!
ILLUMAR ITCUDNAS OMOC!

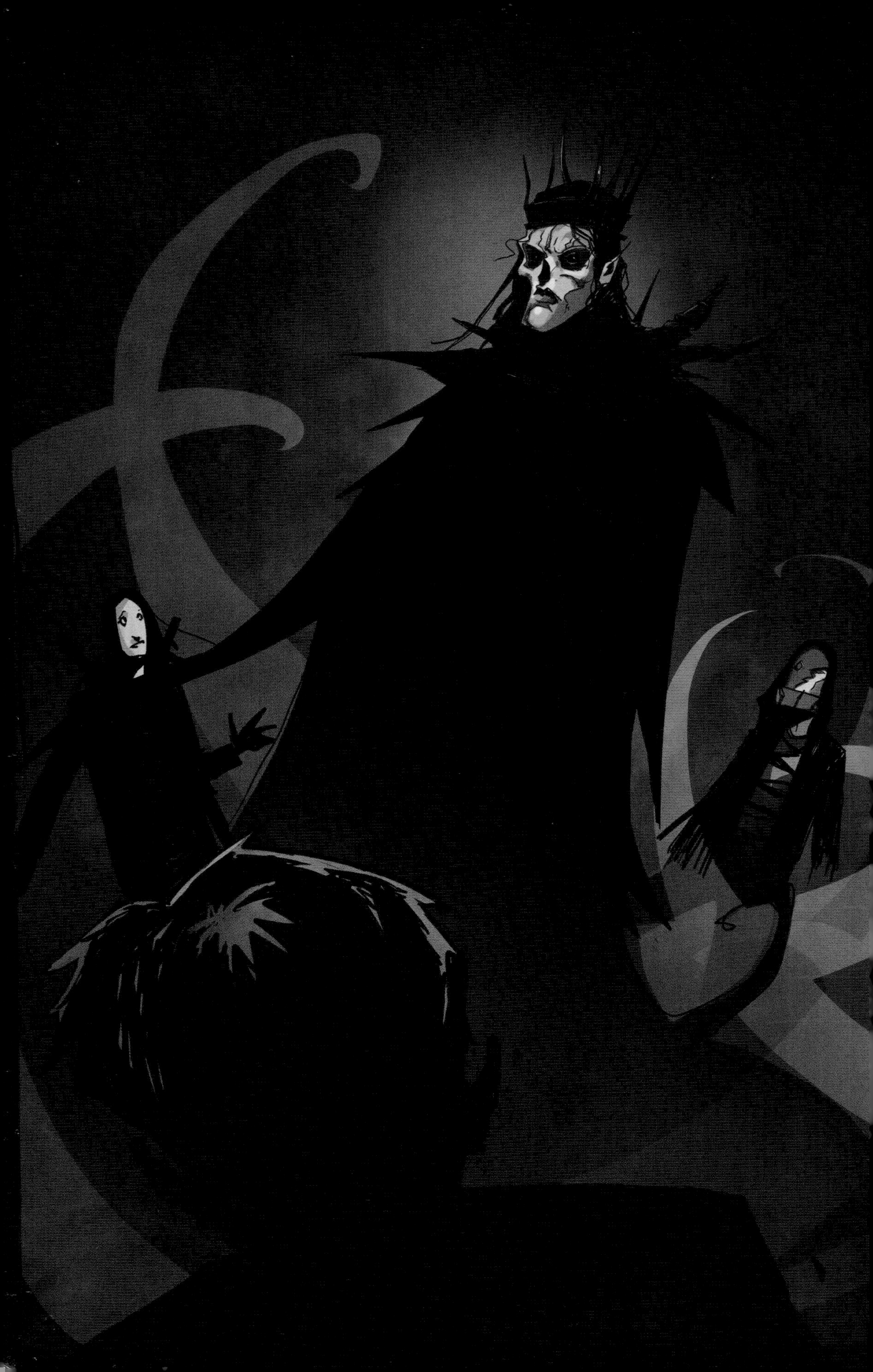

Z

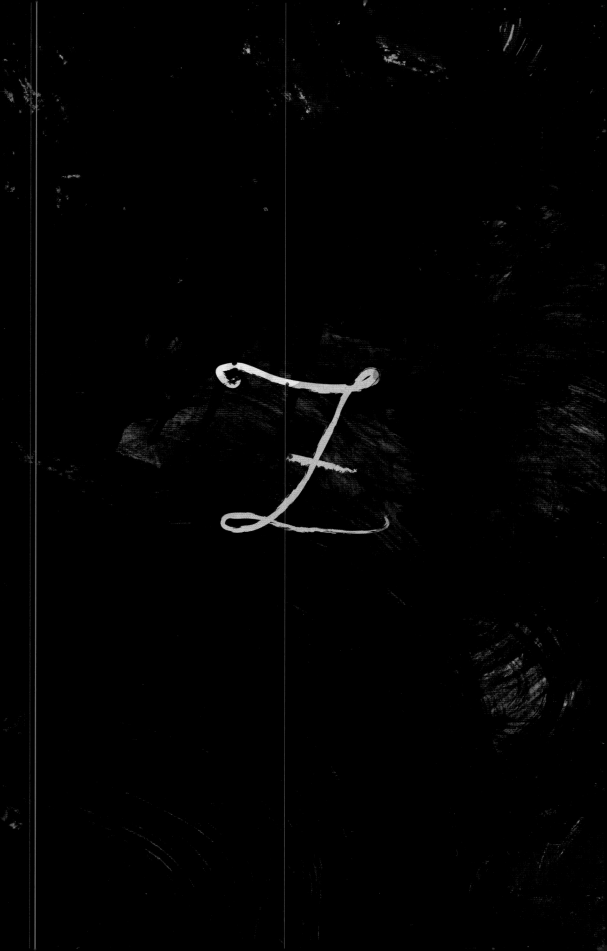

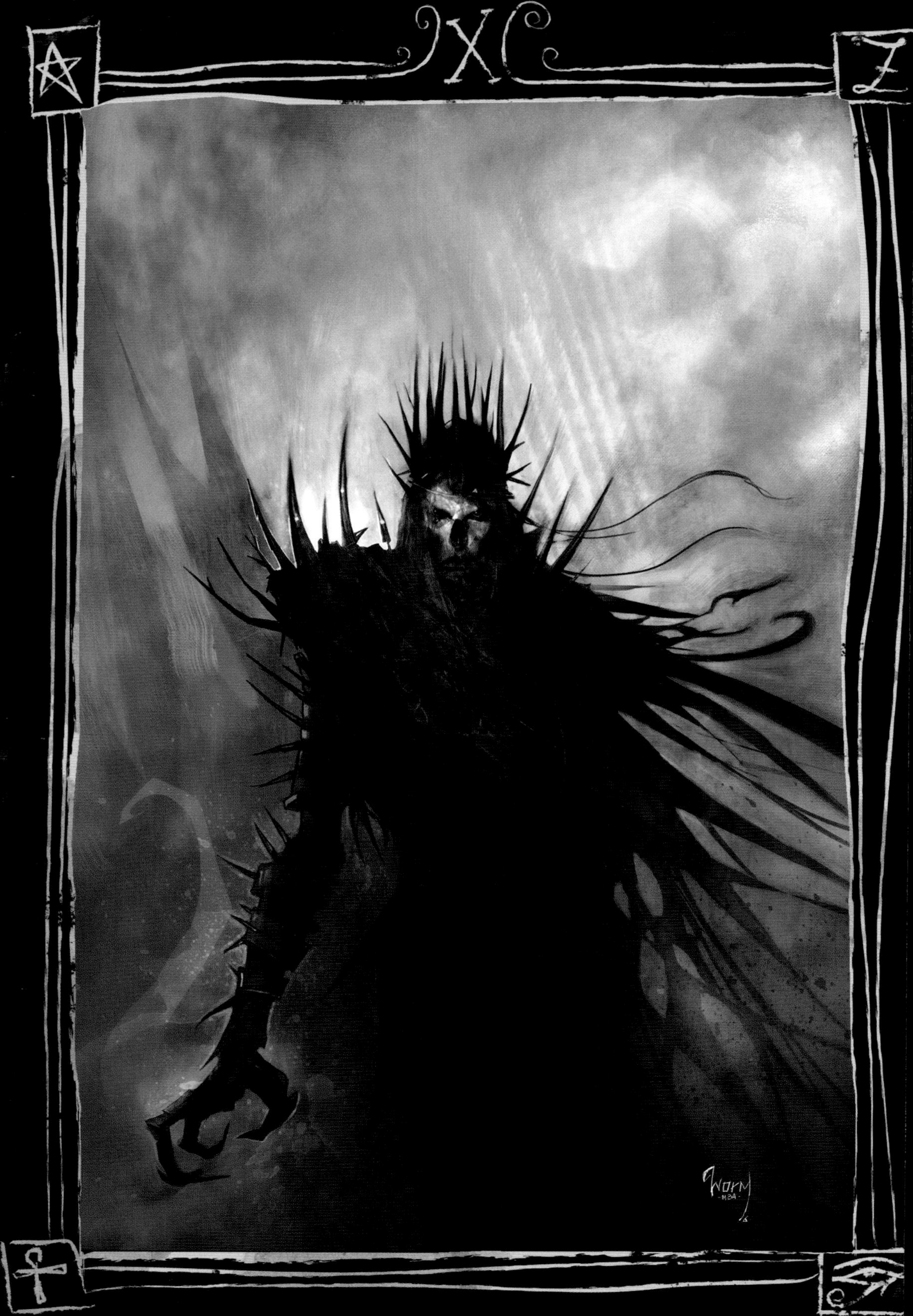
X

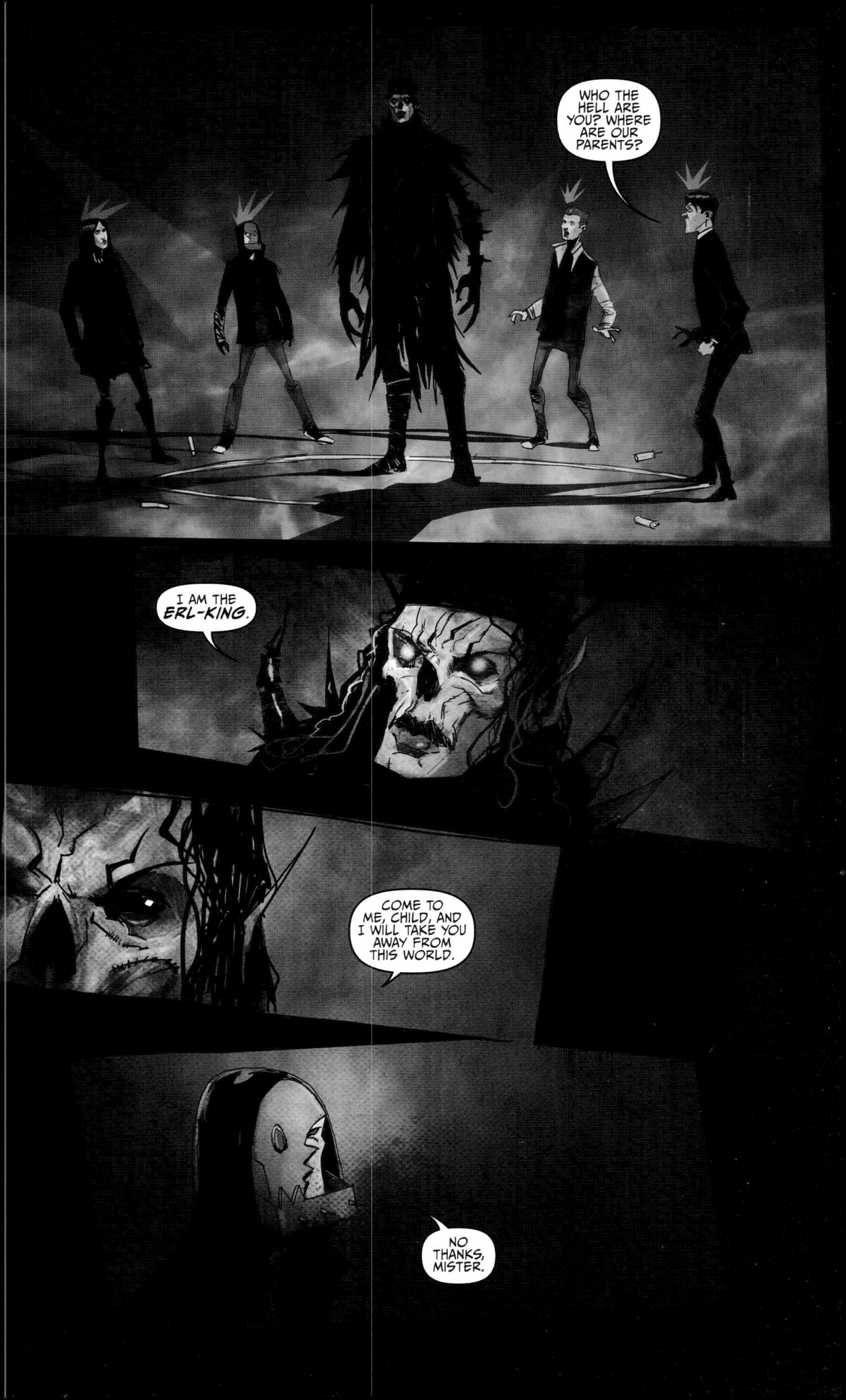
WHO THE HELL ARE YOU? WHERE ARE OUR PARENTS?
I AM THE ERL-KING.
COME TO ME, CHILD, AND I WILL TAKE YOU AWAY FROM THIS WORLD.
NO THANKS, MISTER.

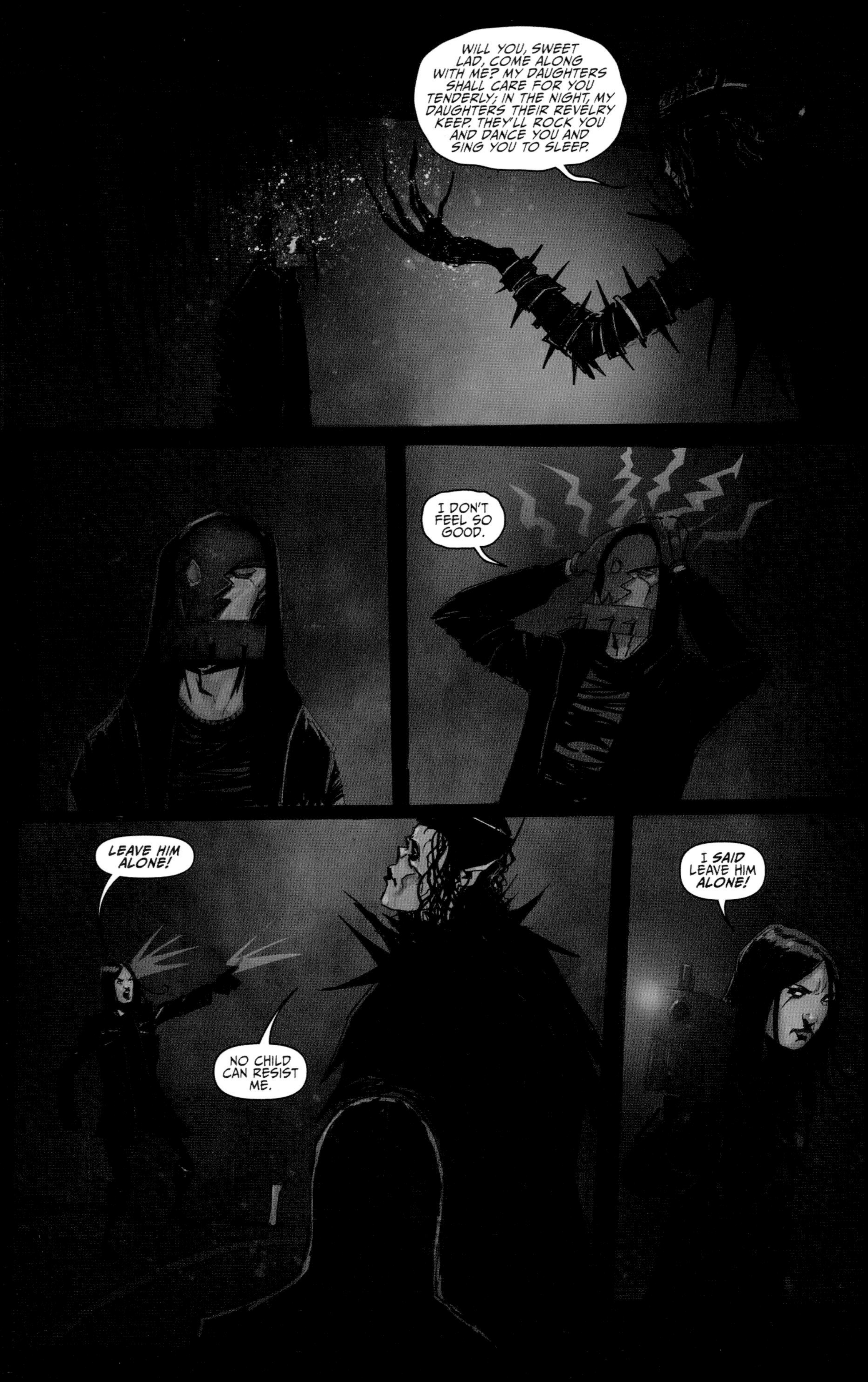
WILL YOU, SWEET LAD, COME ALONG WITH ME? MY DAUGHTERS SHALL CARE FOR YOU TENDERLY; IN THE NIGHT, MY DAUGHTERS THEIR REVELRY KEEP. THEY'LL ROCK YOU AND DANCE YOU AND SING YOU TO SLEEP.
I DON'T FEEL SO GOOD.
LEAVE HIM ALONE!
NO CHILD CAN RESIST ME.
I SAID LEAVE HIM ALONE!

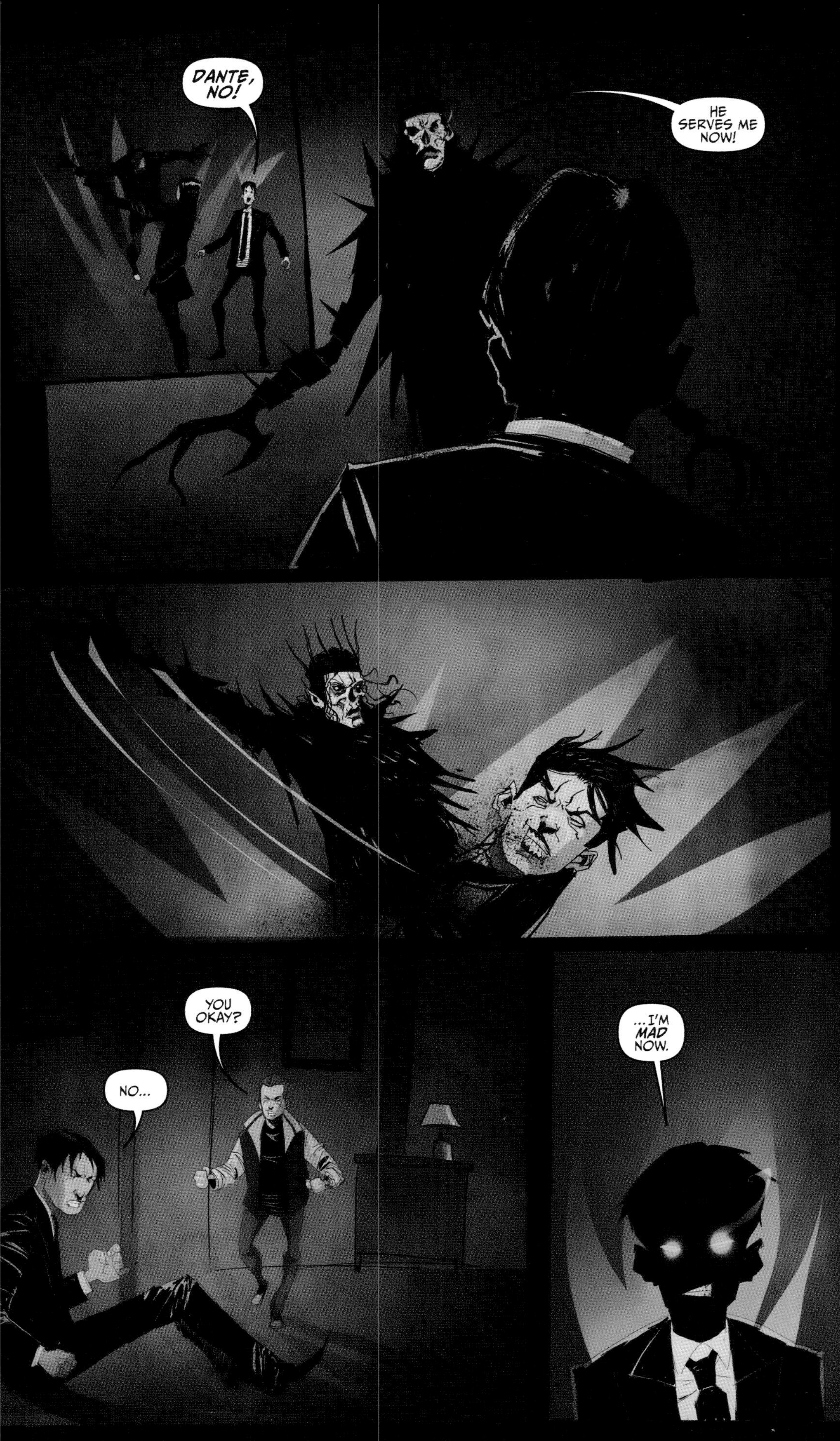
DANTE, NO!
HE SERVES ME NOW!
YOU OKAY?
NO...
...I'M MAD NOW.

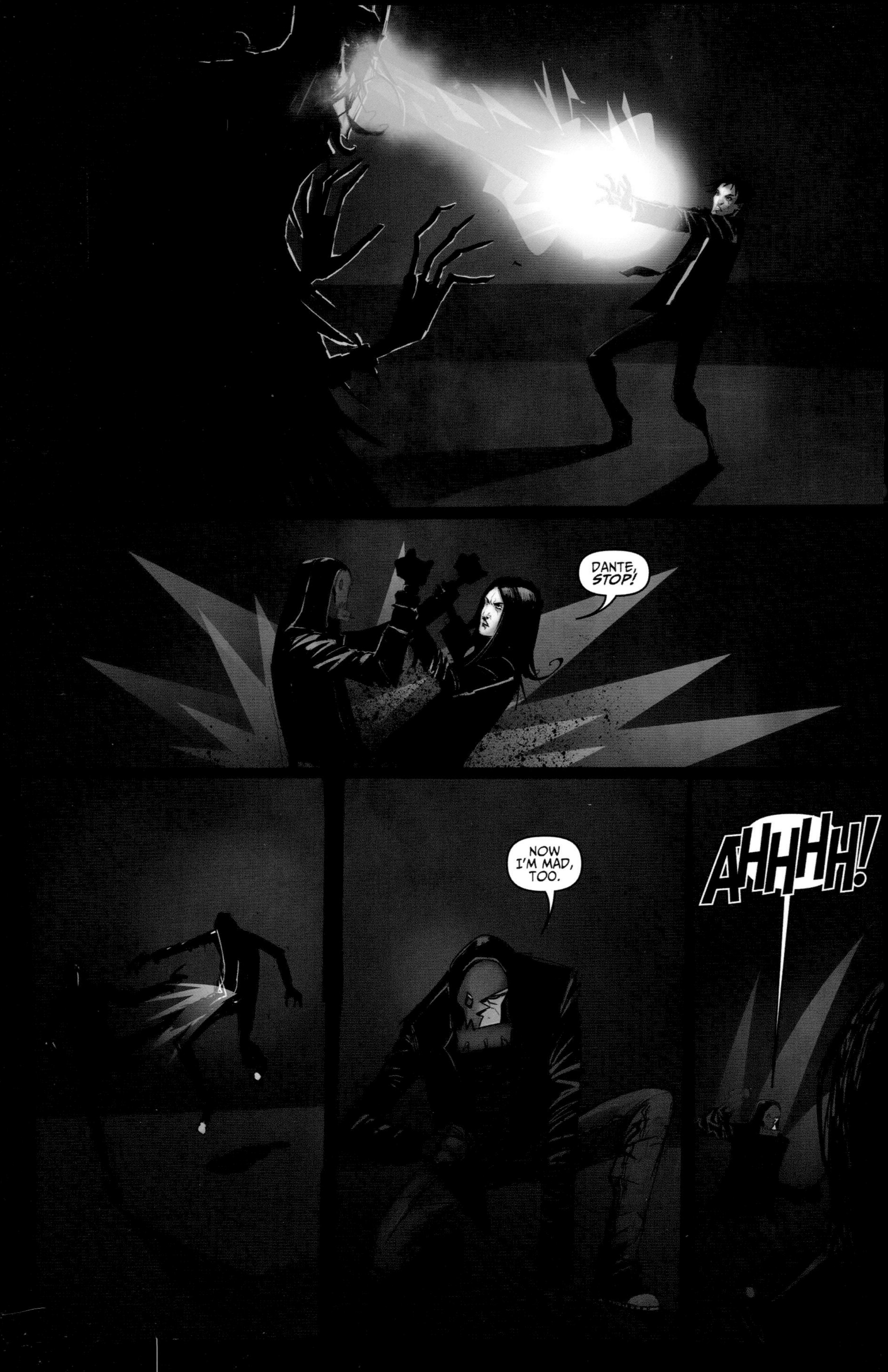
DANTE, STOP!
NOW I'M MAD, TOO.
AHHHH!

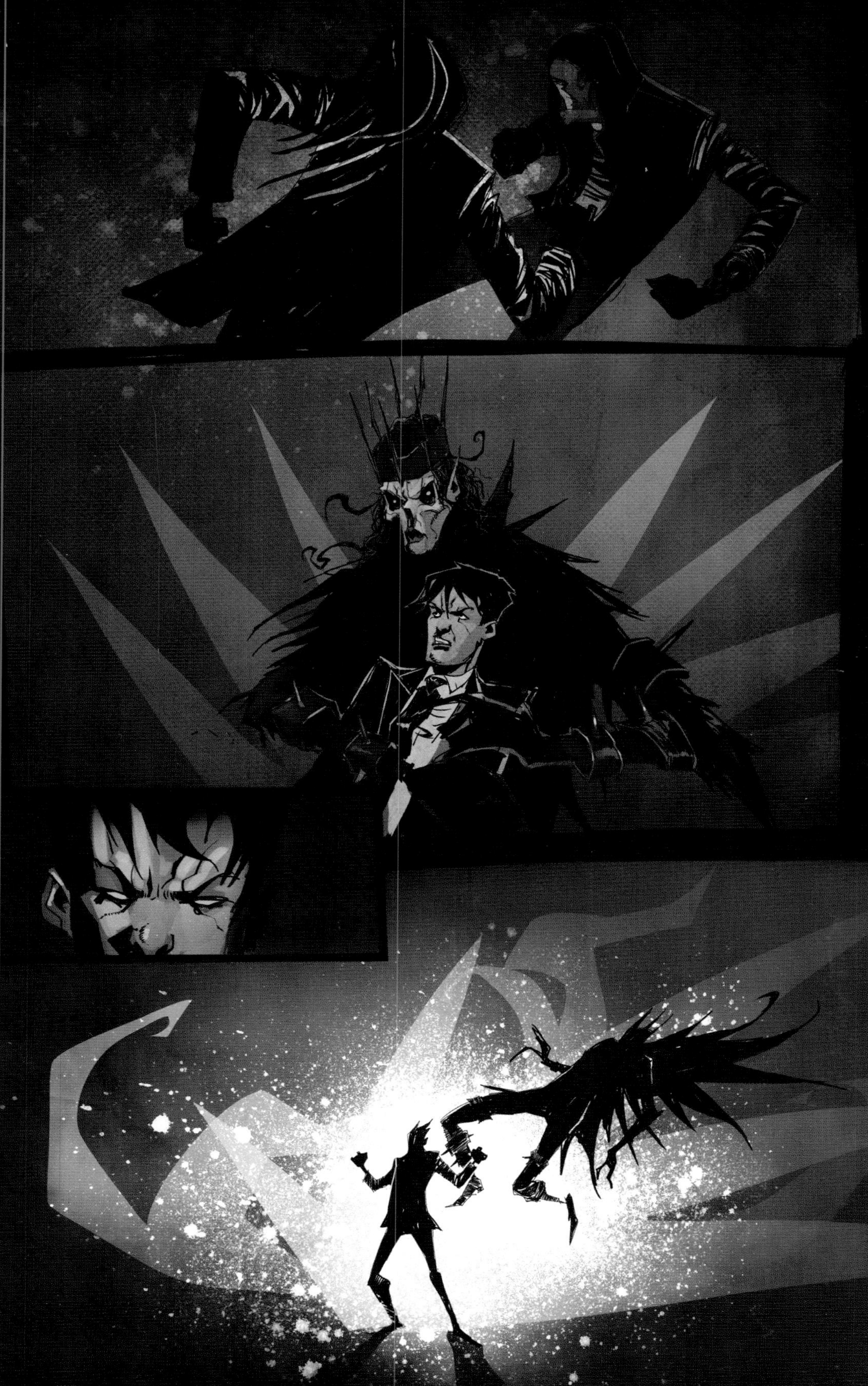

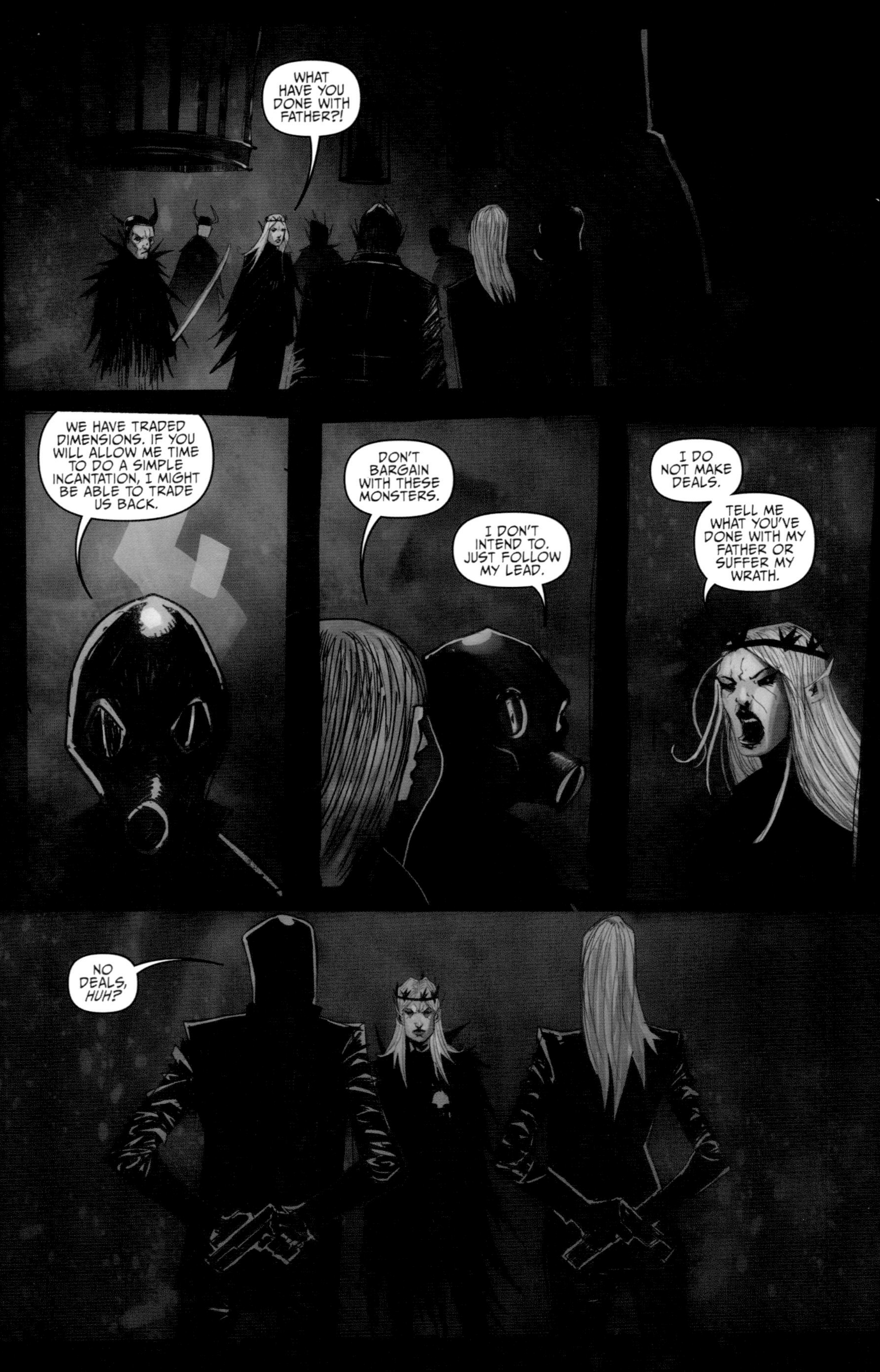
WHAT HAVE YOU DONE WITH FATHER?!
WE HAVE TRADED DIMENSIONS. IF YOU WILL ALLOW ME TIME TO DO A SIMPLE INCANTATION, I MIGHT BE ABLE TO TRADE US BACK.
DON'T BARGAIN WITH THESE MONSTERS.
I DON'T INTEND TO. JUST FOLLOW MY LEAD.
I DO NOT MAKE DEALS.
TELL ME WHAT YOU'VE DONE WITH MY FATHER OR SUFFER MY WRATH.
NO DEALS, HUH?

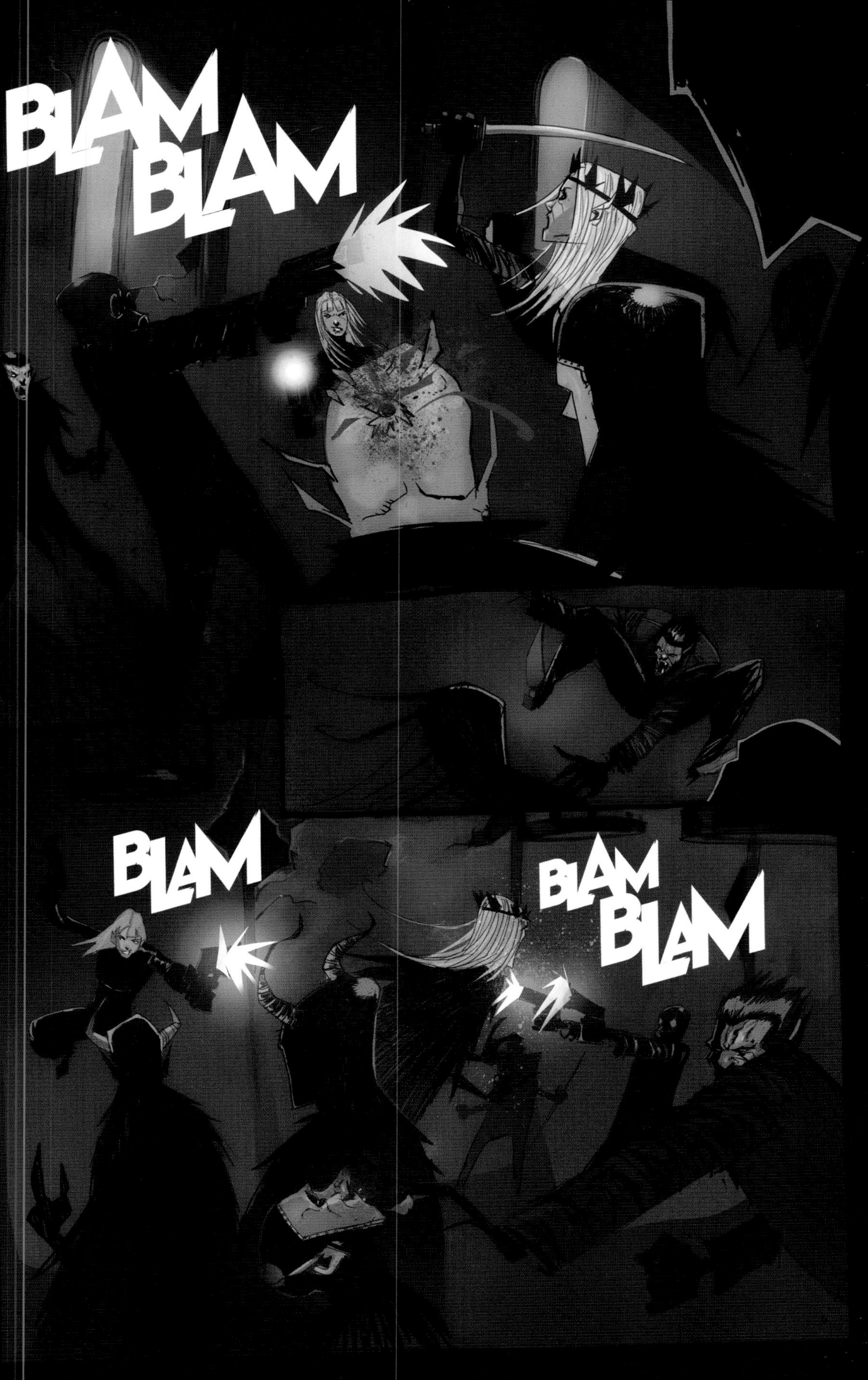
BLAM
BLAM
BLAM
BLAM
BLAM

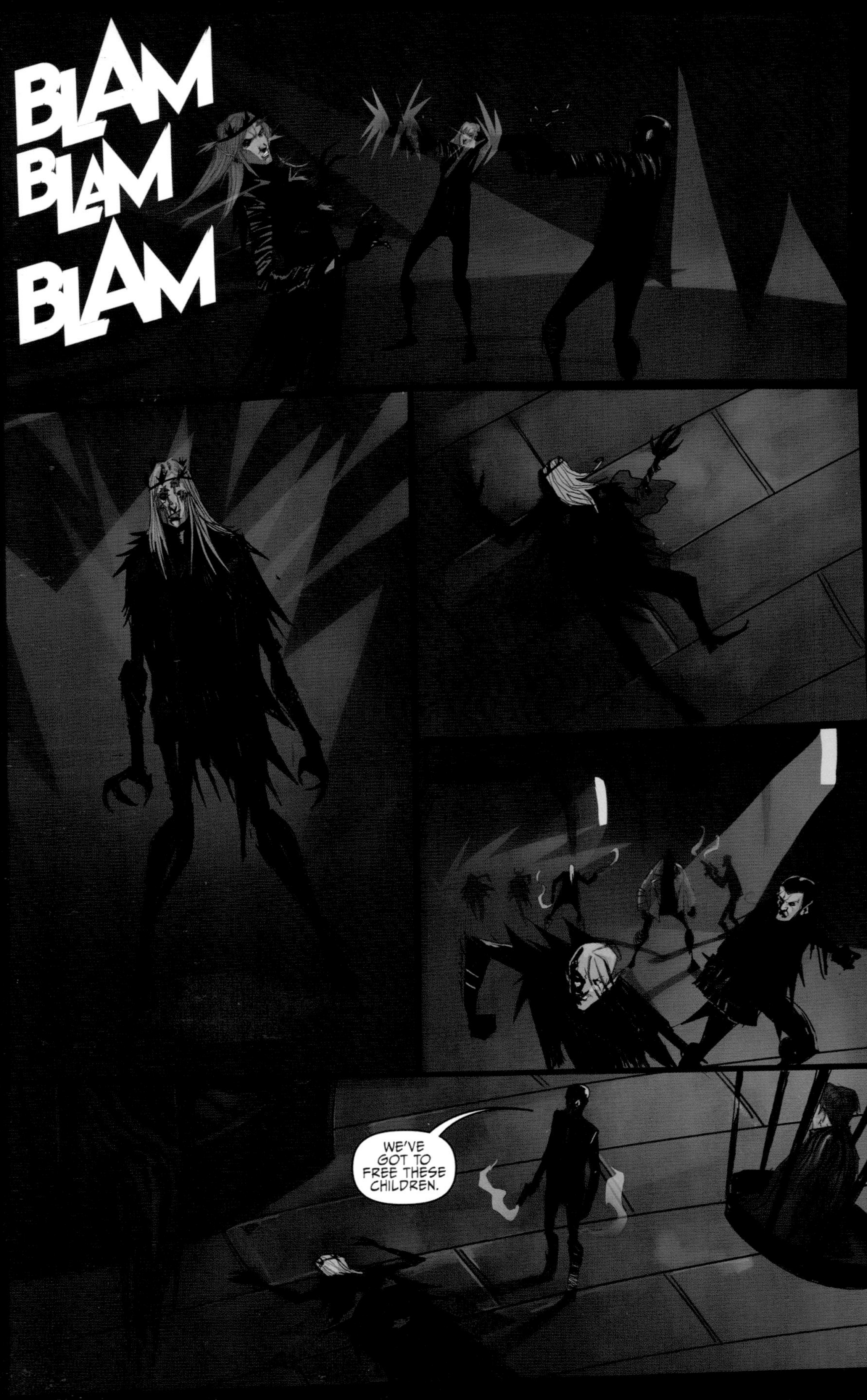
BLAM
BLAM
BLAM
WE'VE GOT TO FREE THESE CHILDREN.

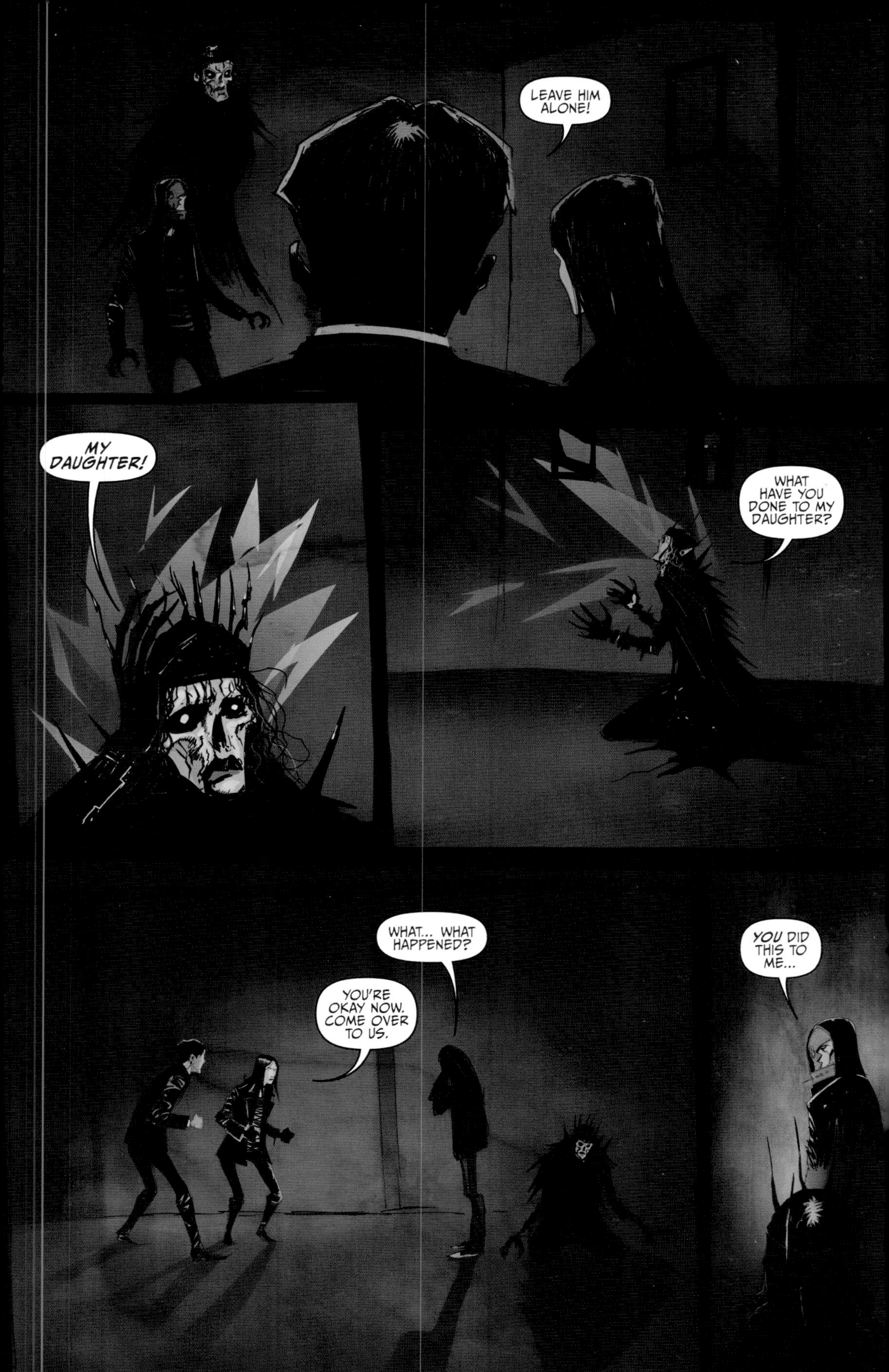
LEAVE HIM ALONE!
MY DAUGHTER!
WHAT HAVE YOU DONE TO MY DAUGHTER?
WHAT... WHAT HAPPENED?
YOU'RE OKAY NOW. COME OVER TO US.
YOU DID THIS TO ME...

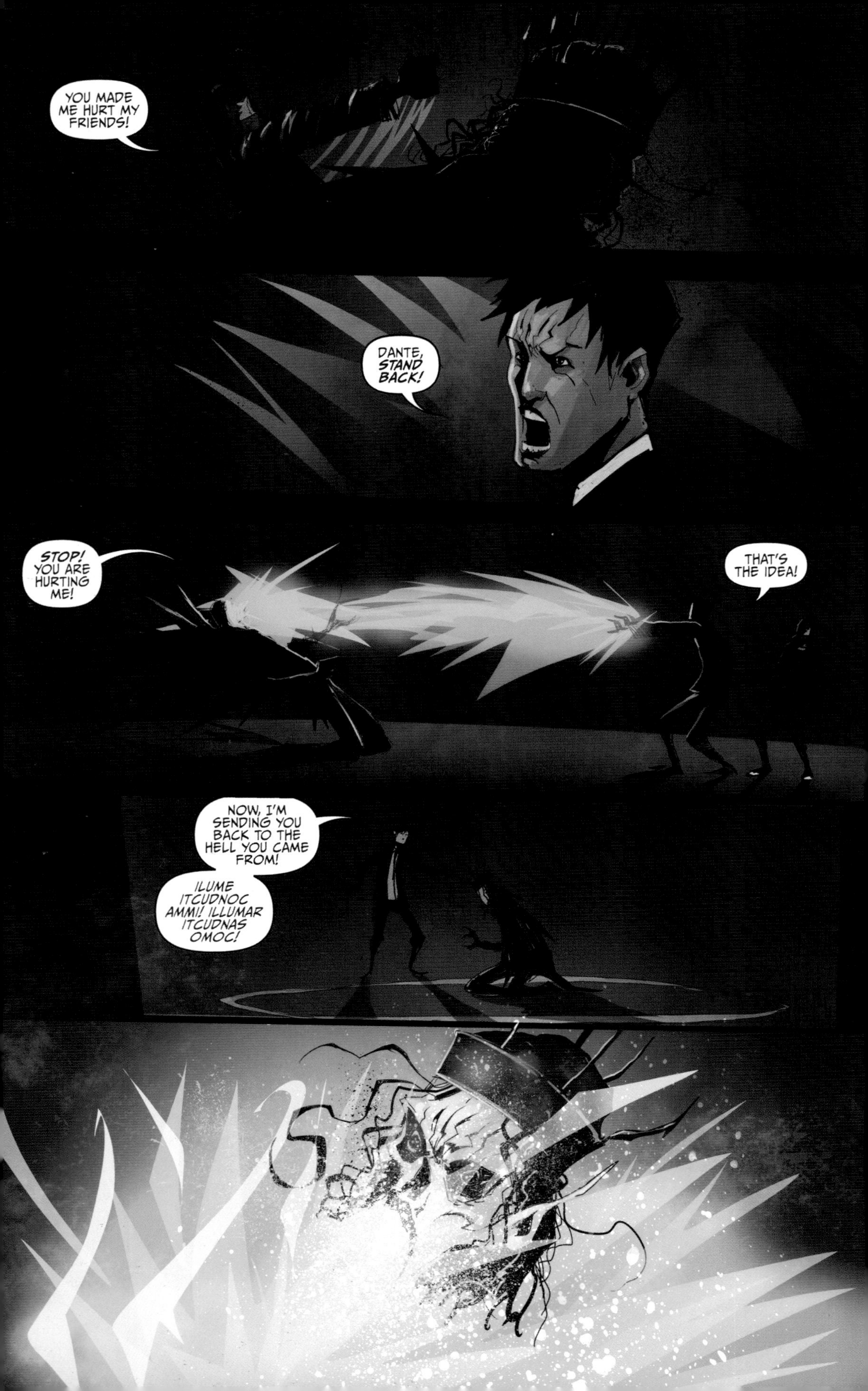
YOU MADE ME HURT MY FRIENDS!
DANTE, STAND BACK!
STOP! YOU ARE HURTING ME!
THAT'S THE IDEA!
NOW, I'M SENDING YOU BACK TO THE HELL YOU CAME FROM!
ILUME ITCUDNOC AMMI! ILLUMAR ITCUDNAS OMOC!

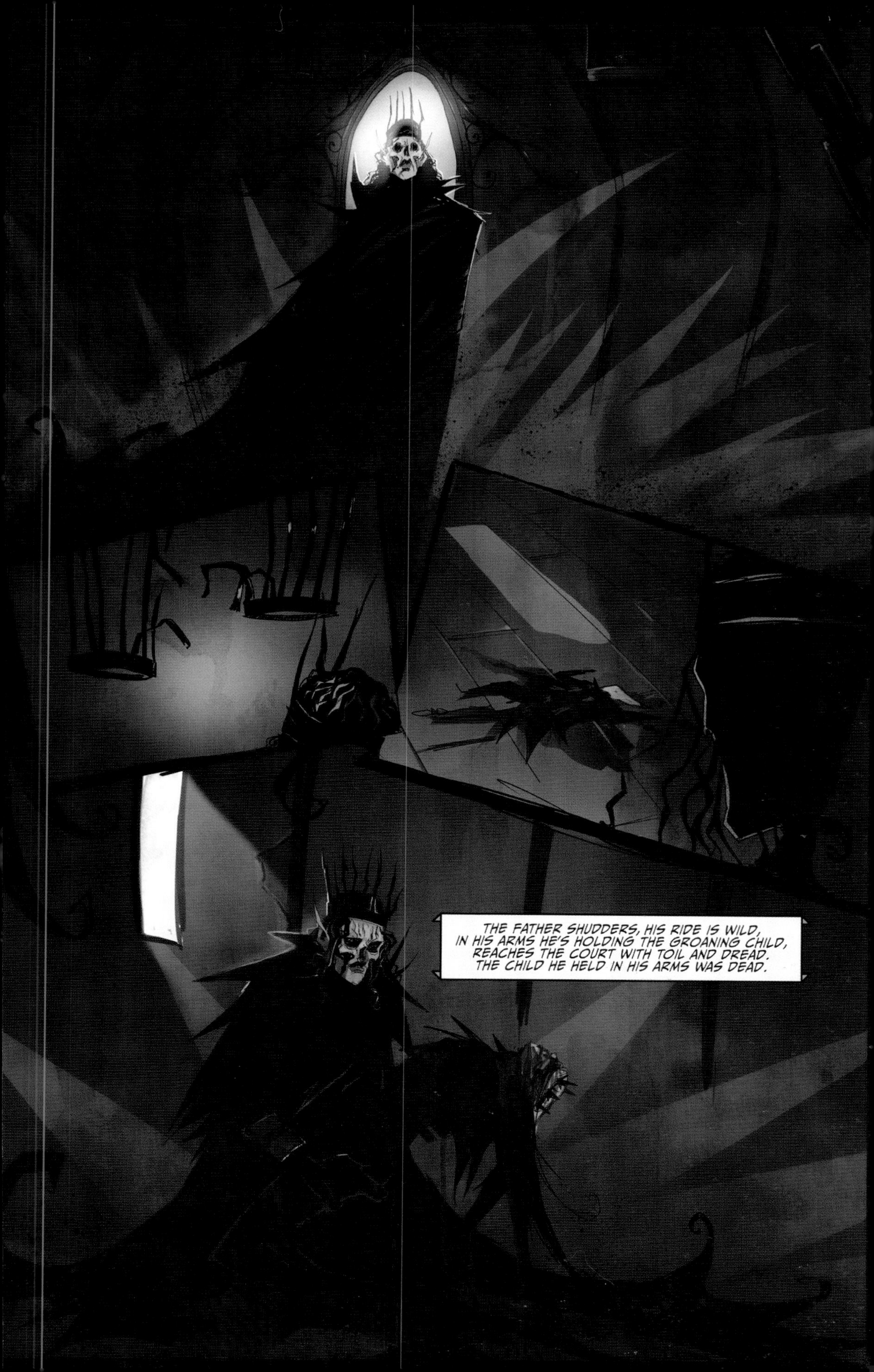
THE FATHER SHUDDERS, HIS RIDE IS WILD,
IN HIS ARMS HE'S HOLDING THE GROANING CHILD,
REACHES THE COURT WITH TOIL AND DREAD.
THE CHILD HE HELD IN HIS ARMS WAS DEAD.

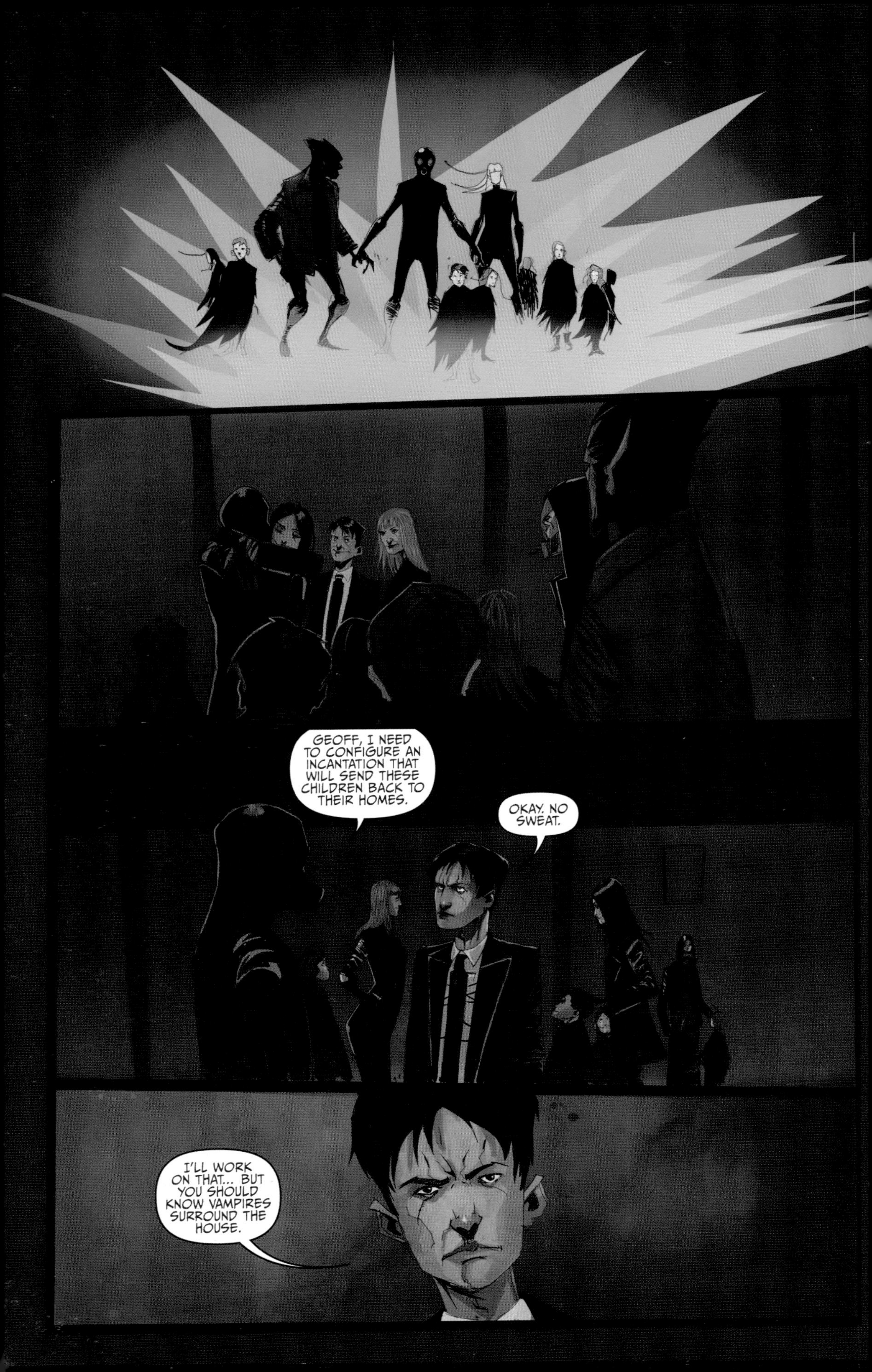
GEOFF, I NEED TO CONFIGURE AN INCANTATION THAT WILL SEND THESE CHILDREN BACK TO THEIR HOMES.
OKAY. NO SWEAT.
I'LL WORK ON THAT... BUT YOU SHOULD KNOW VAMPIRES SURROUND THE HOUSE.

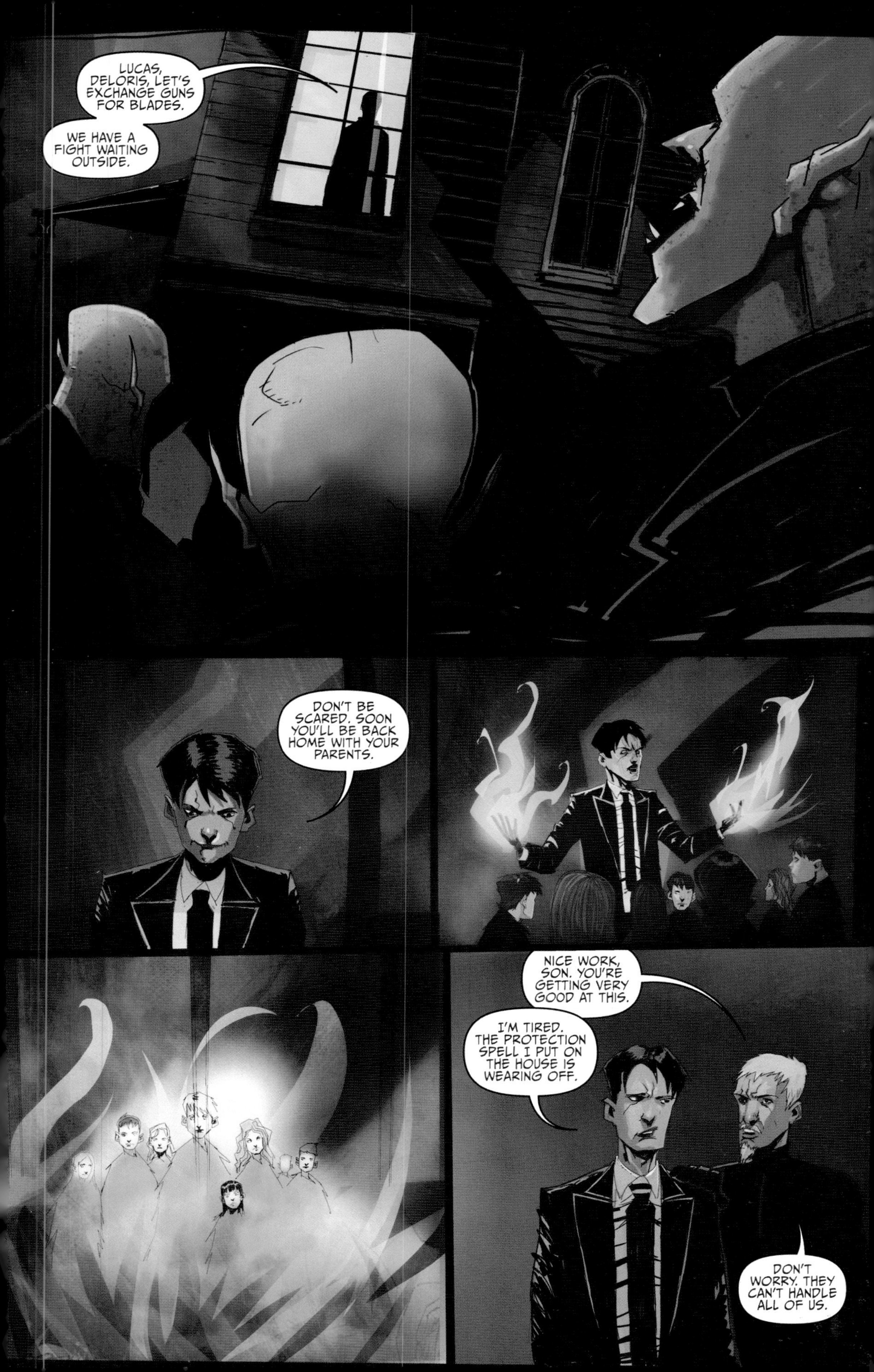
LUCAS, DELORIS, LET'S EXCHANGE GUNS FOR BLADES.
WE HAVE A FIGHT WAITING OUTSIDE.
DON'T BE SCARED. SOON YOU'LL BE BACK HOME WITH YOUR PARENTS.
NICE WORK, SON. YOU'RE GETTING VERY GOOD AT THIS.
I'M TIRED. THE PROTECTION SPELL I PUT ON THE HOUSE IS WEARING OFF.
DON'T WORRY. THEY CAN'T HANDLE ALL OF US.

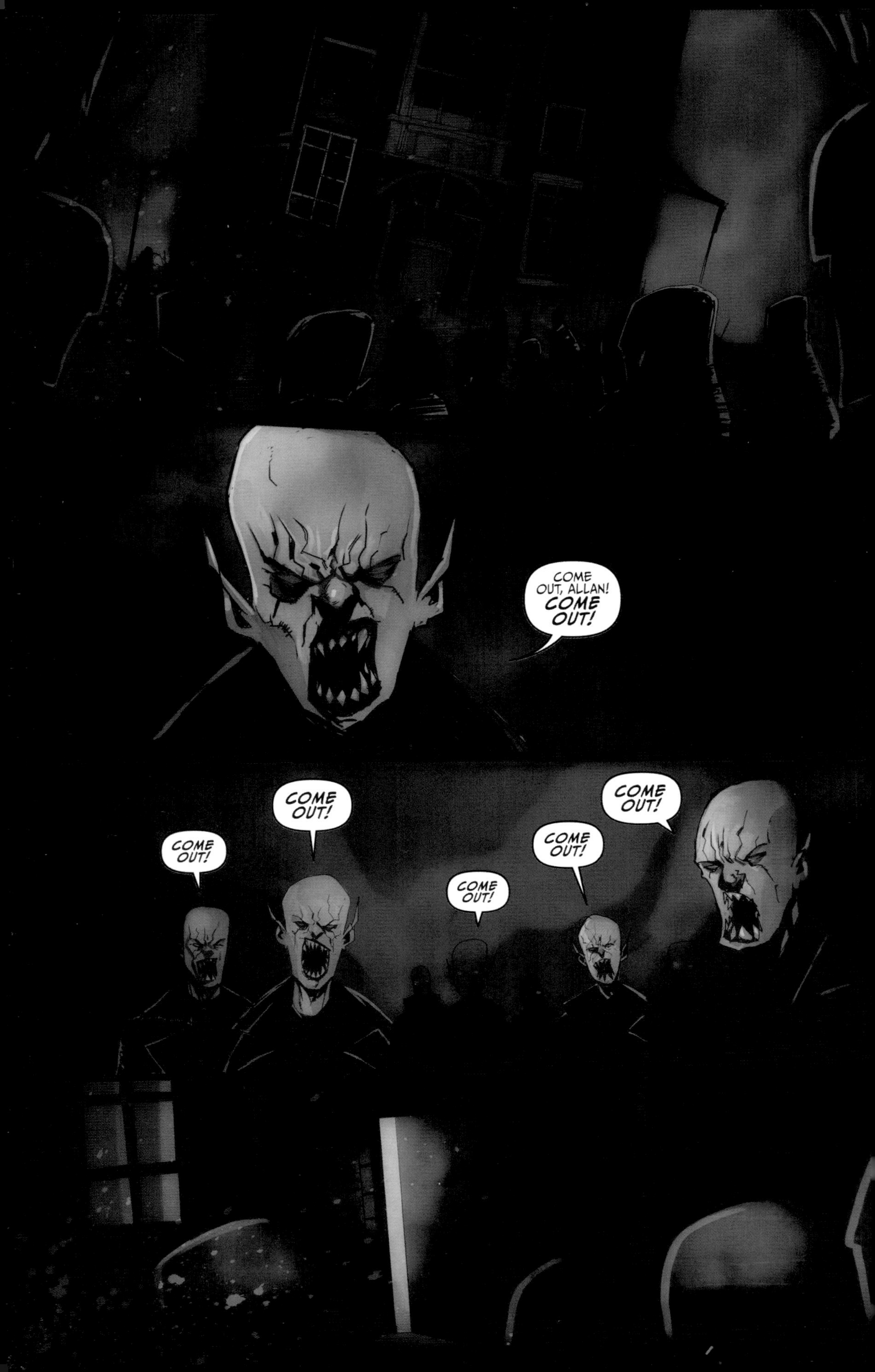
COME OUT, ALLAN! COME OUT!
COME OUT!
COME OUT!
COME OUT!
COME OUT!
COME OUT!

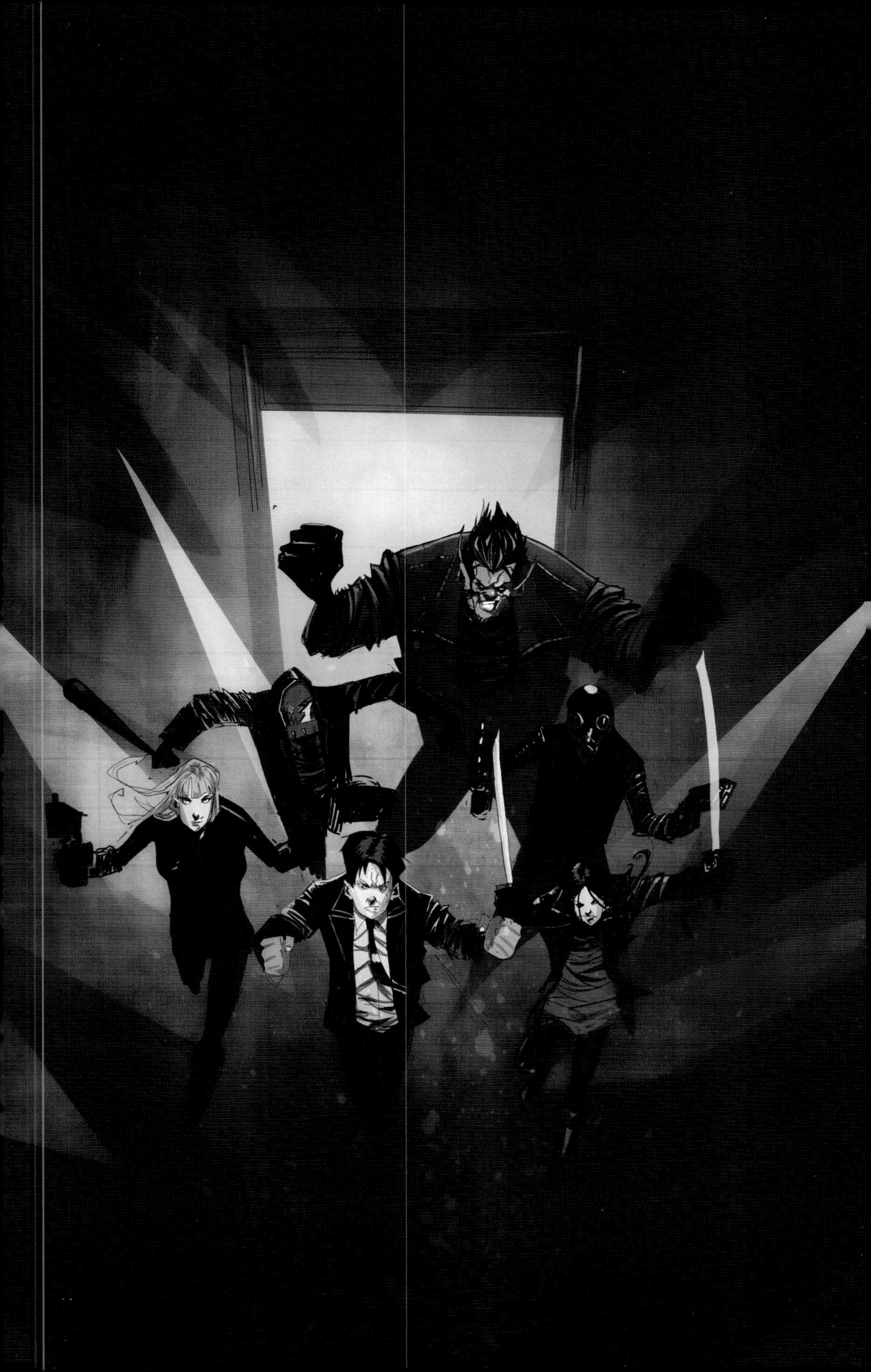

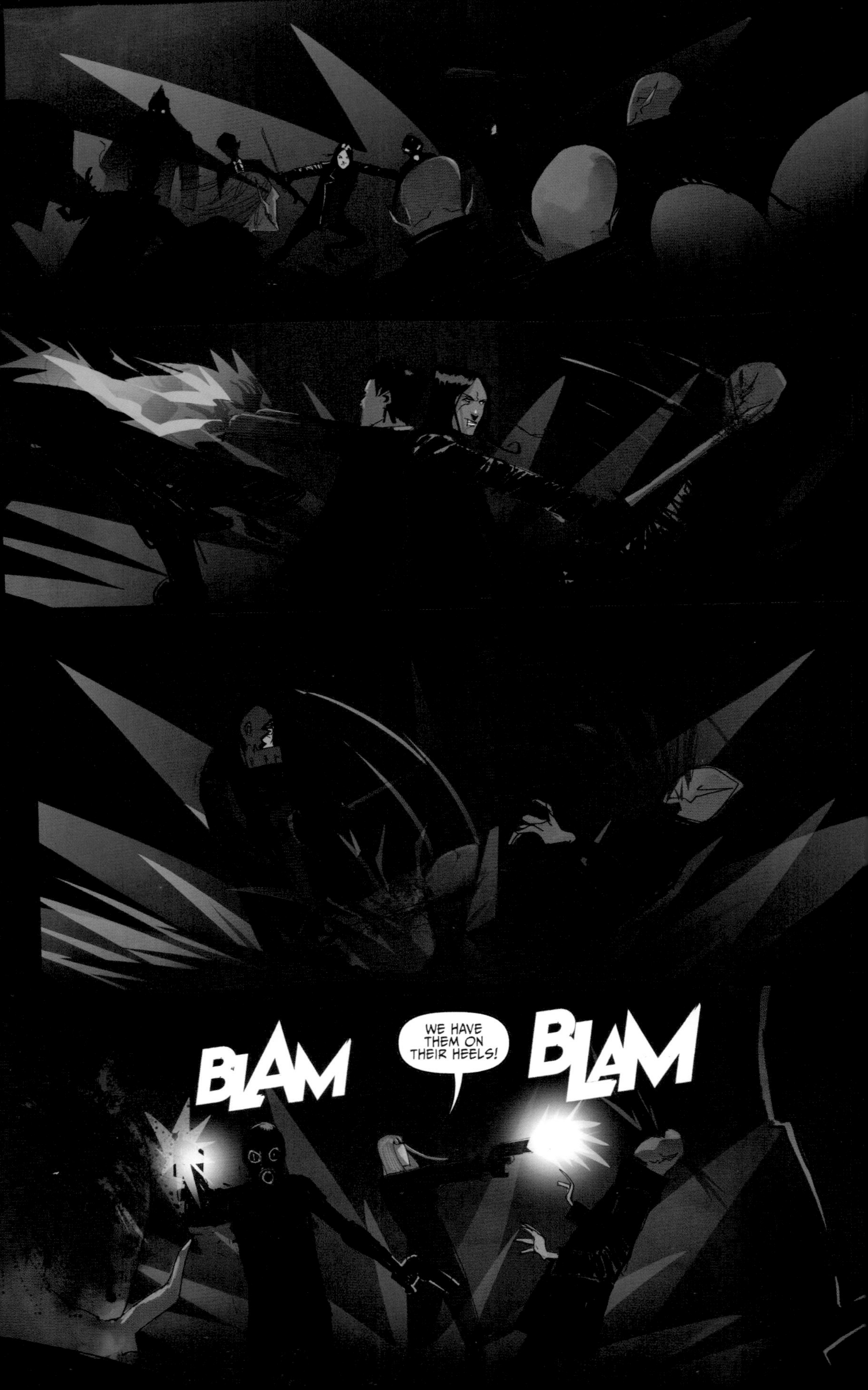
BLAM
WE HAVE THEM ON THEIR HEELS!
BLAM

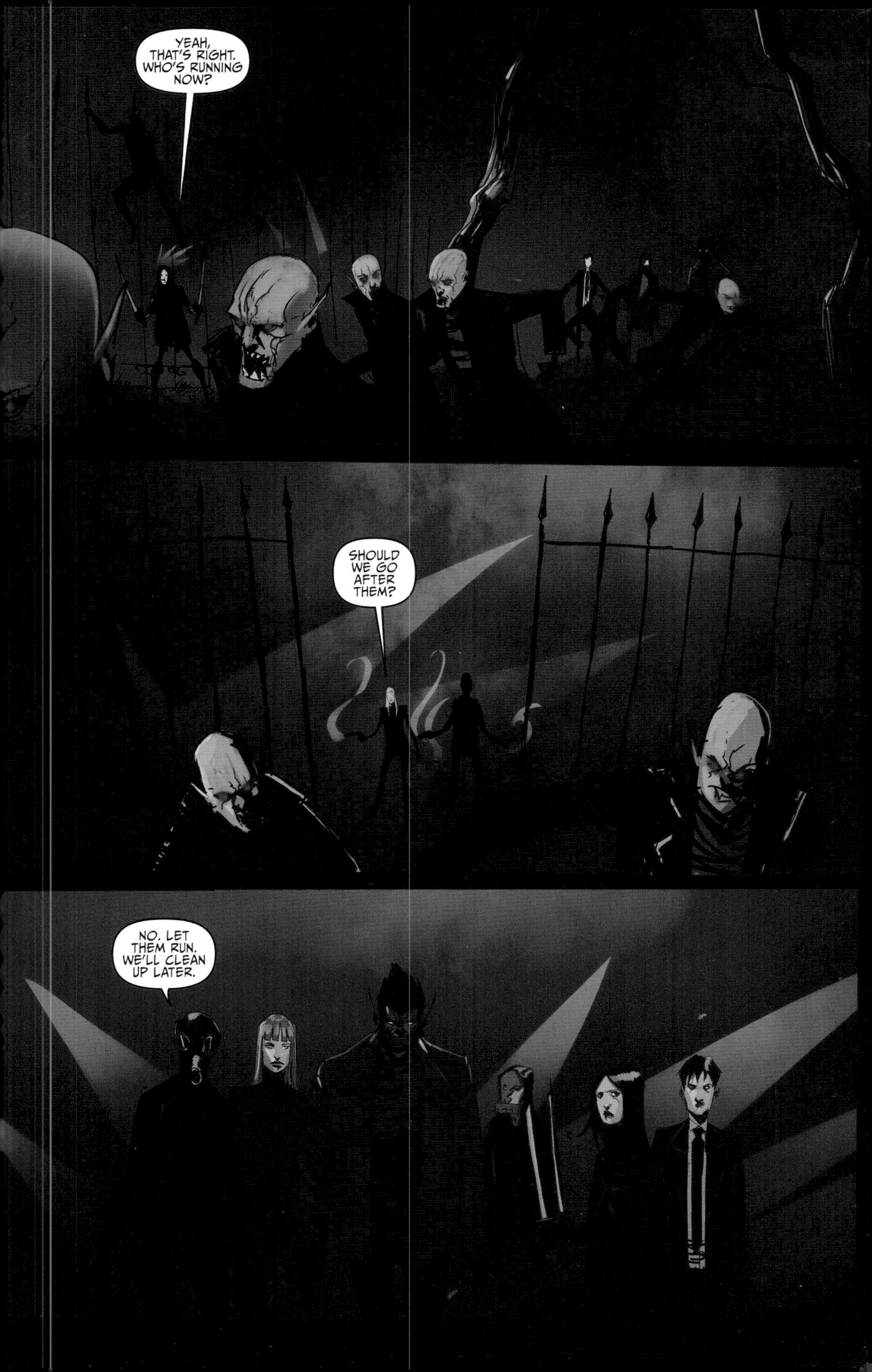
YEAH, THAT'S RIGHT. WHO'S RUNNING NOW?
SHOULD WE GO AFTER THEM?
NO. LET THEM RUN. WE'LL CLEAN UP LATER.

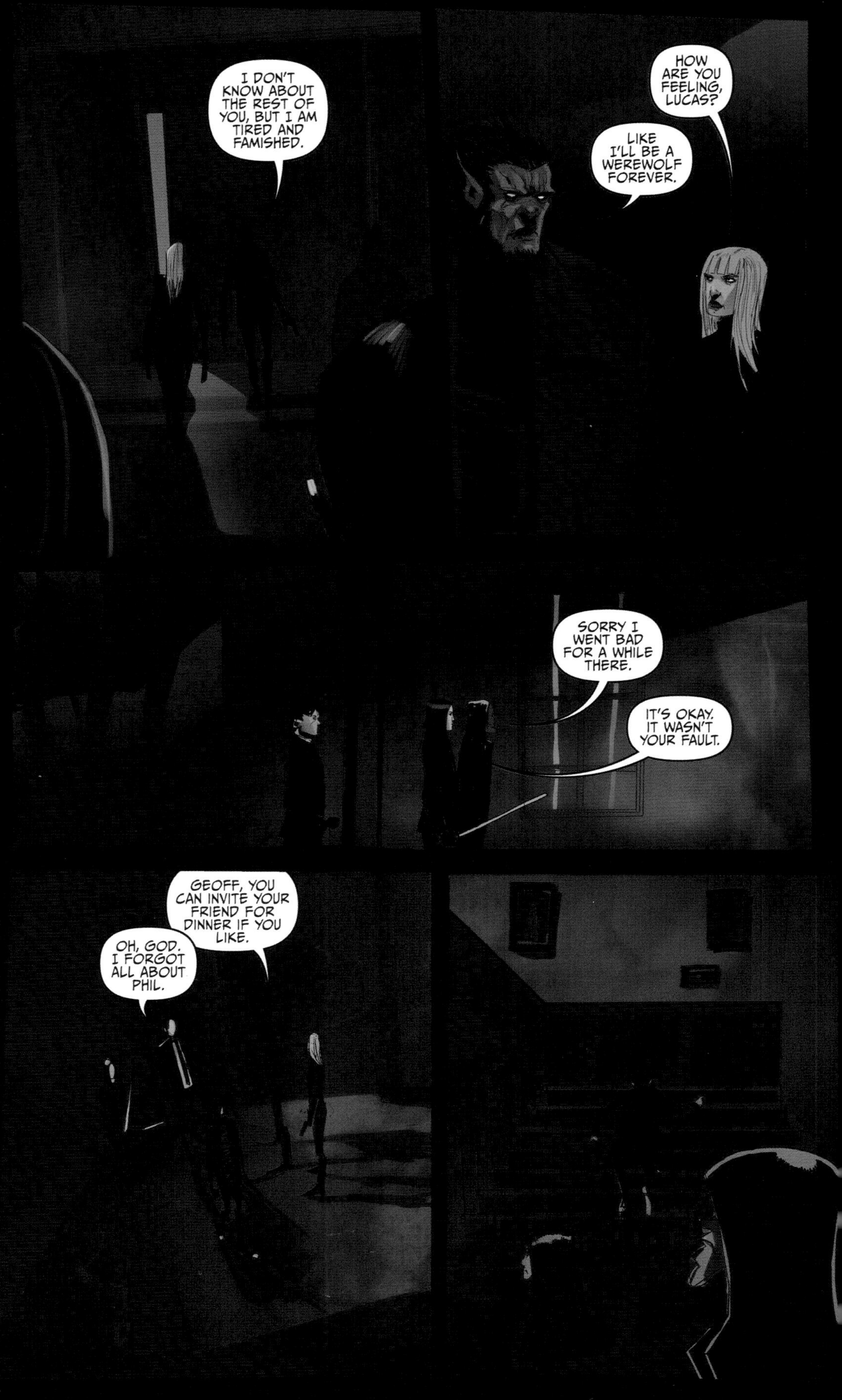
I DON'T KNOW ABOUT THE REST OF YOU, BUT I AM TIRED AND FAMISHED.
HOW ARE YOU FEELING, LUCAS?
LIKE I'LL BE A WEREWOLF FOREVER.
SORRY I WENT BAD FOR A WHILE THERE.
IT'S OKAY. IT WASN'T YOUR FAULT.
GEOFF, YOU CAN INVITE YOUR FRIEND FOR DINNER IF YOU LIKE.
OH, GOD. I FORGOT ALL ABOUT PHIL.

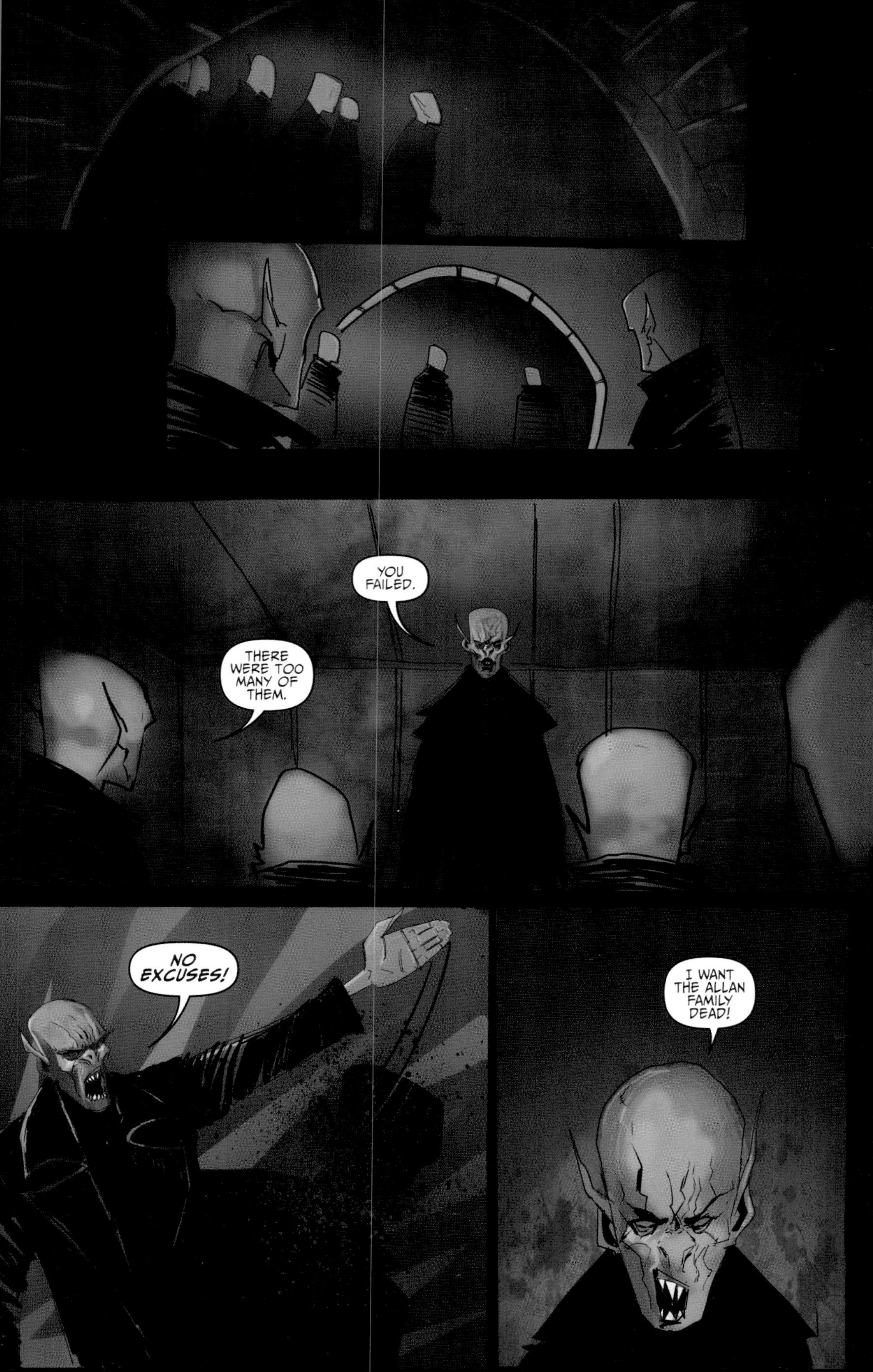
YOU FAILED.
THERE WERE TOO MANY OF THEM.
NO EXCUSES!
I WANT THE ALLAN FAMILY DEAD!

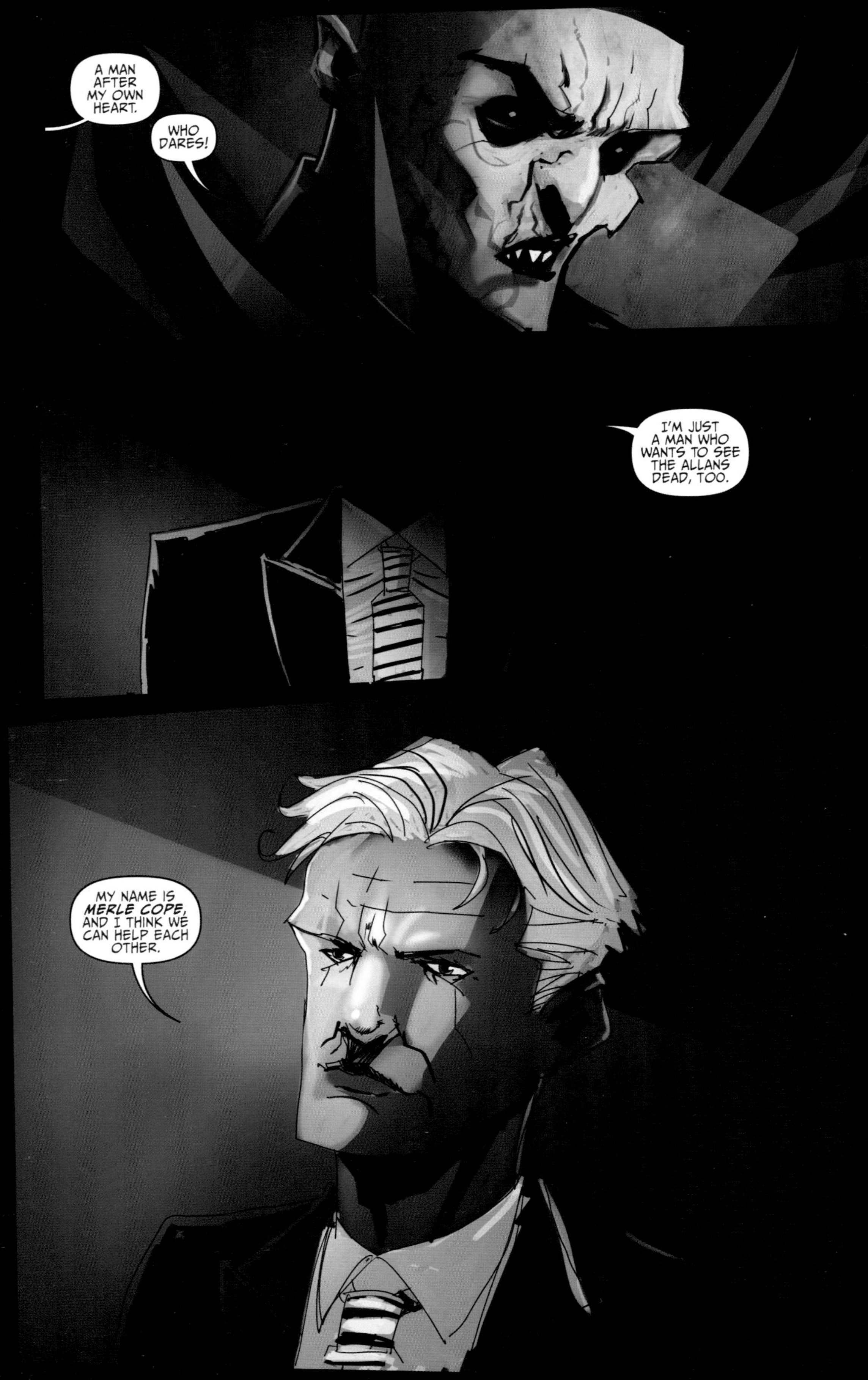
A MAN AFTER MY OWN HEART.
WHO DARES!
I'M JUST A MAN WHO WANTS TO SEE THE ALLANS DEAD, TOO.
MY NAME IS MERLE COPE, AND I THINK WE CAN HELP EACH OTHER.

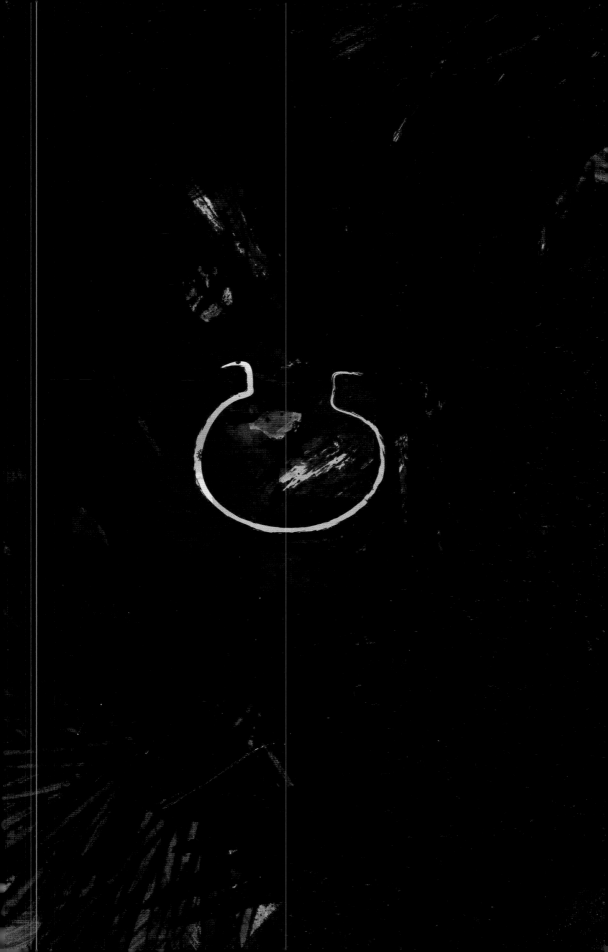

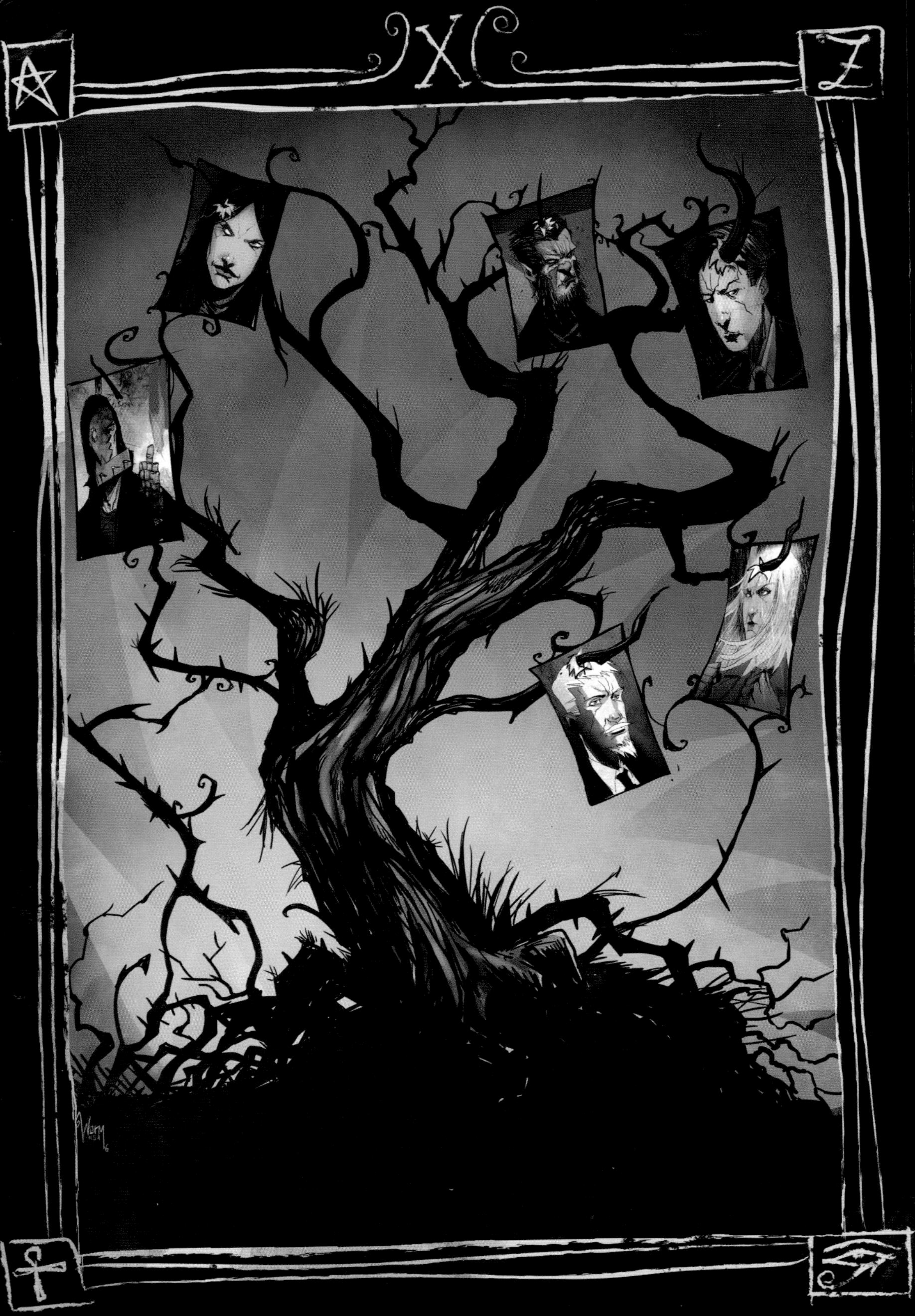
X

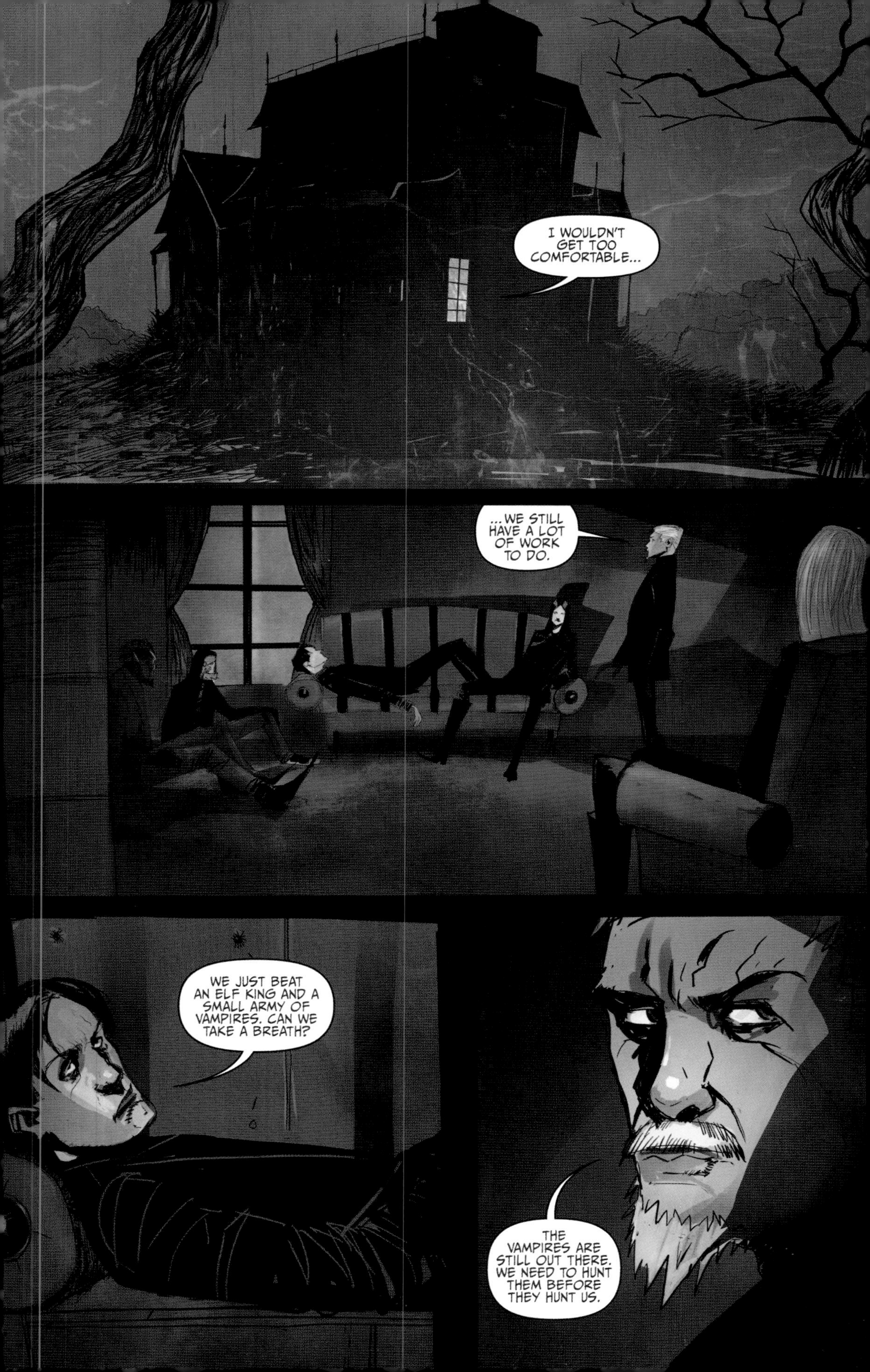
I WOULDN'T GET TOO COMFORTABLE...
...WE STILL HAVE A LOT OF WORK TO DO.
WE JUST BEAT AN ELF KING AND A SMALL ARMY OF VAMPIRES. CAN WE TAKE A BREATH?
THE VAMPIRES ARE STILL OUT THERE. WE NEED TO HUNT THEM BEFORE THEY HUNT US.

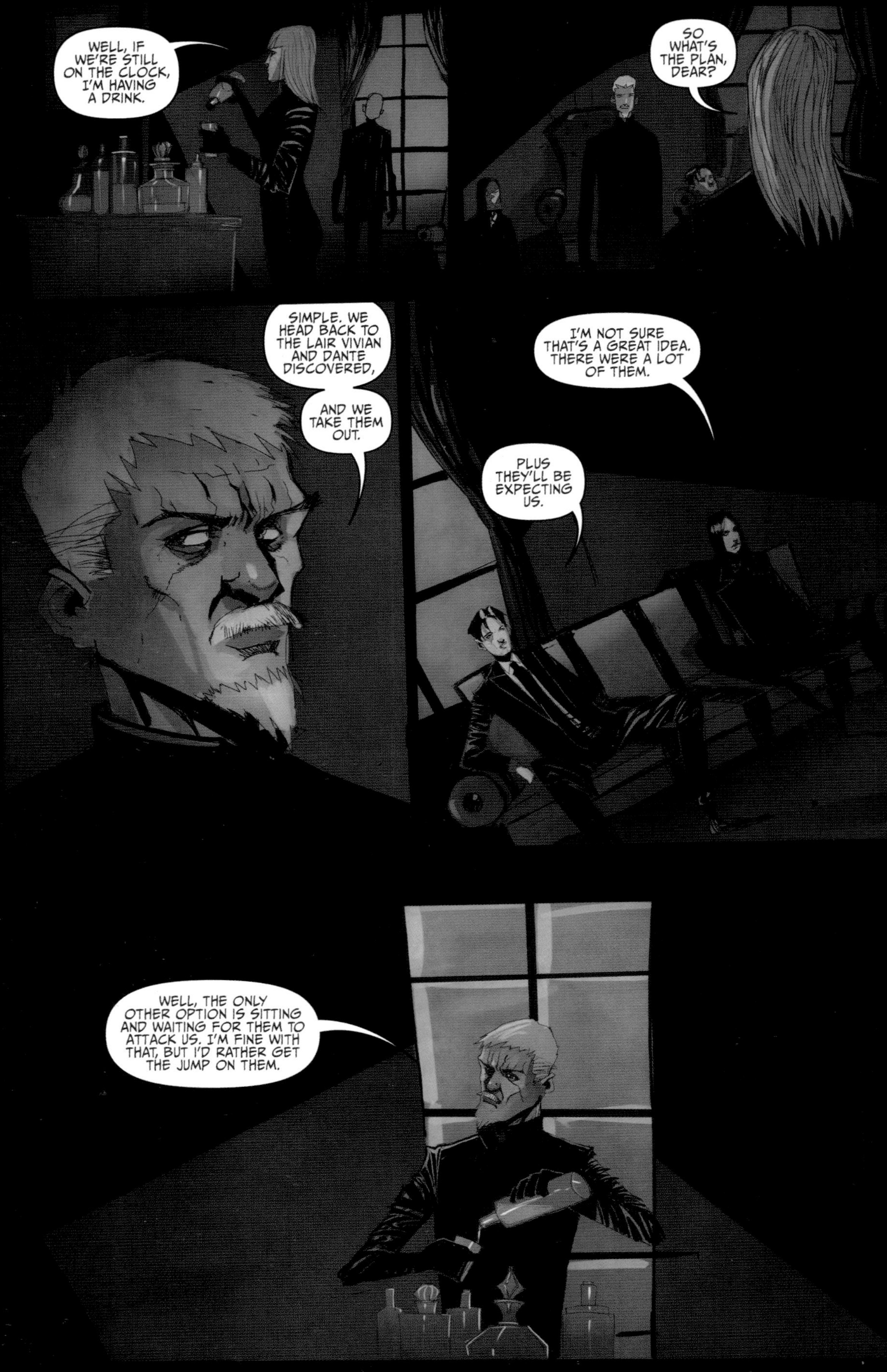
WELL, IF WE'RE STILL ON THE CLOCK, I'M HAVING A DRINK.
SO WHAT'S THE PLAN, DEAR?
SIMPLE. WE HEAD BACK TO THE LAIR VIVIAN AND DANTE DISCOVERED,
AND WE TAKE THEM OUT.
I'M NOT SURE THAT'S A GREAT IDEA. THERE WERE A LOT OF THEM.
PLUS THEY'LL BE EXPECTING US.
WELL, THE ONLY OTHER OPTION IS SITTING AND WAITING FOR THEM TO ATTACK US. I'M FINE WITH THAT, BUT I'D RATHER GET THE JUMP ON THEM.

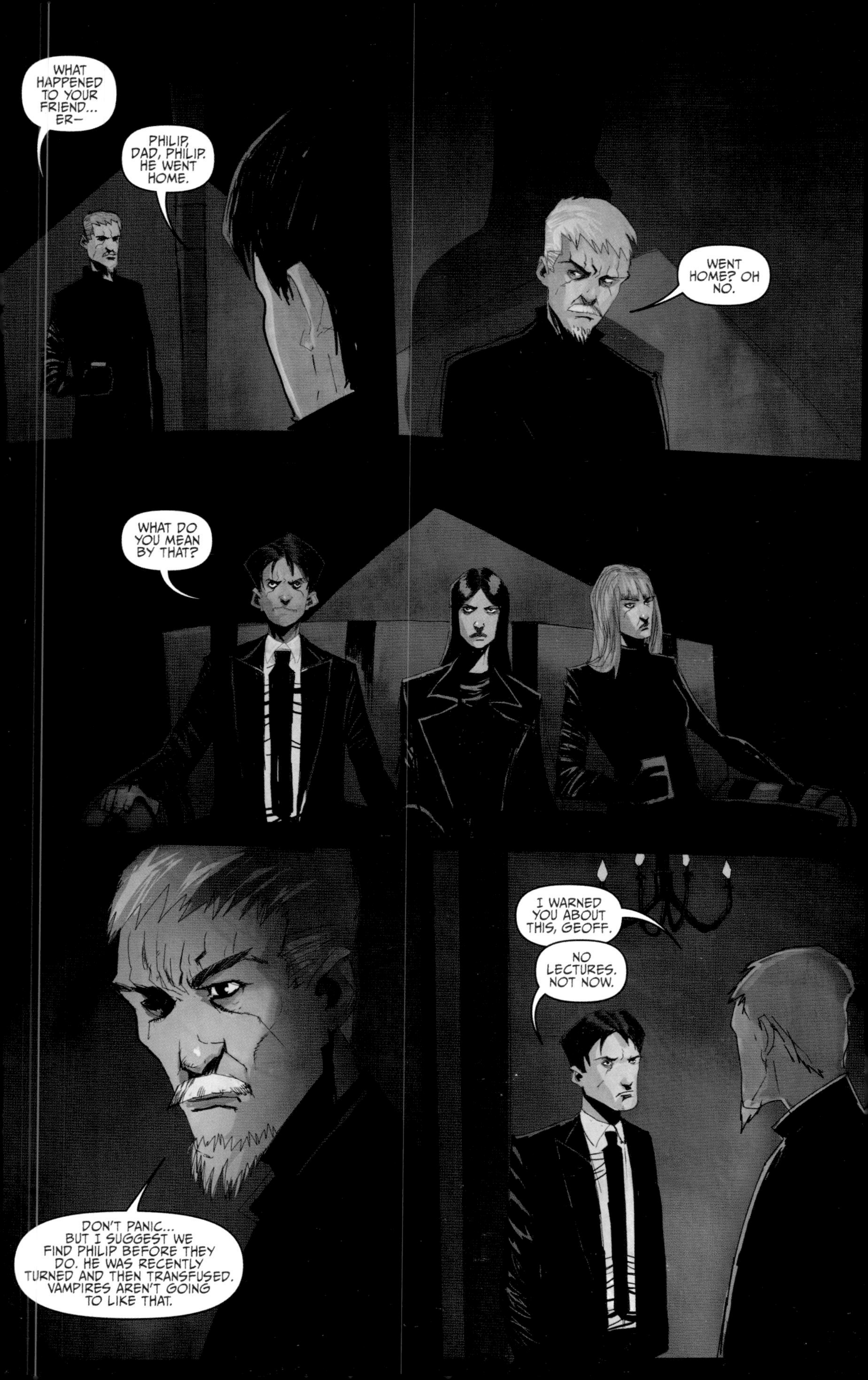
WHAT HAPPENED TO YOUR FRIEND... ER–
PHILIP, DAD, PHILIP. HE WENT HOME.
WENT HOME? OH NO.
WHAT DO YOU MEAN BY THAT?
DON'T PANIC... BUT I SUGGEST WE FIND PHILIP BEFORE THEY DO. HE WAS RECENTLY TURNED AND THEN TRANSFUSED. VAMPIRES AREN'T GOING TO LIKE THAT.
I WARNED YOU ABOUT THIS, GEOFF.
NO LECTURES. NOT NOW.

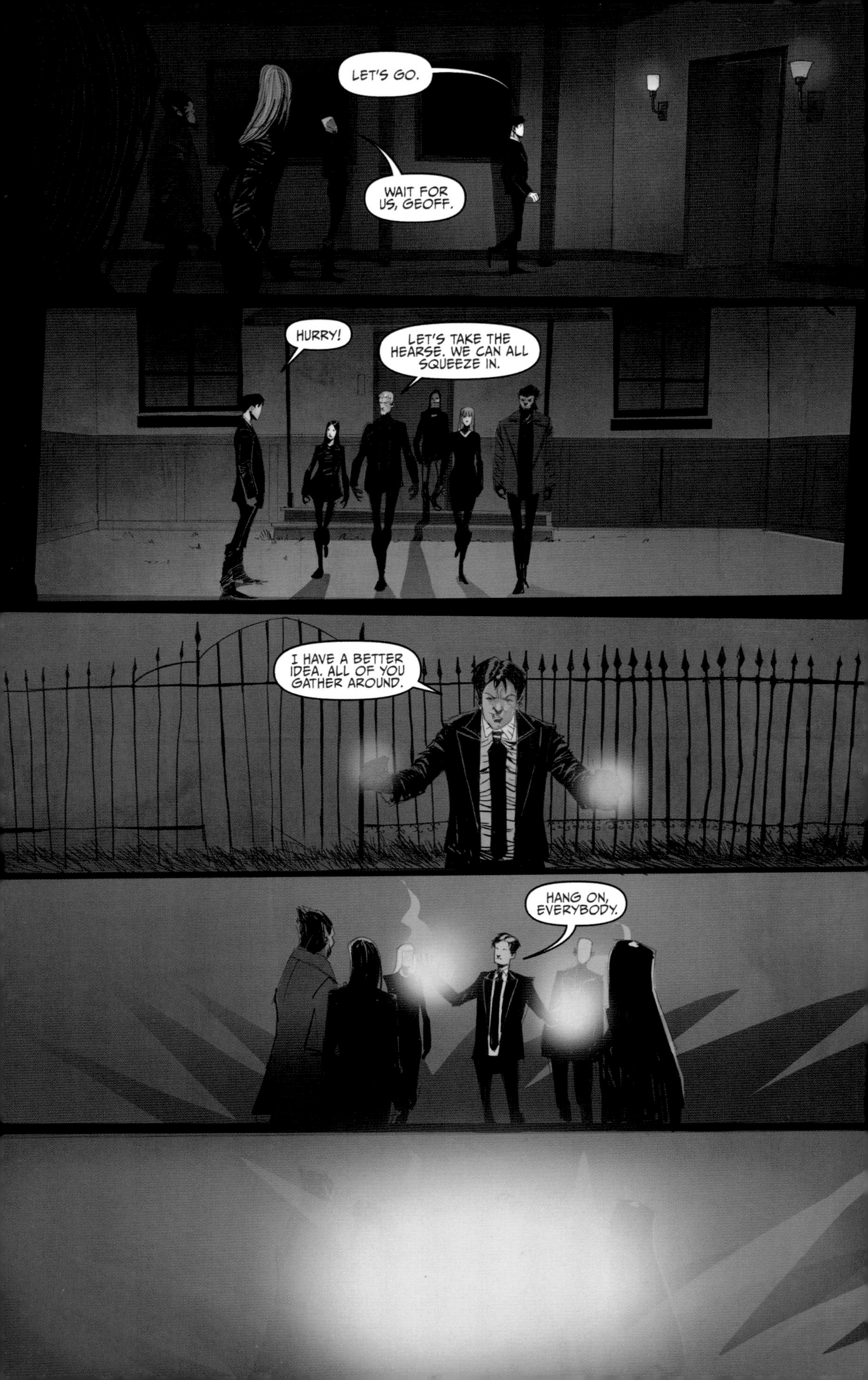
LET'S GO.
WAIT FOR US, GEOFF.
HURRY!
LET'S TAKE THE HEARSE. WE CAN ALL SQUEEZE IN.
I HAVE A BETTER IDEA. ALL OF YOU GATHER AROUND.
HANG ON, EVERYBODY.

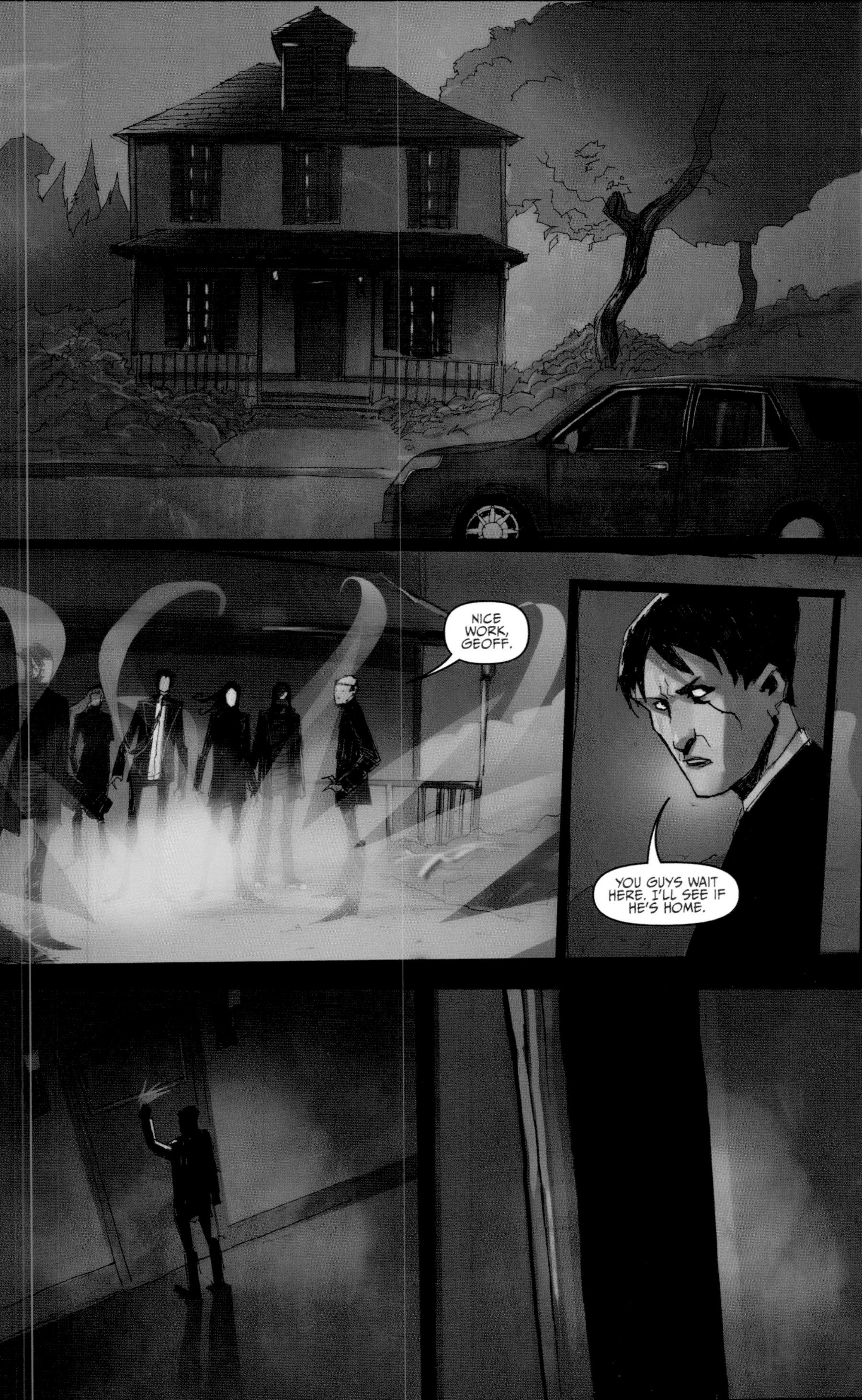
NICE WORK, GEOFF.
YOU GUYS WAIT HERE. I'LL SEE IF HE'S HOME.

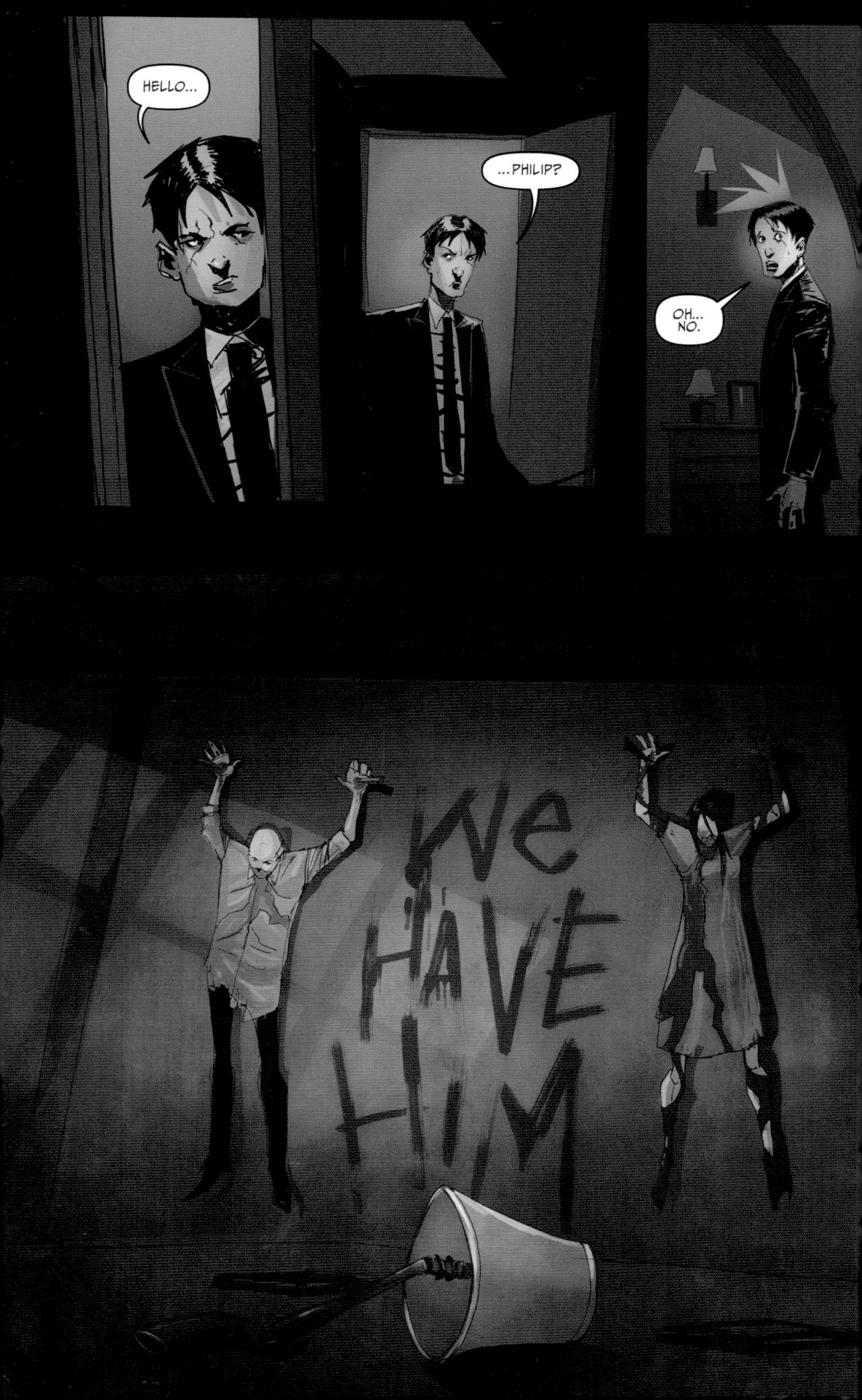
HELLO...
...PHILIP?
OH... NO.
WE HAVE HIM

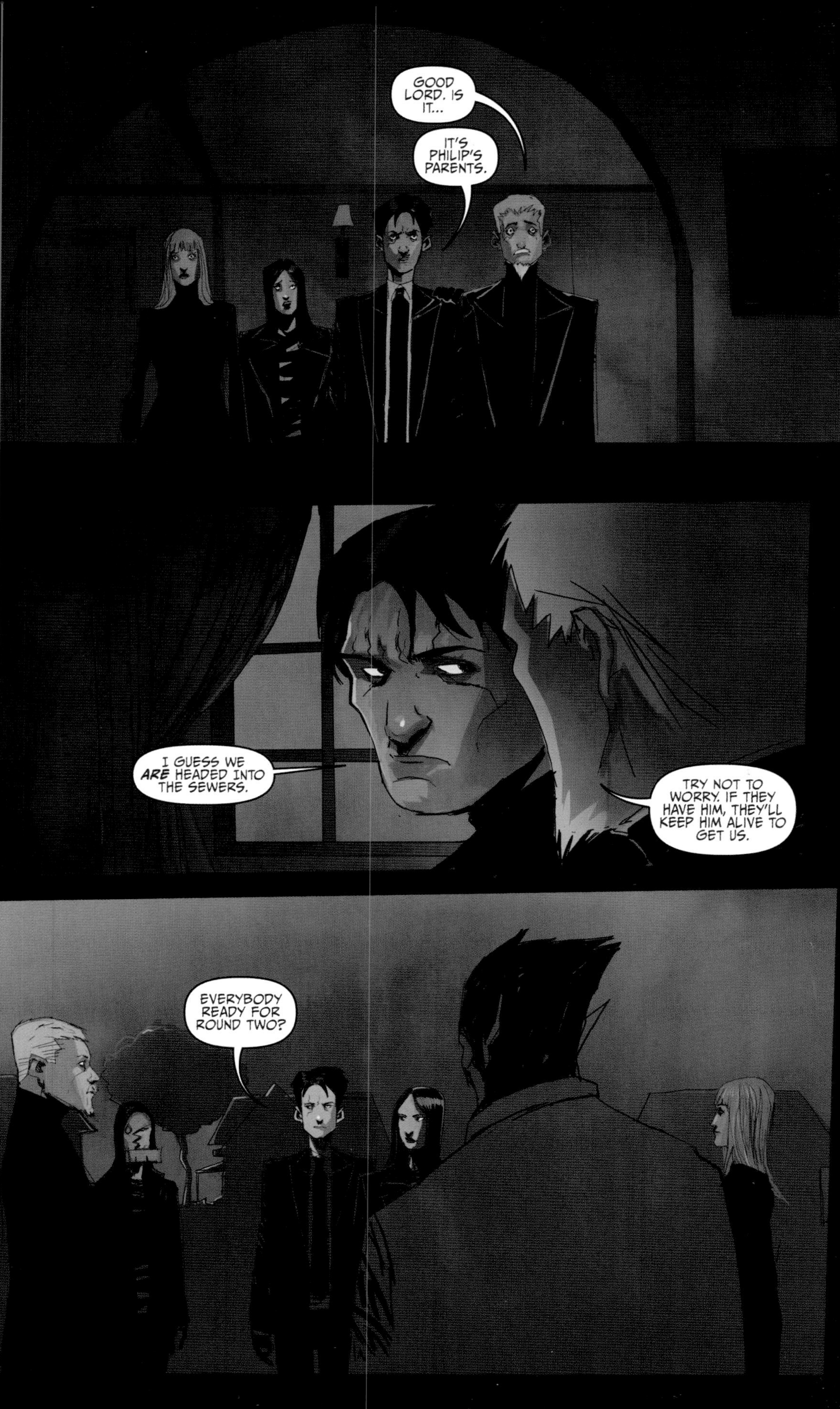
GOOD LORD. IS IT...
IT'S PHILIP'S PARENTS.
I GUESS WE *ARE* HEADED INTO THE SEWERS.
TRY NOT TO WORRY. IF THEY HAVE HIM, THEY'LL KEEP HIM ALIVE TO GET US.
EVERYBODY READY FOR ROUND TWO?

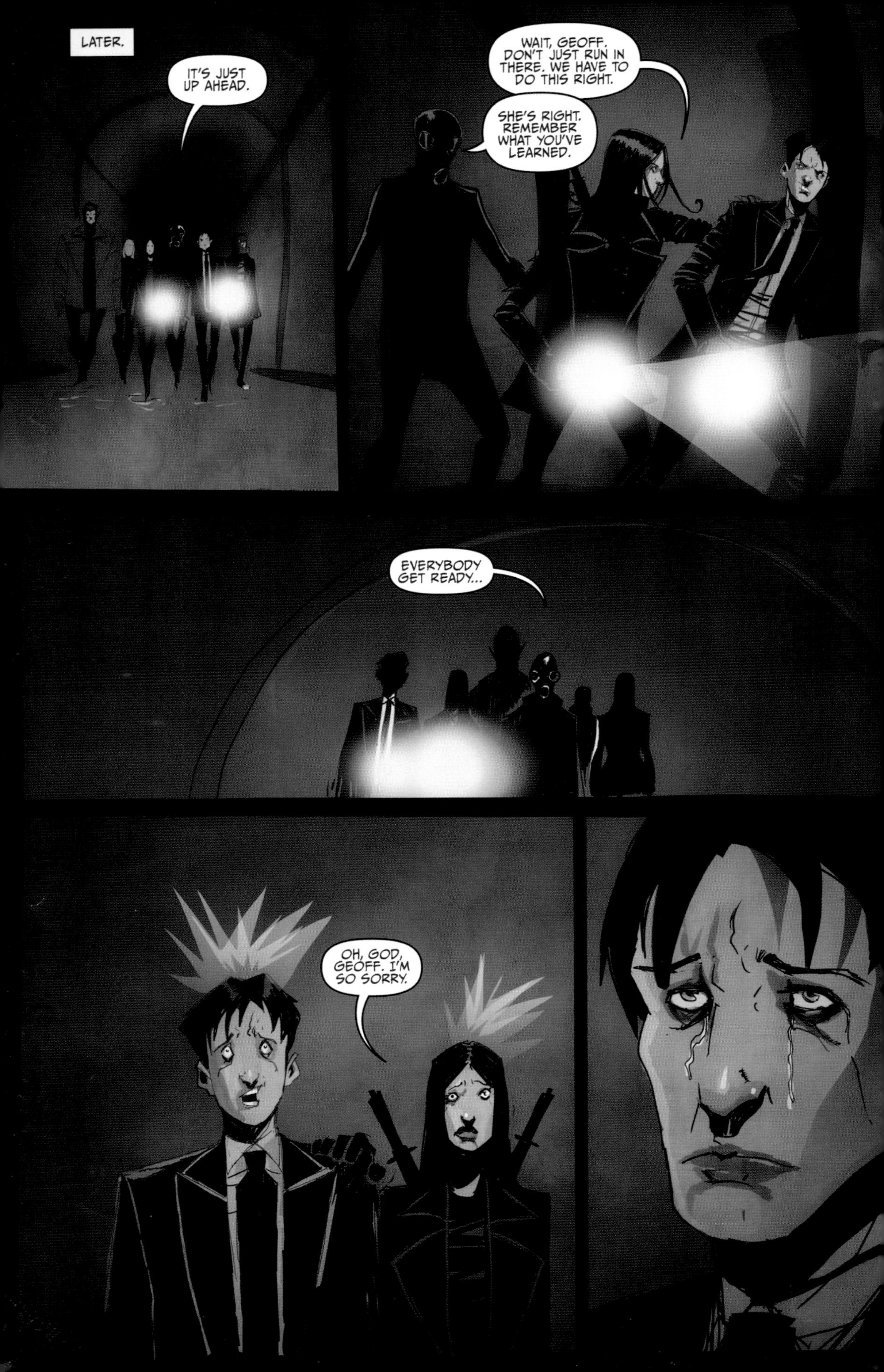
LATER.
IT'S JUST UP AHEAD.
WAIT, GEOFF. DON'T JUST RUN IN THERE. WE HAVE TO DO THIS RIGHT.
SHE'S RIGHT. REMEMBER WHAT YOU'VE LEARNED.
EVERYBODY GET READY...
OH, GOD, GEOFF. I'M SO SORRY.

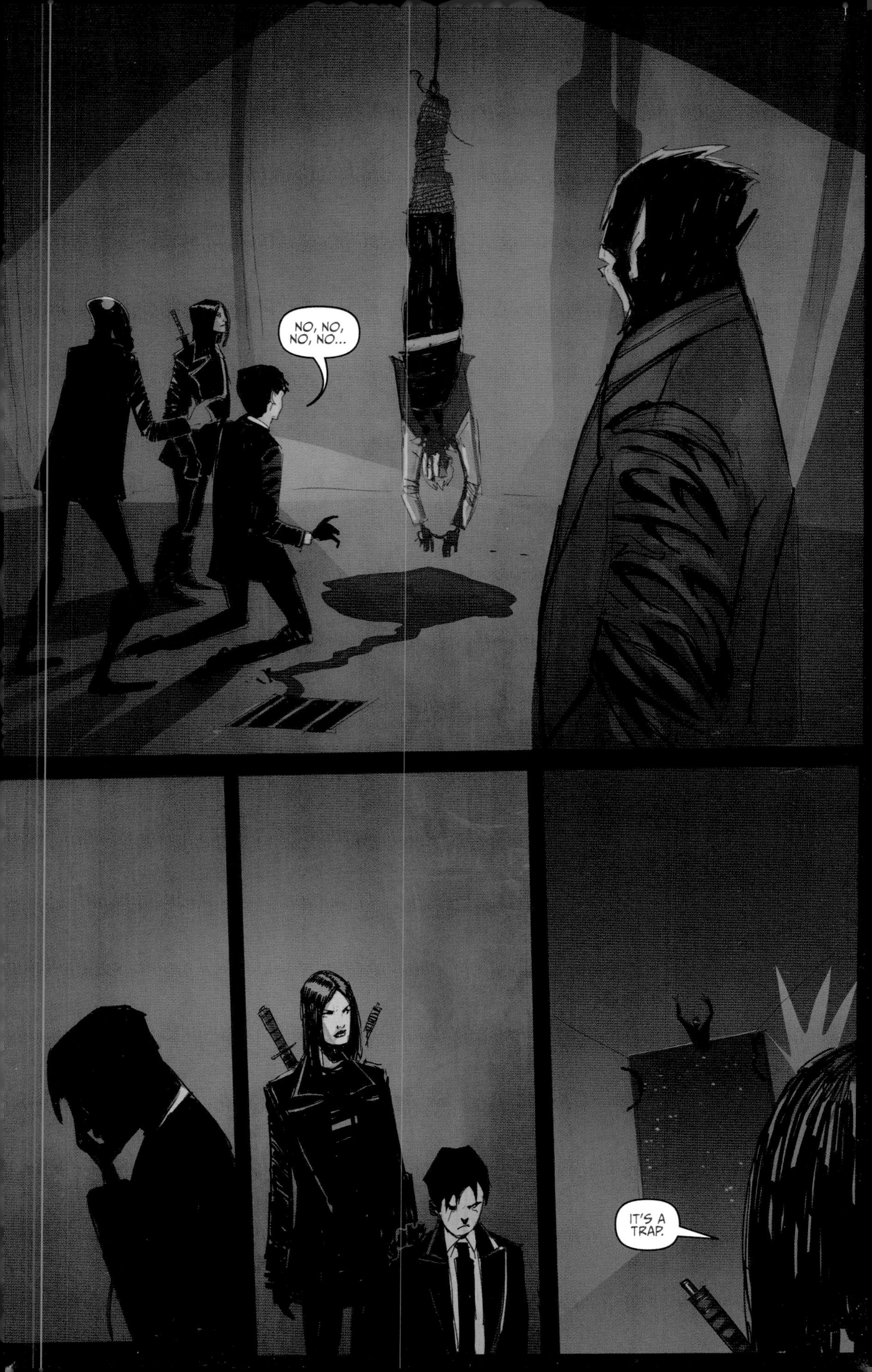
NO, NO, NO, NO...
IT'S A TRAP.

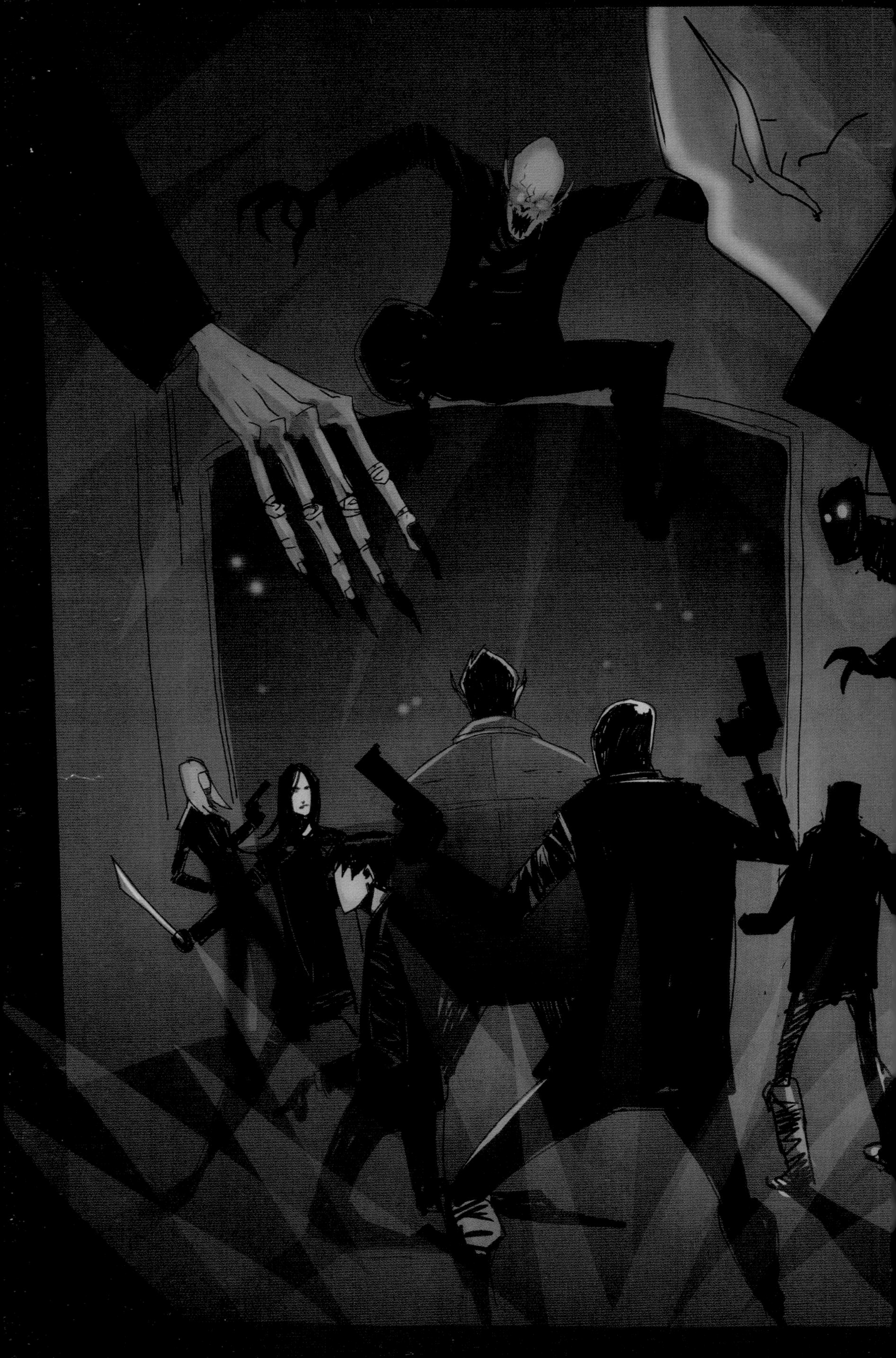

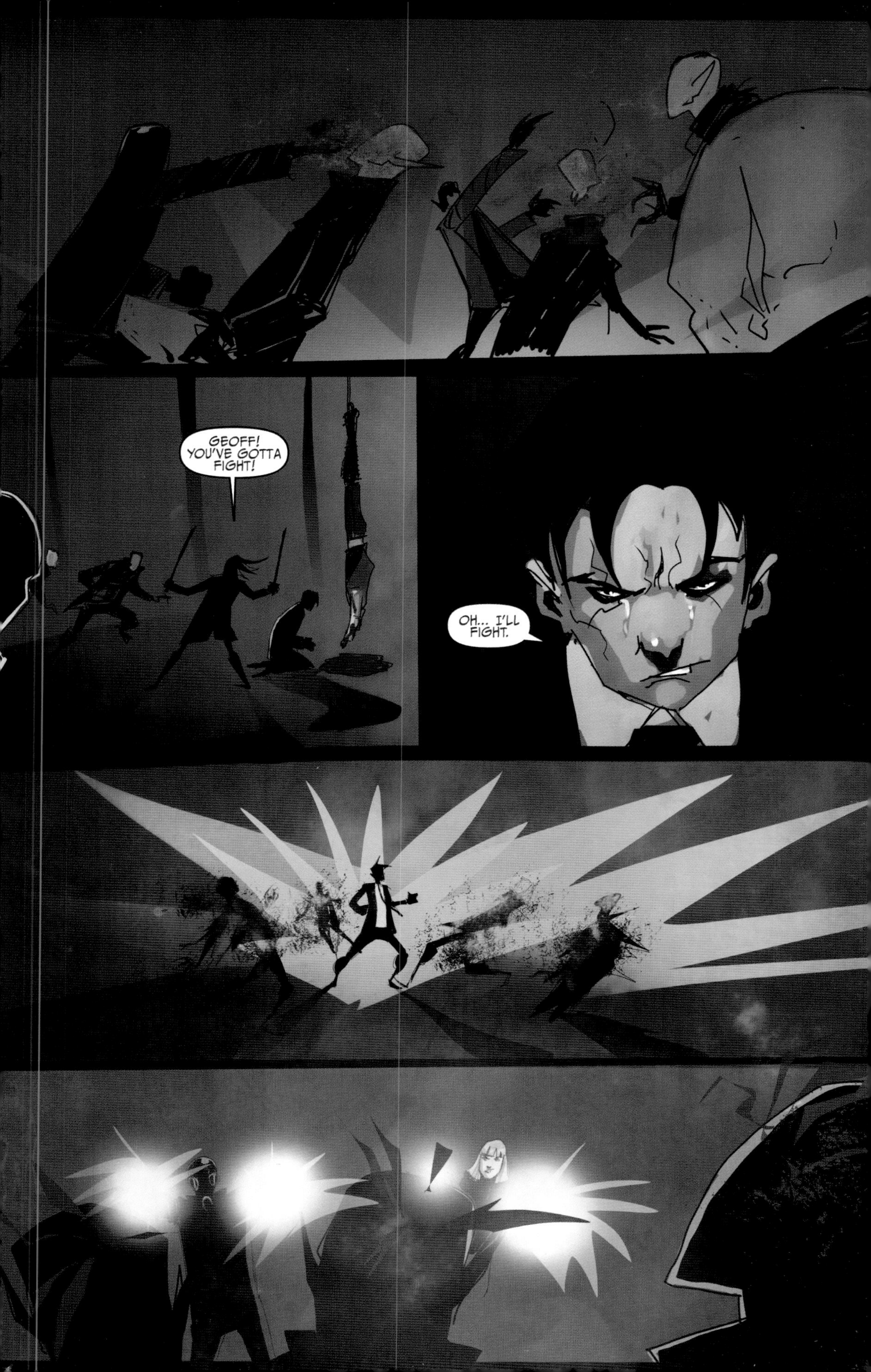
GEOFF! YOU'VE GOTTA FIGHT!
OH... I'LL FIGHT.

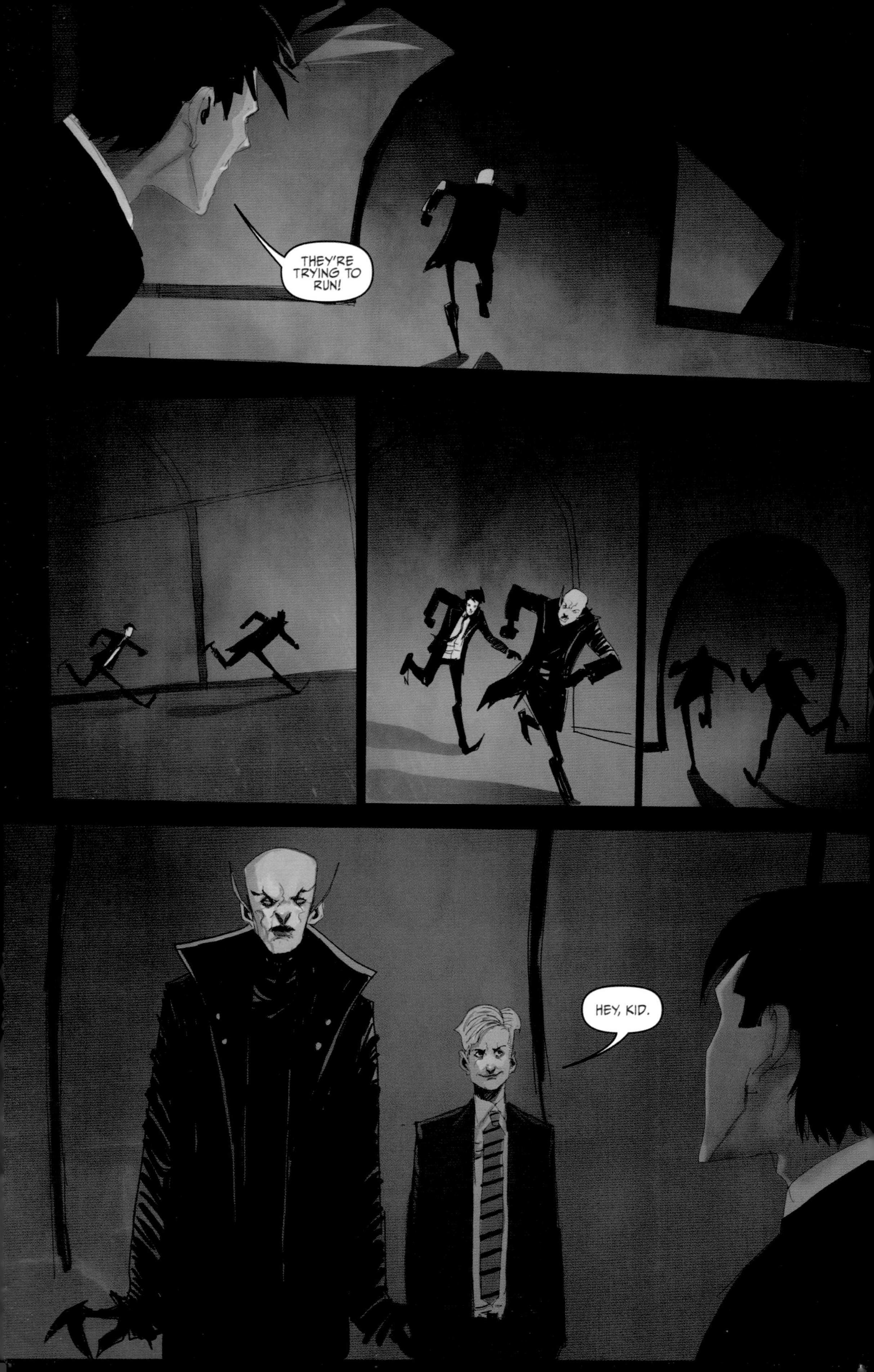
THEY'RE TRYING TO RUN!
HEY, KID.

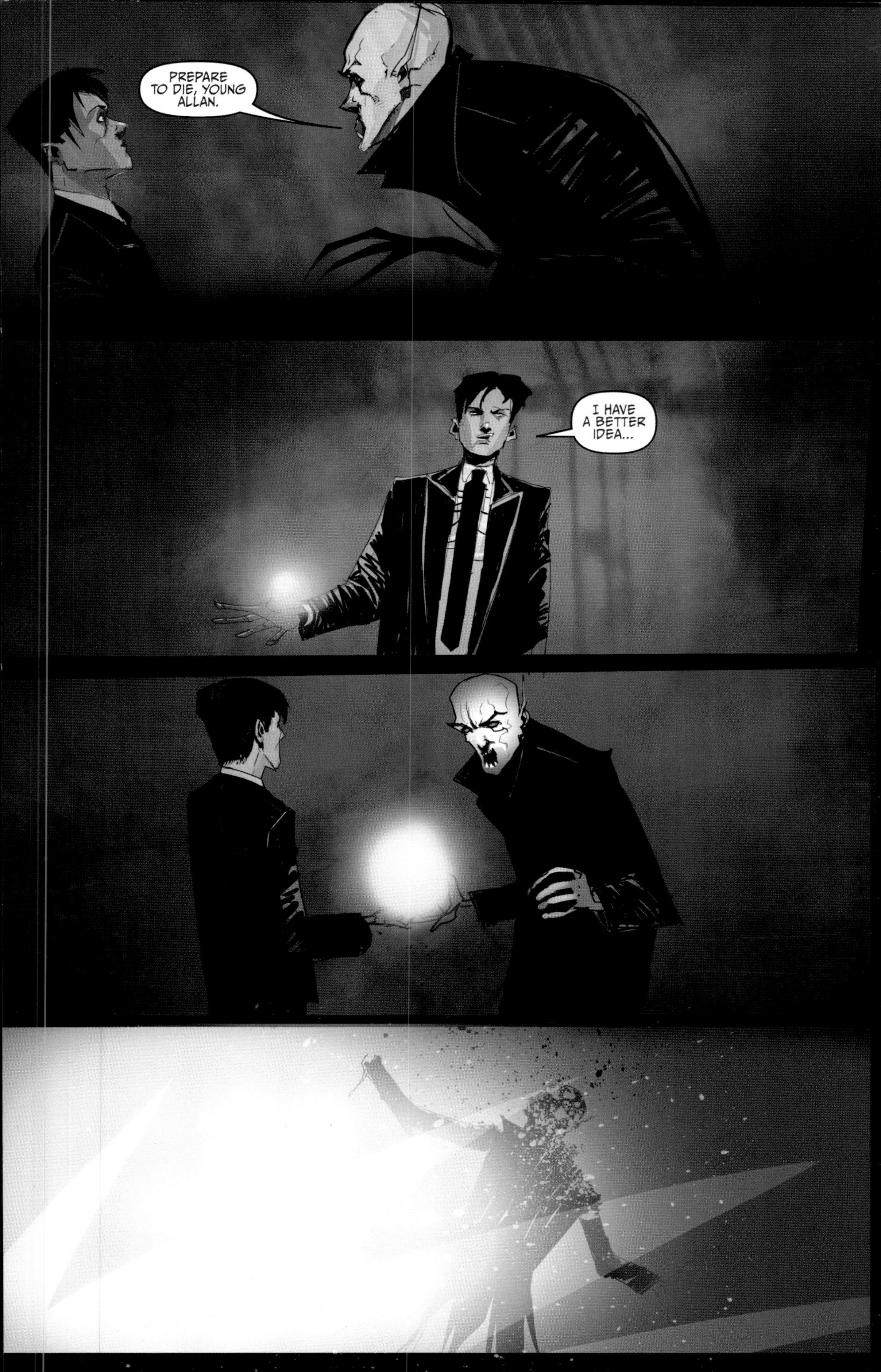
PREPARE TO DIE, YOUNG ALLAN.
I HAVE A BETTER IDEA...

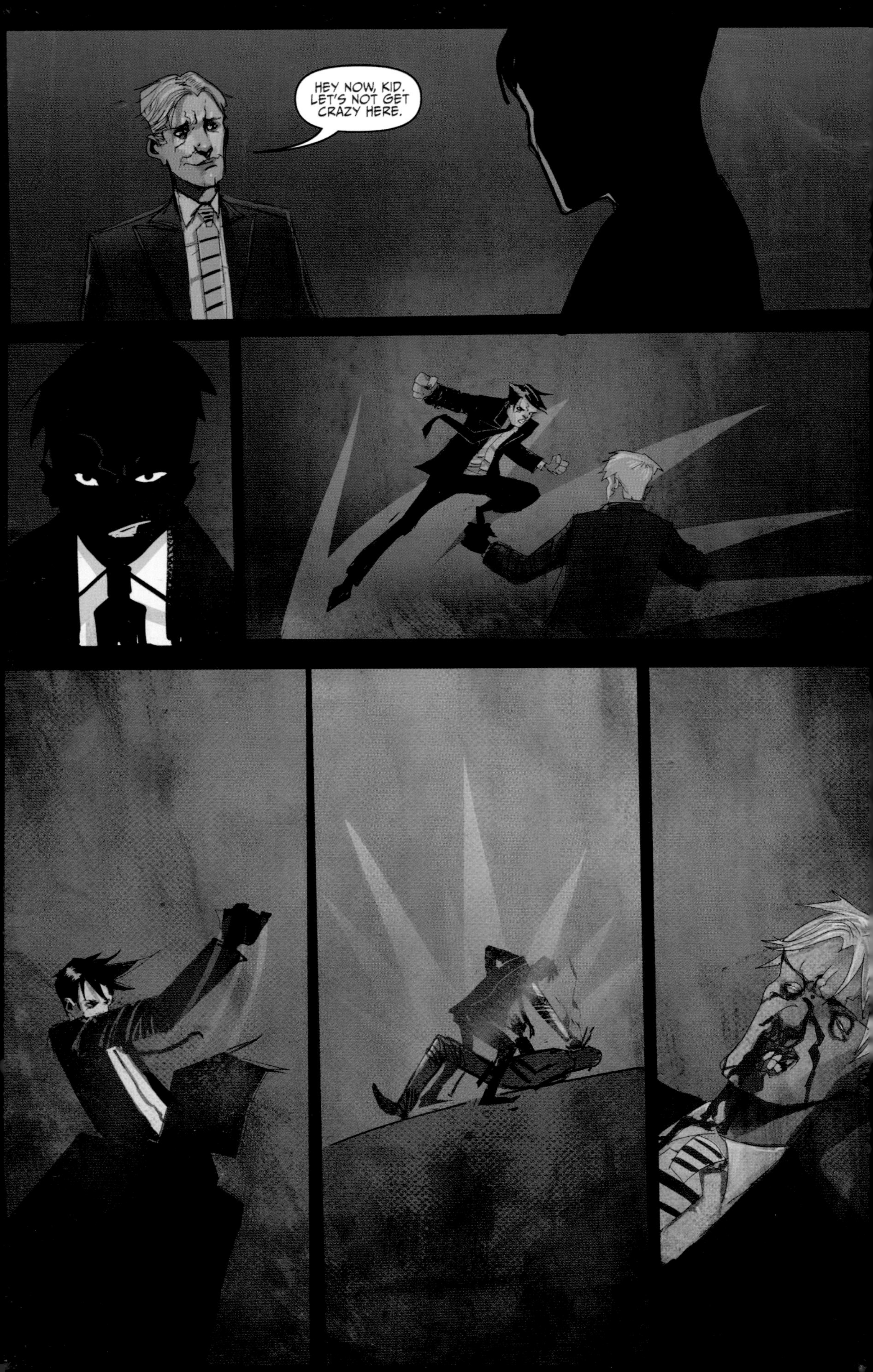
HEY NOW, KID. LET'S NOT GET CRAZY HERE.

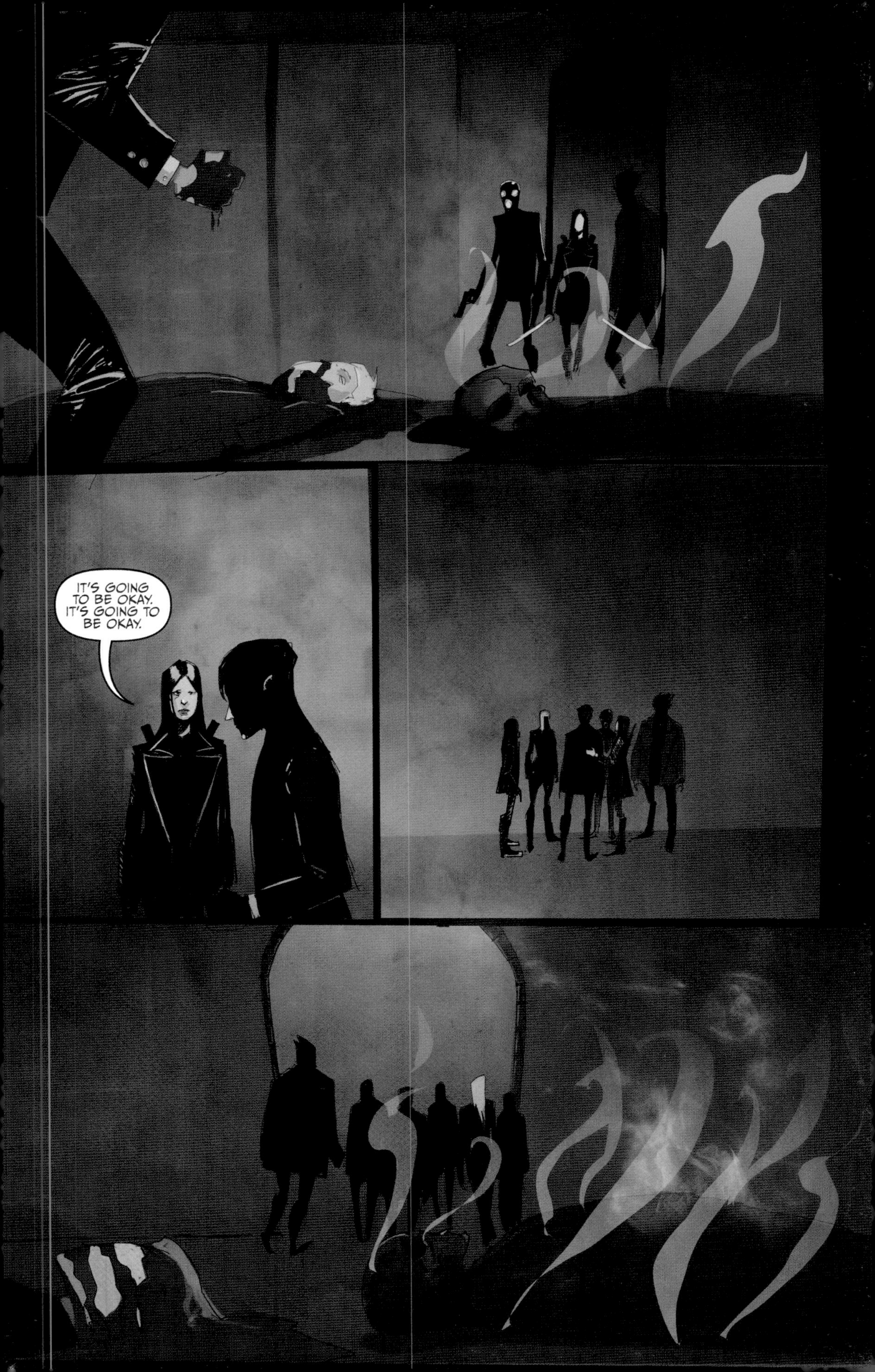
IT'S GOING TO BE OKAY. IT'S GOING TO BE OKAY.

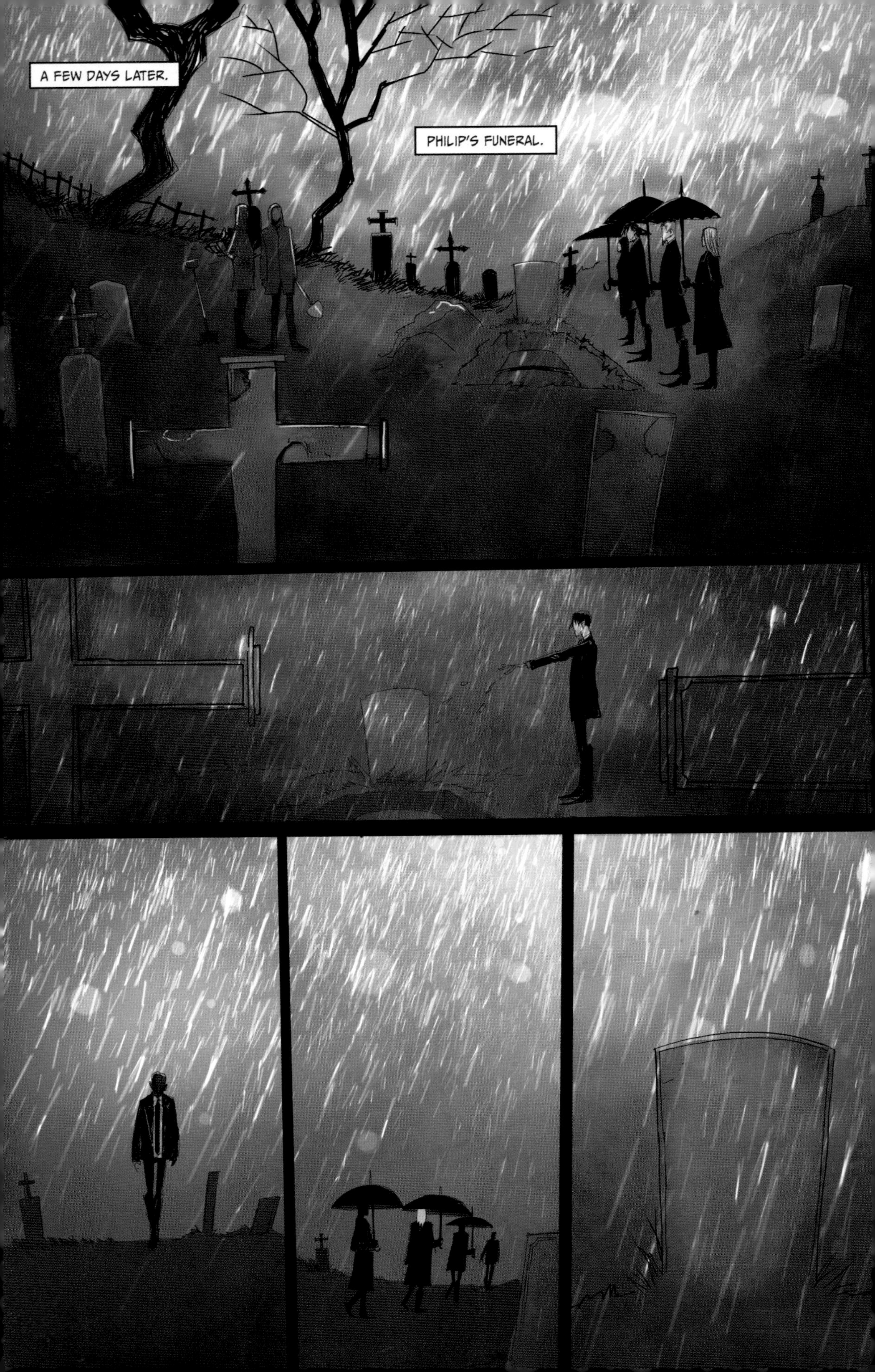
A FEW DAYS LATER.
PHILIP'S FUNERAL.

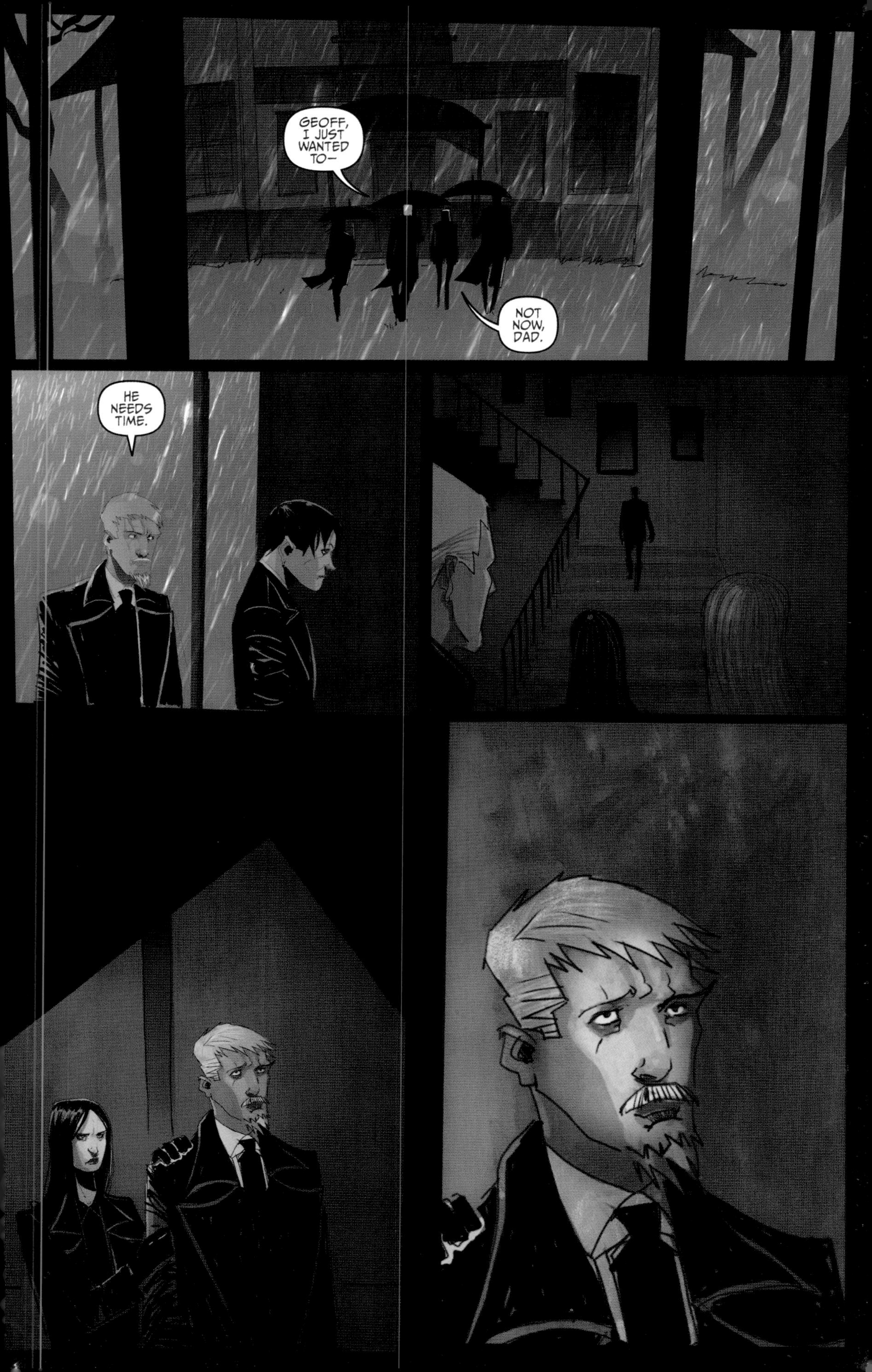
GEOFF, I JUST WANTED TO—
NOT NOW, DAD.
HE NEEDS TIME.

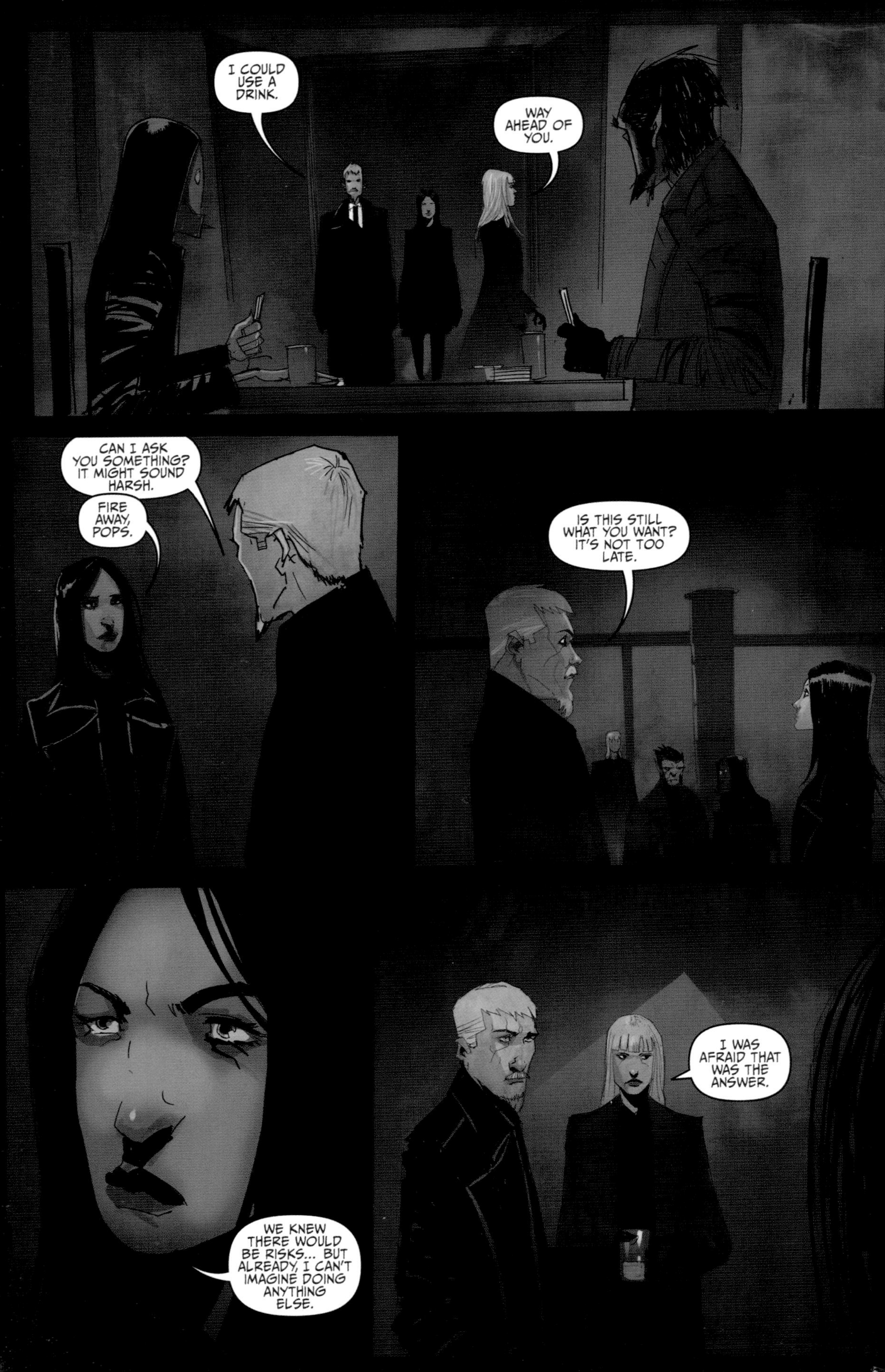
I COULD USE A DRINK.
WAY AHEAD OF YOU.
CAN I ASK YOU SOMETHING? IT MIGHT SOUND HARSH.
FIRE AWAY, POPS.
IS THIS STILL WHAT YOU WANT? IT'S NOT TOO LATE.
WE KNEW THERE WOULD BE RISKS... BUT ALREADY, I CAN'T IMAGINE DOING ANYTHING ELSE.
I WAS AFRAID THAT WAS THE ANSWER.

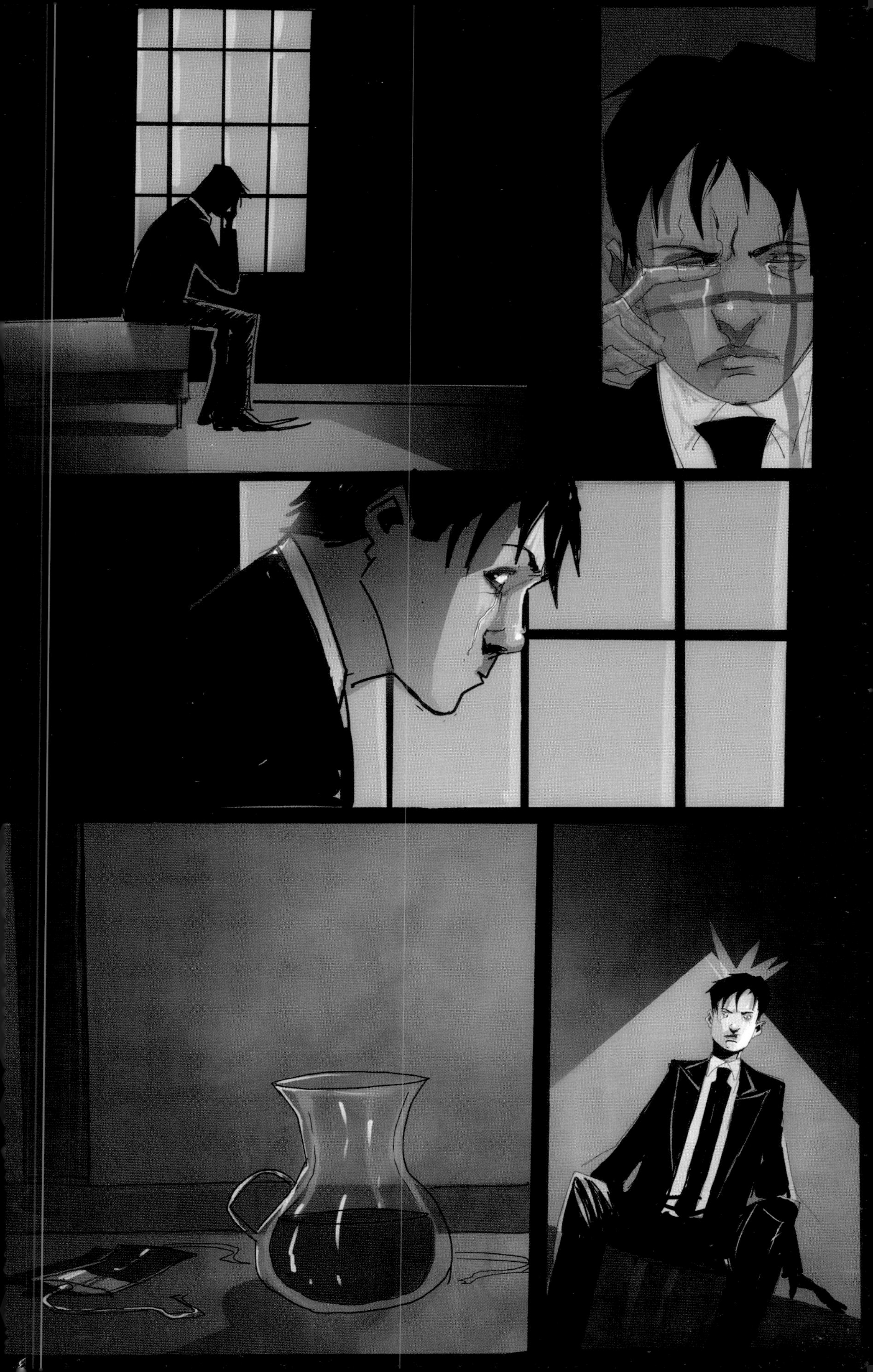

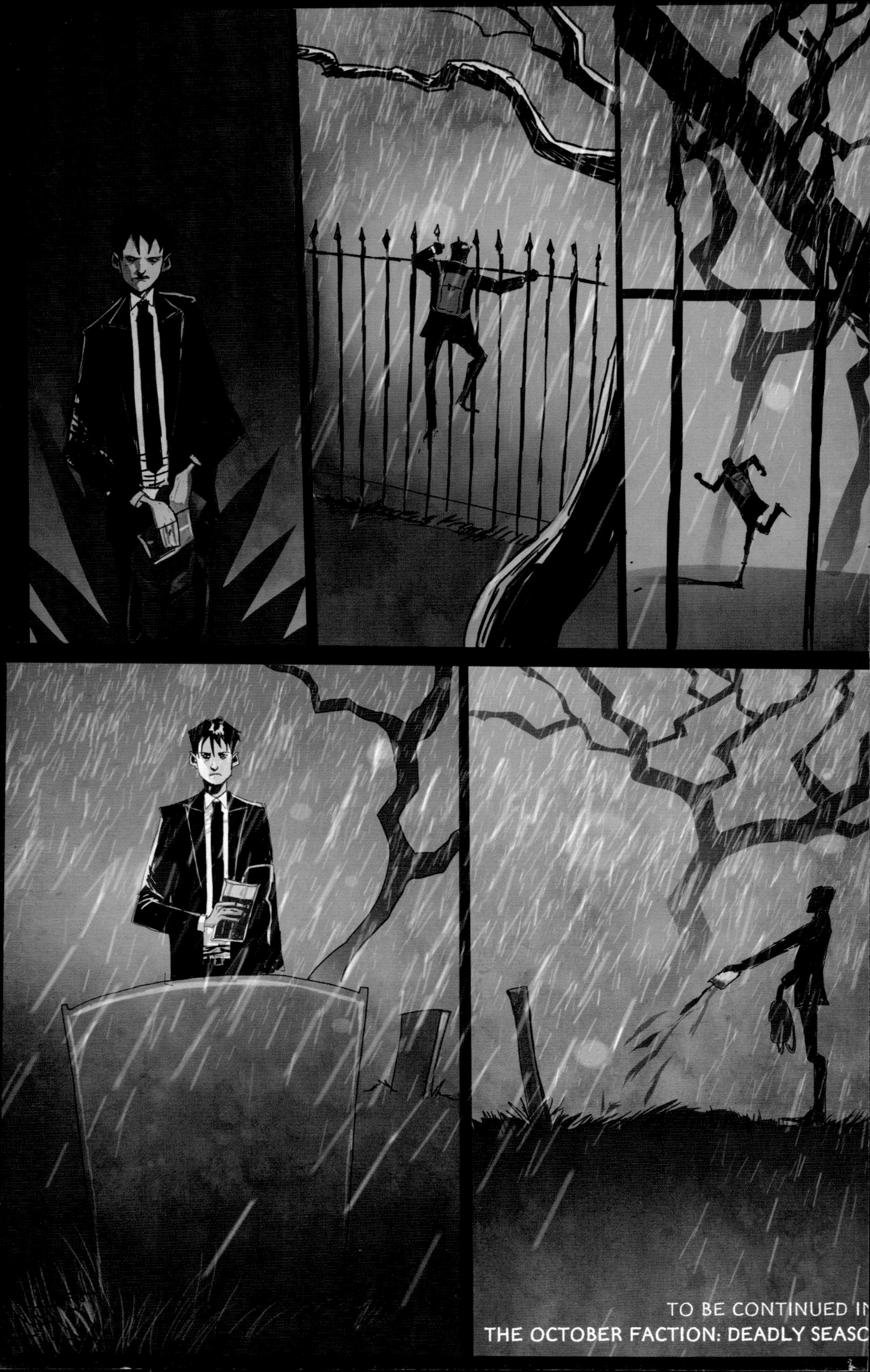
TO BE CONTINUED IN
THE OCTOBER FACTION: DEADLY SEASC

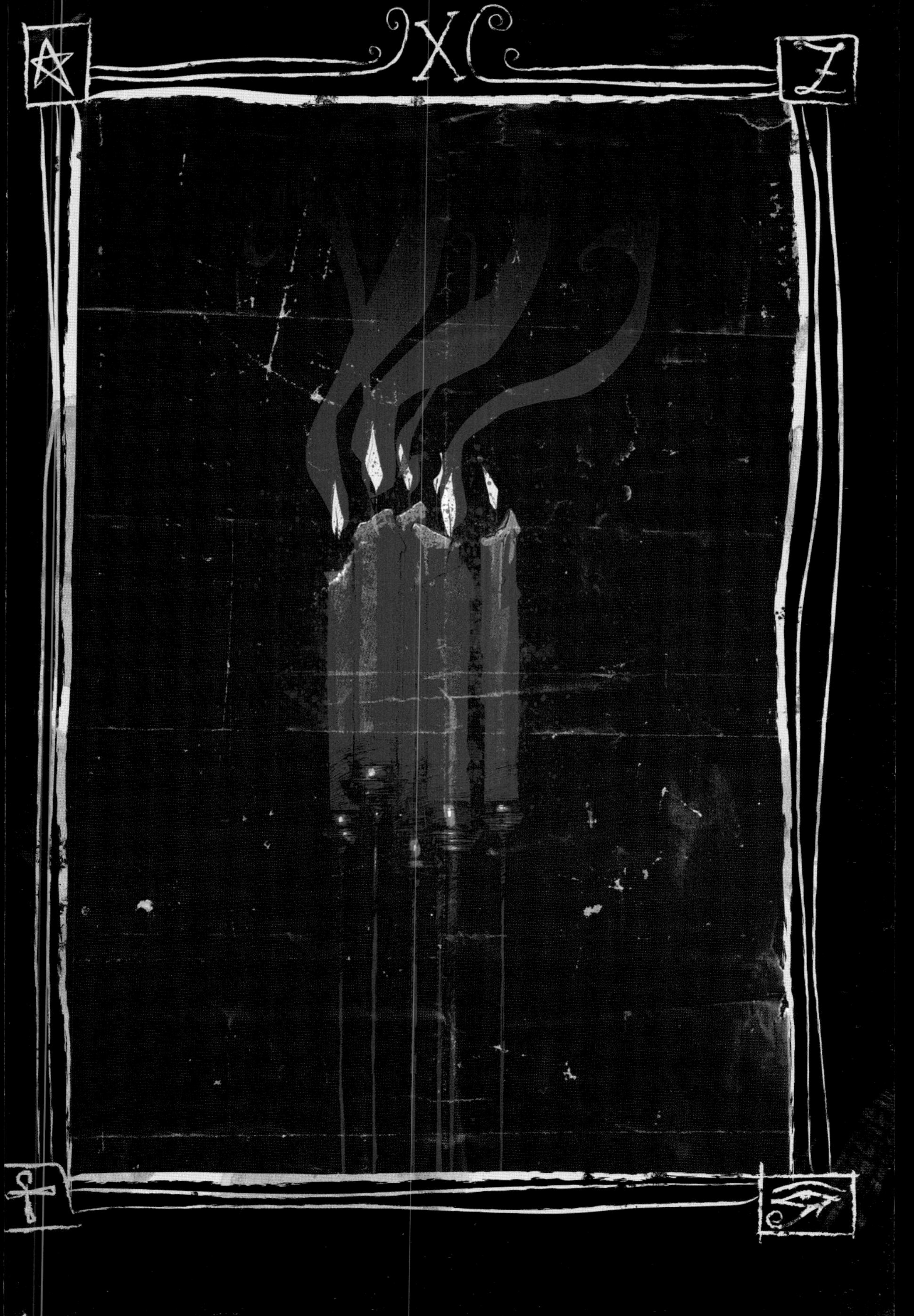
X

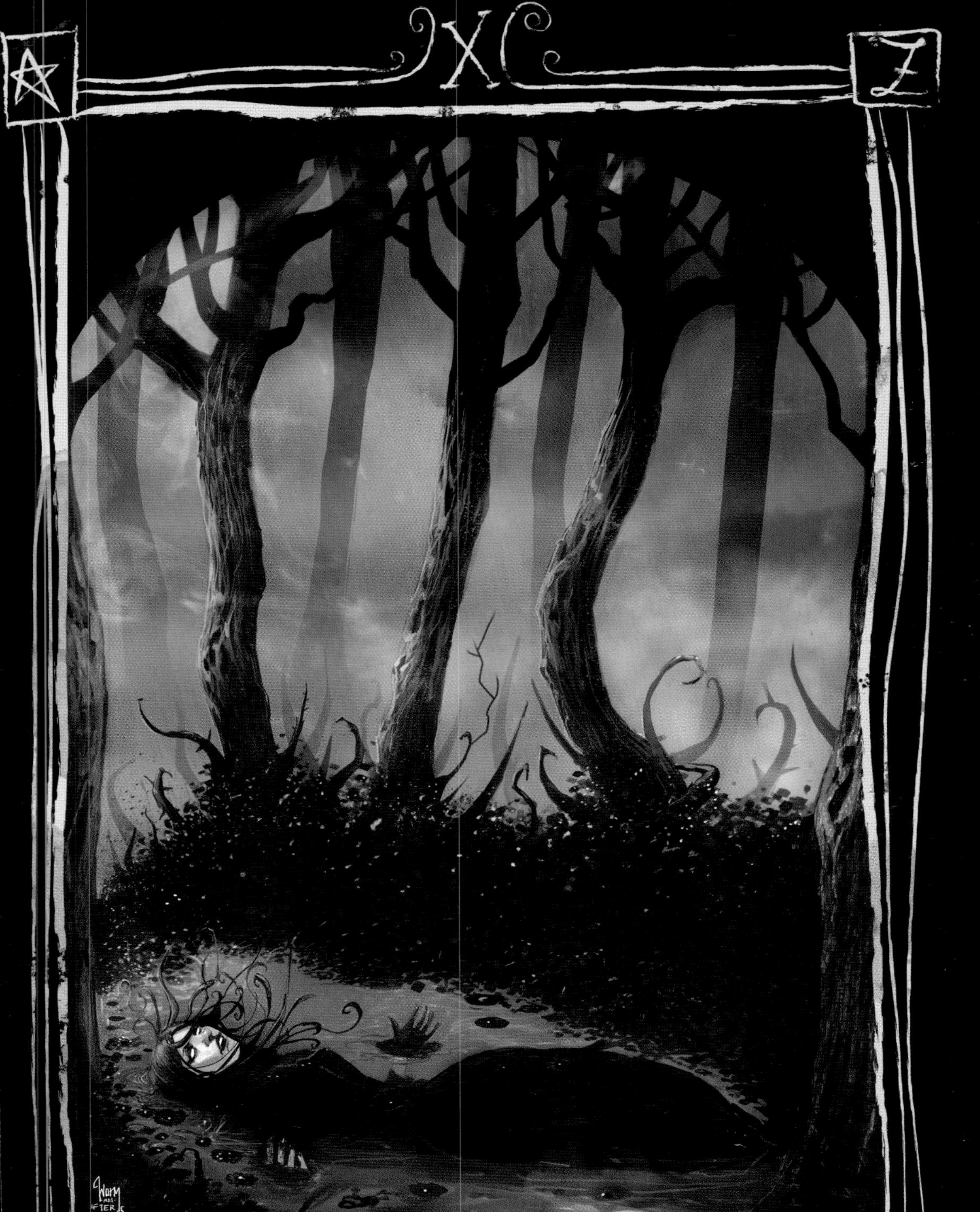
X
Worm
AFTER
FUSELI

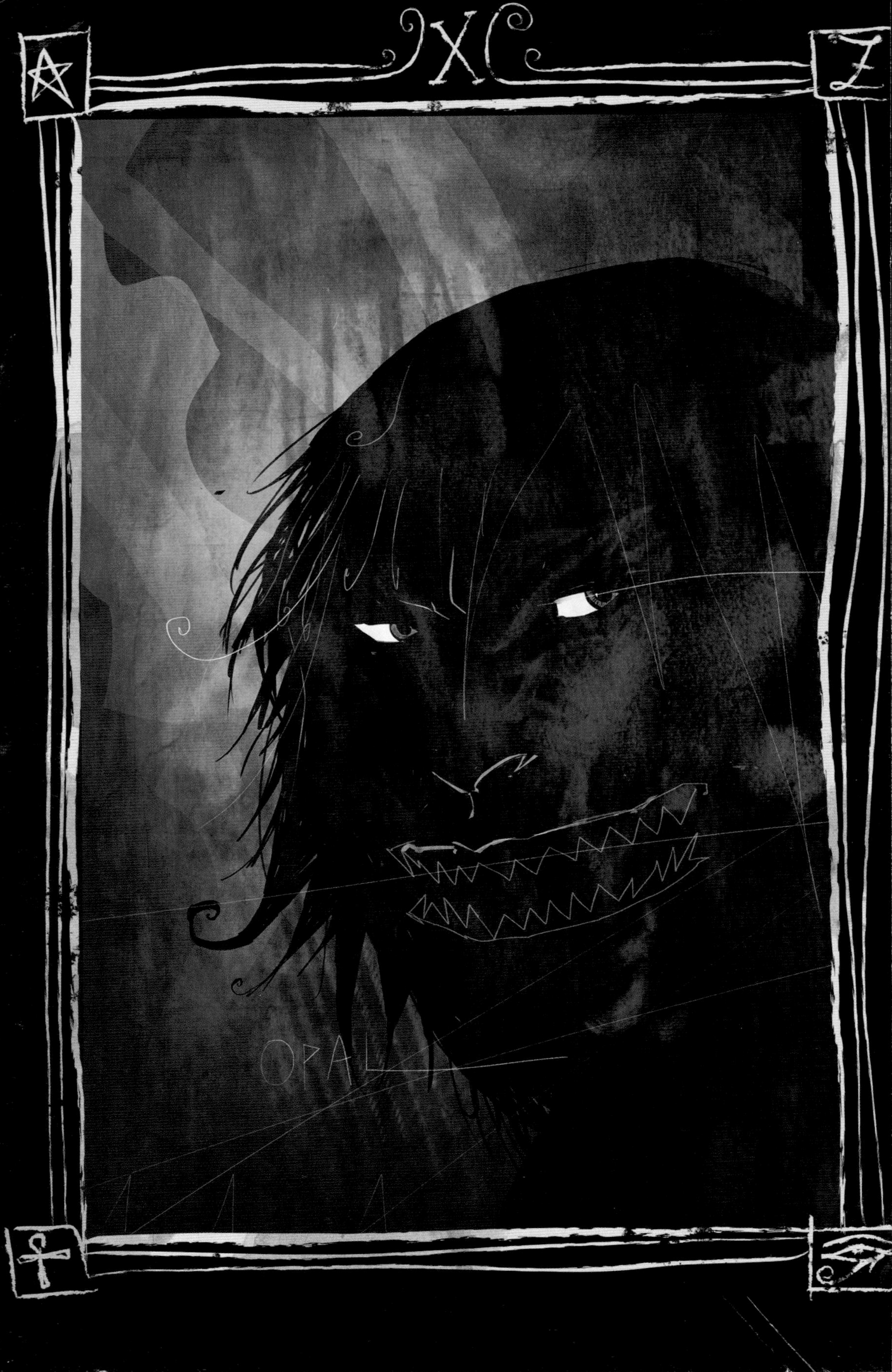
X
OPAL

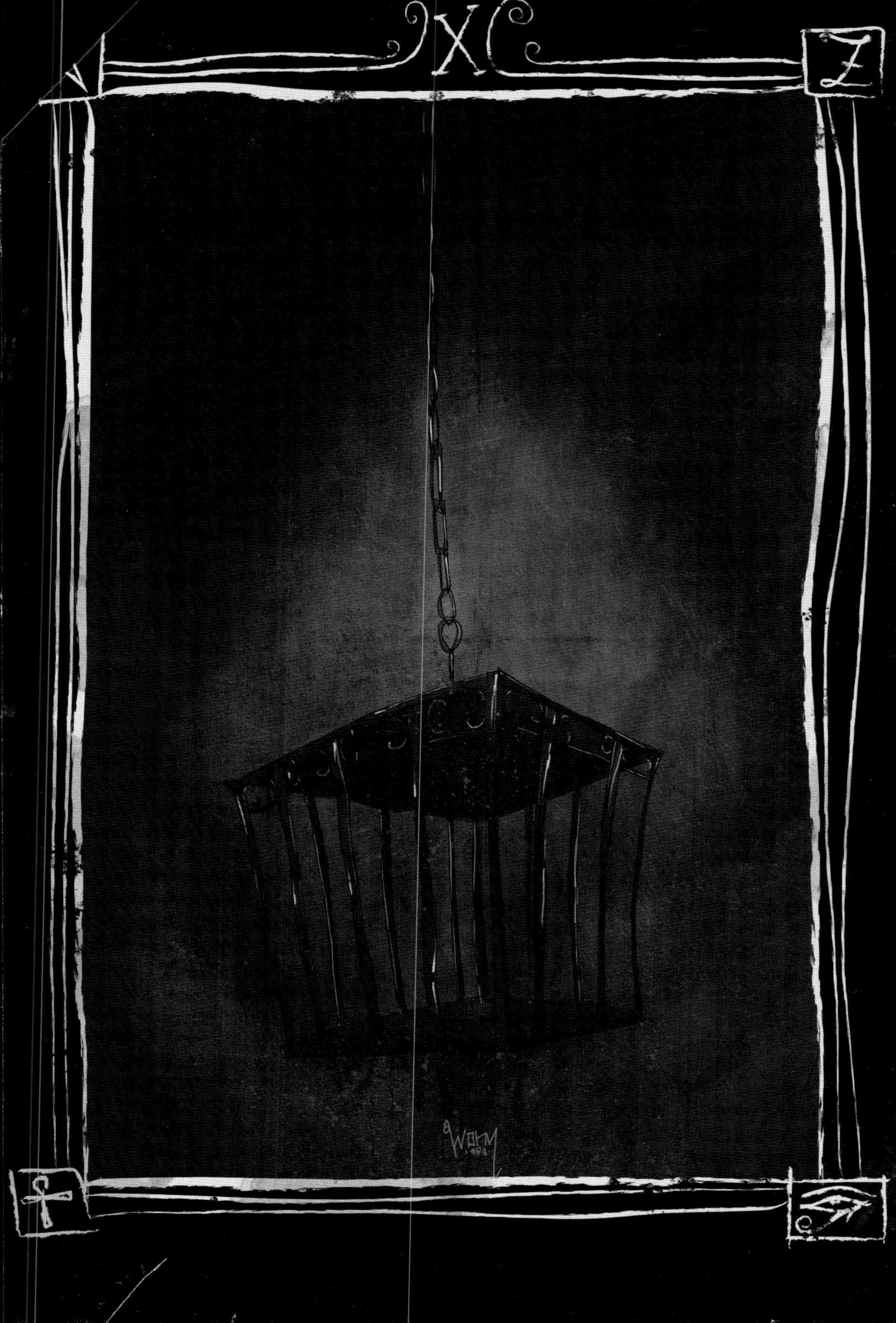
XC
Z

X

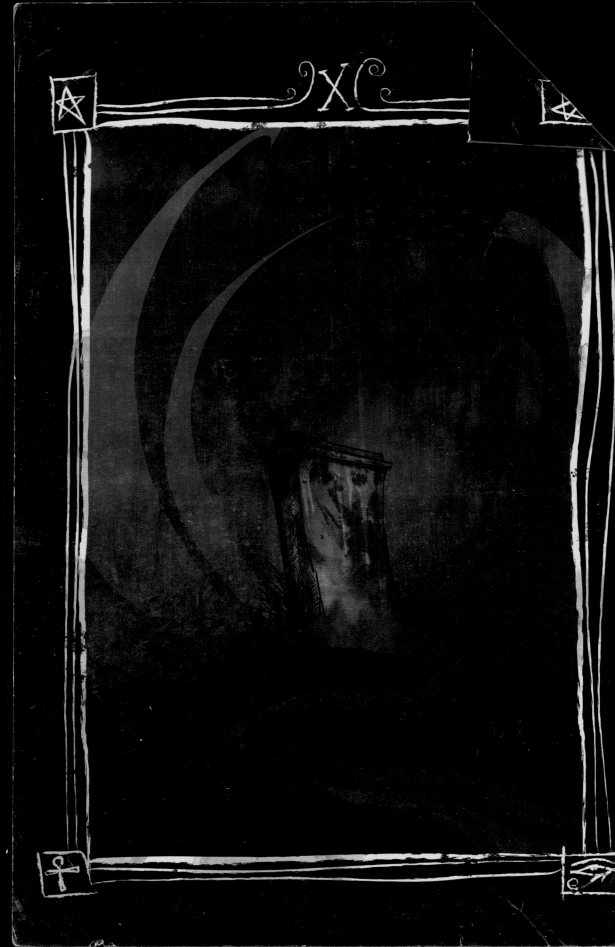